Improving
Service
Quality

Achieving
High Performance
in the Public
and Private Sectors

Michael E. Milakovich

S^t_L

St. Lucie Press

Boca Raton   London   New York   Washington, D.C.

Library of Congress Cataloging-in-Publication Data

Milakovich, Michael E.
    Improving service quality: achieving high performance in the
public and private sectors / by Michael E. Milakovich.
        p. cm.
    Includes bibliographical references and index.
    ISBN 1-884015-45-X
    1. Industrial management. 2. Quality control. I. Title.
HD31.M435 1995
658.5′62—dc20   94-46379
                                                                                            CIP

© 1995 by CRC Press LLC
St. Lucie Press is an imprint of CRC Press LLC

No claim to original U.S. Government works
International Standard Book Number 1-884015-45-X
Library of Congress Card Number   94-46379
Printed in the United States of America   2 3 4 5 6 7 8 9 0
Printed on acid-free paper

DEDICATION

To

Cindy, Nicole, and Tiffany

for their patience and support

TABLE OF CONTENTS

v

PREFACE

All organizations are struggling to improve customer-focused quality in decentralized, individualized, and highly competitive domestic and global markets. Service industries are especially aware of the need to modify manufacturing-based total quality management (TQM) systems to guide their own internal organizational change processes. Better design, implementation, and daily management of customer-focused quality improvement (QI) strategies are essential for survival in rapidly changing business and public service environments.

When thoughtfully applied and appropriately modified to meet all types of customer needs, QI principles are a sound means to respond to customer needs. This conclusion is well-known and often repeated in business circles. However, when various quality and productivity theories and methods are applied, it is very difficult to consistently deliver quality results, especially in quasi-monopolistic, non-competitive, and regulated environments.

Although examples are drawn from successful QI efforts in manufacturing and services, the emphasis in this book is on public and private services not covered by others. These include construction, education, government, insurance, public utilities, and healthcare organizations. Several chapters present step-by-step guidelines, recommendations, and action plans for implementing service quality improvements. This book is not, however, a how-to manual describing the technical details of quality auditing, inspection, planning, statistics, or risk assessment. These types of specialized studies, with self-assessment checklists to determine whether an organization is ready to embark on the QI journey, have already been provided by others (Berry, 1991; Hunt, 1992; Gilbert, 1992; Omachonu and Ross, 1994).

Sound theory and careful strategic planning are always necessary when deciding, among the many alternatives, which QI strategies to follow. One purpose of the book is to assist in developing the wisdom to select the essential elements and design systems that best fit one's own customers' needs.

The early chapters define the general elements necessary to understand and achieve continuous quality improvement (CQI) in services. The integrative concept of total quality service (TQS) is presented as a surrogate for the most effective elements of the many strategies available. Critical components of TQS are described in subsequent chapters and include changing internal management systems, delayering, empowering employees, teamwork, closer customer–supplier relationships, monitoring results, systems thinking, and reducing poor quality costs. It is assumed here that readers are generally familiar with the theories espoused by such experts as W. Edwards Deming, J.M. Juran, and Philip Crosby. Theory-based concepts and principles can and must be used to initiate the organizational changes necessary to promote TQS. An overview of the various theories designed to guide QI efforts is presented in Chapter 3.

The human resource training, rewards, and process monitoring techniques required to achieve the TQS transformation are discussed in Chapters 4 to 6. Chapter 5 details the competitive dimension and the importance of awards and employee recognition in improving customer service. The importance of process improvement and cost reduction and the merging definitions of cost, quality, and productivity are developed in Chapter 6. Throughout the book, theories and methods are integrated with successful service quality examples of internationally recognized service quality leaders such as AT&T Universal Card Services, Federal Express, Ritz-Carlton, and United Service Automobile Association.

This foundation of knowledge and theory prepares the reader for TQS case applications in essential market- and non-market-driven services: public utilities (Chapter 5); construction (Chapter 6); federal, state, and local government and education (Chapter 7); and healthcare (Chapter 8). The concluding chapter summarizes the lessons learned and the leadership skills needed to change internal organizational systems to sustain continuous process improvements.

The knowledge base in this field is expanding so quickly that no one book—no matter how current or comprehensive—can detail all applications in different types of services. The emphasis here is on changing administrative management concepts and promoting leadership principles which guide decision-making and implementation in complex publicly regulated service environments.

Some may read this book to help decide whether or not to invest in the training and organizational changes necessary to compete as a world-class international service provider; others may have already tried one of the many quality approaches and were disillusioned with the results. Still others realize that their choices are limited because TQM, CQI, TQS, or "some other damned acronym" has already been designated "the way" by the direction of the market, the boss, the state, the federal government, or an accrediting association. In many instances, your customers or clients are asking why your organization has not implemented a QI system. They may even be insisting that you demonstrate how your service is better than the competition. Clearly, if your future depends on acquiring the skills to implement service quality improvements in your work environment, then no further encouragement to learn is necessary.

Selecting QI strategies requires a vision that is dynamic, flexible, and focused on exceeding valid internal *and* external customer needs. Current performance appraisal and internal reward systems must be re-examined in relation to achieving this transformation (Milakovich, 1991a; Bowman, 1994). As the quality message spreads, entire organizations are being evaluated (as high, medium, and low performers) in much the same manner as individual performance appraisals are conducted (American Quality Foundation and Ernst and Young, 1992). Many firms are mandating that their suppliers demonstrate a commitment to improved service quality by insisting on higher performance standards and enhanced responsiveness to customer quality requirements. As the quality circle expands, more and more otherwise isolated and protected services are responding to customers by learning how to become more competitive. Therefore, regardless of individual motivation to learn more about improving service quality, the challenge is to understand, design, implement, and monitor the most effective strategy to achieve high-performance status.* If such a commitment does not already exist, it may soon be necessary just to compete in the new service markets or to sell products or services to the quality leaders in the public and private sectors.

Guiding the QI effort requires articulating the mission, setting goals and objectives in future plans, formulating action strategies, and implementing decisions using organization-wide quality control systems to monitor customer feedback and take corrective actions. In a market-driven business environment, this is mandatory. Responding competitively to customers with higher quality goods and services at lower prices is nothing new. All market-driven organizations seek customer input to increase productivity while lowering costs and improving product or service quality. What *is* new in the service quality revolution is that these concepts and principles are being applied locally to access

---

* At this writing, more is known about the attributes of high-performance service organizations in the private sector. Public services, however, are equally concerned about improvement, and many are actively working to define and achieve high-performance status. Creating a high-performance work force means increasing training opportunities, developing new skills for employees, basing pay on skills instead of position, teaching problem-solving skills, and encouraging more effective labor–management communication. (Frank J. Thompson (Ed.), *Revitalizing State and Local Public Service: Strengthening Performance, Accountability, and Citizen Confidence,* San Francisco: Jossey-Bass, 1993.)

markets globally and to improve services in publicly regulated agencies and non-profit organizations. Despite the expansion of capitalism and opening of markets worldwide, increasing numbers of service firms are affected by the decisions of federal, state, and local governments. Therefore, QI initiatives must often be developed and sustained in quasi-regulated rather than unfettered free markets.

Meeting the competitive challenges of service markets in the 21st century requires workers, owners, managers, and suppliers to prepare themselves *now* with the communication, managerial, and technical skills necessary to articulate a "quality vision" for the entire organization. That vision must be translated into an understandable mission for each work group. Each individual within those groups, in turn, must be trained to apply new sets of skills.

There is an even more compelling reason to implement customized and interdisciplinary TQS systems, especially in a recessionary economy. All internal management activities of service organizations must not only be focused, but must also be carefully *integrated* to fulfill *individualized* customer demands for consistent higher quality service, fairness, and courteous treatment. Long-term commitment and support by senior managers, coupled with an understanding of the behavioral and statistical elements of TQS, are rapidly becoming prerequisites for competing in the ultra-competitive domestic and international service markets of the future.

The United States is competing with other nations for an increasing share of emerging world markets. Therefore, improving the quality of American goods and services is quickly becoming a pressing national concern. Knowledge has evolved to the point where a "quality consensus" now exists among many American leaders in the public and private sectors. Effectively responding to changes in global service environments requires an understanding of the complexity of applying total quality concepts in both regulated and free market economies.

The value of free market competition is accepted for those (increasingly few) businesses unaffected by government regulation. At the same time, it is recognized that there is no one best way to manage quality and improve productivity. One virtue of free markets is that they minimize short-term resource allocations to maximize resource efficiency. Businesspeople also tend to ignore the long-term interests of their industries and even their own companies. The latter is reflected in leveraged buy-outs, hostile takeovers, and efforts to maximize quarterly profits over long-term investments in research and training of employees. Thus, there exists a need for governments to ensure the long-term competitive advantages of certain industries, especially those more likely to be affected by international competitive pressures.

This book is written for current and future managers in private corporations, public agencies, and non-profit organizations who share a common need to know how the service quality revolution personally affects them and their daily work environments. If there is a bias in the presentation, it is in the argument for the formation of multi-level "quality constituencies" or organized interest groups demanding higher quality public and private services.

It is my hope and expectation that the experiences, information, and observations contained in these pages will assist leaders of American firms in providing better product support and services to world markets, thereby improving U.S. competitiveness abroad and job security at home. My goal is to help all those in competitive as well as regulated and controlled markets to better serve their customers and guide fellow citizens, employees, managers, owners, and stockholders in the turbulent business, economic, political, and social climate ahead.

ACKNOWLEDGMENTS

No book is ever the sole effort of one individual. The concepts, ideas, insights, and suggestions for improvement contained in the following pages benefitted from the critical and supportive reviews of many readers. This collaborative effort would not have been possible without the thoughtful comments, reviews, and material contributed by Carlos Atienza, Evan Berman, Jason Blunt, John Fargher, Howard S. Gitlow, Albert C. Hyde, Vincent Omachonu, Laura Palmberg, Olga Quintana, John Rondinelli, David Sumanth, Bill Werther, Jonathan West, and Kostas G. Zografos. I owe a special debt of gratitude to my faculty colleagues Jose Eulogio Romero-Simpson and Malcolm Golden, who contributed unpublished papers and reviewed earlier drafts of the book. Thanks also to Kenneth Sedell, who offered insights to Chapters 3 and 6.

The author also acknowledges the valuable support of a close circle of professional associates who reviewed earlier drafts. They include Gen. Robert L. Dilworth (retired), Virginia Commonwealth University, Richmond, Virginia; Lincoln Forbes, Dade County Public Schools, Miami, Florida; Carol Greebler-Schepper, TQMPlus, Lucerne, California, who contributed original material for the final chapter; V. Daniel Hunt, President of Technology Research Corporation, Springfield, Virginia; Dr. Jack Miller, M.D., M.B.A., Quality Management Director, Mercy Hospital, Coconut Grove, Florida; and Gordon Roston, Senior Advisor, Treasury Board of Canada Secretariat, Innovative and Quality Services, Ottawa, Canada. Their willingness to share experiences, frustrations, and insights about the challenges of daily leadership for service quality greatly strengthened the book.

While the author accepts full responsibility for conclusions and interpretations, he gratefully acknowledges the support of all those who helped improve earlier drafts of the text. This includes Dennis Buda, President of St. Lucie Press, for his encouragement and support for the project. Sandy Pearlman is recognized for her patience in preparing the final draft as well as her editorial, copyediting, and proofreading skills.

Last, but not least, I would like to offer a special thanks to the many colleagues, friends, and students with whom I have worked in executive briefings, public policy seminars, workshops, and training sessions. Without your encouragement, this work would not exist.

MEM
Coral Gables, Florida

ABOUT THE AUTHOR

Dr. Michael E. Milakovich (Ph.D. Indiana, 1972) is Professor of Business Administration in the Political Science Department at the University of Miami, Coral Gables, Florida. He has served as Coordinator and Project Director for the University of Miami Institute for the Study of Quality in Manufacturing and Service. His areas of specialization are quality management and productivity improvement, health services administration, and business–government relations.

He is a Life Member of the American Society for Public Administration, serves as an expert witness in state and federal courts, and advises numerous public and non-profit organizations on policy analysis and quality improvement strategies. He serves as a member of several editorial boards, including the Board of Directors of the National Center for Public Productivity.

Dr. Milakovich has authored and co-authored several books, and his research has been published in top-ranked refereed journals such as *National Productivity Review, Health Care Management Review, Public Productivity and Management Review, North Carolina Review of Business and Economics, National Civic Review,* and *The Justice System Journal.* He has conducted extensive research in American court cost management, public sector quality management, and healthcare quality improvement. He is co-author with George Gordon of *Public Administration in America* (St. Martin's Press, 1995) and has consulted with various judicial, governmental, and healthcare agencies both in the United States and abroad.

LIST OF ABBREVIATIONS

AQL	Acceptable quality level	FQI	Federal Quality Institute*
BLS	Bureau of Labor Statistics*	GAO	General Accounting Office*
BPR	Business process reengineering	GNP	Gross national product
CFM	Cross-functional management	GPRA	Government Performance and Results Act
CQI	Continuous quality improvement	HMO	Health maintenance organization
CWQC	Company-wide quality control	IPA	Independent provider affiliate
DoD	Department of Defense*	IRS	Internal Revenue Service*
EAP	Employee assistance plan	ISO	International Standards Organization
EOP	Executive Office of the President*	JCAHO	Joint Commission on Accrediting Healthcare Organizations
FADE	Focus-analyze-develop-execute	JIT	Just-in-time delivery
FPL	Florida Power & Light Company	JUSE	Union of Japanese Scientists and Engineers

MBO	Management by objectives	PPBS	Planning-programming-budgeting-system
MBQA	Malcolm Baldrige Quality Award	PPO	Preferred provider organization
MSC	Management by self-control		
NAFTA	North American Free Trade Agreement	QA	Quality assurance
		QCC	Quality control circle
NPR	National Performance Review*	QDW	Quality in Daily Work
		QI	Quality improvement
OMB	Office of Management and Budget*	QIP	Quality Improvement Program
OPM	Office of Personnel Management*	QIT	Quality Improvement Team
PAA	Personal application assignment	SPC	Statistical process control
		SQC	Statistical quality control
PACE	Planning-activation-control-evaluation	SSA	Social Security Administration*
PCMI	President's Council on Management Improvement*	TCC	Total care concept
		TQC	Total quality control
PD	Policy deployment	TQM	Total quality management
PDSA	Plan-do-study-act	TQS	Total quality service
PIP	Productivity Improvement Program	USAA	United Services Automobile Associaton

---

* Denotes United States government agency, branch, or commission.

INTRODUCTION: THE NEED FOR IMPROVED SERVICE QUALITY

The United States emerged as a world leader in industry and manufacturing during the early 20th century. The Industrial Revolution, the assembly line, mass production manufacturing, abundant natural resources, and the assumption of a world leadership role in response to international events shaped the country's Manifest Destiny. By mid-century, America was the dominant economic power in world markets. In the years following World War II, the United States produced over one-half of the world's manufactured goods and controlled nearly all of its markets; the manufacture of industrial products provided most American jobs and generated two-thirds of the country's gross national product (GNP). Manufacturing is still a vital component of the national economic strength of the United States, but the composition of the GNP and growth sectors of the economy have changed dramatically.

Today, only one in seven Americans still works in a manufacturing job. Under current economic forecasts, that number is likely to fall even lower by the turn of the century. Services now produce over two-thirds of the U.S. GNP, and 80 percent of the American population is employed directly in service industries. If those working in manufacturing service support are included, that number jumps to 86 percent. The trend is unmistakable: over 90 percent of the work force will soon be employed in the public, private, and non-profit service sector.

Despite this irreversible shift from factories to offices, the management practices, quality control processes, and productivity improvement systems used in most service industries are still based on models designed for the pre-information age, mass production, manufacturing era.

In the early 20th century, the American economy was dominated by a smaller number of large, highly centralized organizations that were capable of turning out millions of identical "widgets" in cookie-cutter fashion at maximum efficiency and lowest cost. One of the problems facing American industry since the late 1970s has been that competitors from Asia and Europe have been able to produce more higher quality and lower cost products for world markets. With help from the United States, Germany and Japan—America's two major competitors—dramatically altered their political and social systems following World War II. Changes in management systems naturally followed. Increasing international competitiveness combined with consumer frustration with the quality of American goods and services prompted a re-examination of U.S. quality and productivity management systems in the 1980s.

To meet the challenges of intensified international competition, many U.S. manufacturers initiated changes variously known as total quality control (TQC), total quality management (TQM), continuous quality improvement (CQI), and business process reengineering (BPR). The major reason for applying these quality improvement (QI) strategies was as an effort to respond to the needs of customers and manage the complex interrelationships between costs, competition, market share, productivity, and profit. For thousands of American firms, the application of TQC/TQM/CQI/BPR has resulted in impressive gains in productivity, increased market share, and improved global competitive position. For other less fortunate firms, including many service organizations, the experience with "off-the-shelf" industry-based quality systems has produced mixed results.

The last decade witnessed a profound restructuring of basic productive enterprises. Large multinational enterprises literally "reinvented" themselves from the inside out using TQM and CQI principles. Many literally were broken up into smaller, more manageable, decentralized units in order to establish closer working relationships with customers and suppliers. Given the sheer size and scope of the effort, mistakes were inevitable.

Many TQM and CQI programs failed or were poorly executed, especially when imposed from the top down in a rote and mechanized "do it or else" fashion that was reminiscent of early 20th century industrial bureaucracies. In some instances, the principles of TQC and CQI (or other related acronyms) were misunderstood and misapplied. Early efforts to apply quality theories in services often met with initial successes, followed by frustration, resistance, and eventually layoffs as the quality demanded by management could not (or would not) be internalized and delivered to customers. Nonetheless, TQM was "the thing to do" in corporate America during late 1980s.

Deploying these (then) innovative management strategies raised product quality and productivity but did little to forestall the downsizing of the labor force in many U.S. industries. In fact, BPR is generally recognized as an implicit means to rationalize the loss of jobs. In other instances, unrealistic expectations and controversial quality bureaucracies were created. Predictably, a TQM backlash has dampened enthusiasm and further limited service applications (Forbes, 1994).

In what may be a longer-lasting legacy, this period also witnessed the formation of a national quality constituency which successfully promoted a federal quality award (the Malcolm Baldrige National Quality Award), raised hopes for the restoration of American industry, and spawned the growth of numerous quality consulting firms with "instant expertise" in applying various QI theories in both manufacturing and services. In the end, the well-intended efforts to provide better quality service often did not match the motivation or capacity to consistently meet customer expectations.

DEMANDING TOTAL QUALITY PUBLIC AND PRIVATE SERVICE

Concern about quality issues has become heightened in all types of service organizations. Competitive service providers such as accounting firms, airlines, banks, import–export firms, insurance companies, and private hospitals, as well as regulated monopolies such as local governments, schools, and utilities, are being asked to demonstrate at least minimum QI application. In most cases, success is still defined by the bottom-line return on investment, better customer satisfaction, and increased market share. Nonetheless, greater numbers of tax-supported agencies are now seeking ways to transform organizational cultures and improve service to customers as well. Given the bewildering "acronym-soup" of choices, and hoping to avoid the pitfalls of earlier post-industrial misapplications, this can be a daunting task.

There is now a general industry-wide awareness of various QI strategies, some with exotic-sounding buzzwords such as *kaizen*, ISO 9000, *poka-yoke*, and Hoshin Planning. Despite intense interest, however, most service organizations are still only vaguely aware of the potential impact of the quality revolution on their daily work environments. Only a few very select multinational world-class competitors (listed in Tables 3.1 and 5.1) recognize the competitive advantage of quality and productivity strategies for improving market share *and* motivating the work force. Significantly, those regulated and non-market services most in need of improved customer service quality are not as yet faced with the same competitive challenges as manufacturers in the 1980s.

The service quality revolution is impacting the daily operations of public and non-profit agencies as well as private organizations; definitions of service quality are merging, and business environments change almost daily. Information, capital, products, and services flow across international borders at speeds unheard of just a few months ago. As larger numbers of nations subscribe to open markets and liberal free trade policies, competition increases and more governments (including the United States) "de-monopolize" and deregulate their own service markets. Providers of critical public, private, and non-profit services such as education, healthcare, law enforcement, and corrections increasingly recognize that a new economic reality exists.

Often protected by quotas, tariffs, or favorable government regulations that isolate them from the rigors of "do-or-die" competition in international markets, regulated service monopolies have had fewer incentives to change. Without competition, inefficiencies in service delivery processes are protected, costs increase, and customer complaints are more likely to be ignored (cable TV service is a prime example). Despite the relative security of regulated local markets, many public agencies are increasingly aware that their jobs as well as their organizations could disappear overnight as rules change and world markets continue to merge.

The service quality revolution requires massive changes and will be "catalyzed and guided" by government policy and action (Bassett, 1992; Osborne and Gaebler, 1992). Once considered bastions of stubbornness and resistance to change, governments are now deregulating outmoded laws, empowering employees to act in the best interest of the citizen/taxpayer/customer, privatizing non-essential services, and streamlining procurement processes (Kelman, 1990). Public agencies are further responding to customer needs as suppliers of essential services for millions of people who cannot or will not purchase them from private providers. The trend toward customer-oriented, decentralized, and deregulated public and private service markets is accelerating worldwide as attention is focused on recommendations for change and success stories from a wide range of public agencies and private industries (Gore, 1993; Ingraham et al., 1994; Levin and Sanger, 1994; Spechler, 1993).

Consider the changes that have occurred in Asia since the 1980s, in Europe since the early 1990s, and in North America following the opening of free trade between Canada, Mexico, and the United States.

Passage of the North American Free Trade Agreement (NAFTA) in late 1993 has created tremendous opportunities for entrepreneurial ventures undreamed of just a few years ago. Those with the vision to see the potential of those changes will benefit. At the same time, the consequences of neglecting shifts in the global market are becoming more severe for all types of service organizations. Changes likely to occur in the future will surprise some and shock others. In the immortal words of Juliette Lowe and Lord Baden-Powell: *Be prepared!*

If those providing services lack the tools and training necessary to do the job, are not backed by management, and are disinterested in even meeting—much less exceeding—customer needs, then dissatisfied customers, if they have the choice, will turn to a competing provider. For customers unwilling or unable to purchase services from a competitor, continued neglect of quality could lead to frustration and eventually negatively impact a provider's bottom line. One of the strengths of free markets is that competition among service providers has been shown to reduce costs. However, so-called "managed competition" in quasi-regulated services such as education, government, and healthcare does not guarantee increased productivity or better service to customers.

Those who depend on government agencies or non-profit "third sector" voluntary associations (the American Heart Association, YMCA, or United Way, for example) often do not have a choice of competitive providers (nor can they switch providers if the service they receive is less than acceptable). For increasing numbers of recipients, the politically regulated sector provides essential services such as emergency disaster relief, job counseling, retirement assistance, unemployment insurance, education, healthcare, and public safety, typically *without* market competition. Continued neglect of service quality principles in these non-market services not only short-changes those who pay (directly and indirectly), but further alienates taxpayers and undermines confidence in government institutions. These so-called "public service monopolies" offer special challenges for learning and applying quality and productivity improvement principles and concepts. This theme is expanded in Chapters 5 to 8, in which competition in government, educational, and healthcare services is discussed.

Reduction of tariffs and quotas, free trade agreements, and information technology enhance the ability of all customers to shop internationally to find the highest value, best quality products and services, often at much lower prices than those offered by providers closer to home. This trend is irreversible: service organizations can no longer hide from domestic or global competition. *Whether purchasing goods or services, all consumers want more value for their scarce resources.* Plainly, any distinction (if one ever existed) between the quality and value received when purchasing a manufactured product and buying a service has all but disappeared.

To survive, *all* organizations must respond to customer dissatisfaction as well as understand fundamental problems associated with changing economic cycles. Traditionally, this has meant reacting to customer complaints, restructuring debt, and often laying off employees in order to reduce costs. In the short run, this response may have protected corporate profits, but it caused severe disruptions for displaced workers and their families. As Henry Ford observed at the beginning of the mass production era, this strategy is ultimately self-defeating, as people need jobs to buy products and services, which in turn fuels the economy. Firing workers not only reduces the number of potential buyers, but also increases costs by shifting the burden of retraining and unemployment compensation from the private to the public sector. Retraining for those whose jobs have been eliminated has emerged as a major national priority in the effort to reorient the current unemployment compensation program.

What is new in the quality movement is the awareness that successfully responding to customer demands for improved service quality requires correcting the root causes of system flaws which cause the dissatisfaction (among both customers and employees) that is so common in today's service encounters. Total quality service (TQS) principles offer an alternative to reducing the work force, ignoring complaints, or increasing costs. That strategy is to become more customer responsive, less bureaucratic, and more efficient. In order for this to occur, however, changes in the work environments and organizational structures for delivering services are critical.

Traditional vertical hierarchies (corporate or governmental) isolate managers, centralize authority, and distance those accountable from their customers. Such hierarchies must be flattened. Barriers to cooperation between departments *within* organizations must be eliminated, leadership roles redefined, and, in the latest jargon, processes reengineered. Customer contact personnel at all levels must be empowered and trained to respond positively and effectively to customers. Everyone must adopt a "process" approach in an effort to eliminate non-value-added (unnecessary) steps to meet customer-defined needs and requirements.

If initiated solely as a short-term response to financial crises or as a reaction to customer complaints, these reforms, like earlier attempts, are destined to fail. Internal changes are necessary, but insufficient by themselves, to deliver customized, customer-designed services. They must be accompanied by a commitment from leaders, owners, and senior managers to change the way in which services are delivered. Organizations must initiate fundamental structural changes accompanied by rewards, resources, and training in order to learn how to sustain QI goals.

LEARNING CUSTOMER-DRIVEN TOTAL QUALITY SERVICE

As more and more service providers compete for greater shares of expanding domestic and international markets, customer-driven quality management is fast becoming the preferred method for improving organizational performance. This change comes just in time for some, but too late for others.

In the mid-1980s, Karl Albrecht and Ron Zemke sounded the alarm by identifying the "lack of a consistent model or framework for managing service" as the reason most often cited for customer dissatisfaction (Albrecht and Zemke, 1985). For most services, the means to consistently manage and monitor TQS to achieve customer success, empower employees, and improve productivity have still not been fully developed or consistently applied.

With the exception of specialized fields such as industrial engineering, operations research, or production management, few books deal with the application of quality and productivity improvement principles to services. Moreover, when compared to manufacturing, there are less *integrated* service quality improvement cases, examples, or self-study materials available for learning how to apply quality management concepts to specific services. There is a gap between the statistically based quality and productivity improvement manufacturing models and the human relations, marketing-based, labor-intensive customer relations approaches used in services. The result is a dearth of training materials available to current and future service industry leaders, especially in small (under 150 employees) and medium-sized (under 1500 employees) service firms.

Only those recently graduated from one of a very few select colleges or trade schools will be well-versed in the newly emerging subject of TQS.[1] The reason for this is that faculty members at most major research universities teach courses and conduct research in narrow specialty fields. Course textbooks are written in accordance with accrediting association guidelines within traditionally defined academic units such as accounting, business law, computer information systems, economics, finance, management, marketing, or public administration, where specialties prevail. Faculty who step outside the well-worn paths of their disciplines do so at considerable professional risk. Thus, any relationship between traditional academic structure and the real world of service providers is purely coincidental.

This neglect is more than ivory tower isolation, although some academicians will always disdain the practical applications of their theories. There are fewer incentives to approach topics such as quality and productivity management from an interdisciplinary or team perspective. Higher education institutions, especially large research universities, survive on research grants, reputation, and alumni support rather than market-driven, competitively based teaching and research quality.[2] Consequently, few research universities encourage the interdisciplinary cooperation necessary to apply quality concepts to various business, educational, healthcare, governmental, or engineering services.[3] Team-taught courses are offered occasionally, but academic reward systems, such as grading students in the classroom and individual performance rankings in business, reflect traditional specialties and discourage participation in interdisciplinary projects.

Not surprisingly, specialization and fragmentation of curriculum restricts course offerings and results in a lack of self-study material for learning these concepts. Such neglect runs counter to industry trends, where teamwork and cross-functional (horizontally integrated) organization are valued as a means to successfully implement TQM, CQI, or TQS. For other service firms, unlike higher education, this often means the difference between extinction and long-term competitive survival.

The absence of a quality focus in higher education may also explain why so many larger research universities are losing support, downsizing, and coping with increased customer (i.e., faculty, parents, students, alumni, and, if state supported, taxpayers) dissatisfaction with the service provided (Seymour, 1992). This neglect is especially harmful to recent graduates who have earned advanced degrees without acquiring a basic understanding of the importance of quality and productivity improvement for the future of the United States in a competitive global economy (see Chapter 5 for details).

REDEFINING TOTAL QUALITY SERVICE

The spectacular success of Japanese industry in producing higher quality, lower cost, and more reliable products using statistical quality control methods forced U.S. manufacturing leaders to rethink their own perceptions about the relationship between cost, quality, productivity, and customer satisfaction. Efforts by U.S. manufacturers to catch up in the 1980s were in direct response to Japanese and, to a lesser extent, European competition for greater shares of international markets.

While competition from Europe and Japan prompted North American managers to improve the quality of manufactured goods, free trade policies, technology, the threat of litigation, and increased consumer activism *within* the United States simultaneously focused attention on the need for TQS. Providers of poor quality goods and services were more likely to be sued in the mid-1980s, which made some of them defensive about initiating the system changes necessary to eliminate the causes of poor quality. Manufacturer's neglect prompted consumer anger over shoddy work and defective products and resulted in the continuing liability insurance crisis. Perspectives are slowly changing, but some service industry leaders are still skeptical about the costs and commitment required to learn, redesign, and apply TQS principles. More recently, a TQM backlash, which reflects a failure to understand the complexities of quality improvement, has forced many firms to rethink their approaches to TQM.

Quality is still viewed by too many as a luxury or a subjective "warm and fuzzy" term. It is often used loosely to describe a goal or an objective (usually increased profits or sales) rather than a continuous activity toward a final destination—a reward or prize instead of a never-ending journey. The quest for workable systems to improve service quality at the point of customer contact has been described more realistically as a pilgrimage rather than a panacea. Like so many other clichés, these have some basis in truth.

TQS is defined as a powerful, yet simple, method of process improvement for achieving customer satisfaction, without the need for substantial additional resources. Readers are guided to anticipate future customer needs by systematically evaluating and validating customer requirements, streamlining internal processes, and merging customer satisfaction data with existing management control systems. TQS anticipates customer needs and encourages employee participation and ownership of work processes. It is an essential first step, which allows an organization to define its own quality standards, compete on a higher level, exceed customer expectations, and increase market share. While there is little agreement about the precise definition of the term, there is value in accepting the diversity of definitions for TQS offered by others (Albrecht, 1992; Brown, 1992; Gilbert, 1992).

While industrial-era quality control methods often required statistical knowledge and applications, no previous exposure or extensive experience with advanced statistics is necessary to learn how to implement TQS. Concepts and principles are aimed at encouraging employee responsibility, reducing internal competition, promoting teamwork, improving decision-making processes, and lowering costs. When the organizational changes and simple statistical techniques that comprise the TQS approach are combined, remarkable gains in market share, productivity, and competitive position can be achieved.

There are many different types of service organizations, ranging in complexity from the corner grocery store to multi-billion-dollar insurance firms. (In today's economy, the local grocery may offer better quality service and be the more efficiently run business!) Although they vary in size, ownership, locality, and type of service provided, all service firms share the common *lack of tangible product output* that distinguishes them from manufacturing industries.

For the reasons outlined above, fewer service firms have consistently applied TQS systems that are capable of integrating, managing, monitoring, and improving all aspects of customer service satisfaction. Therefore, less is known about quality applications in such important competitive and non-competitive, market and non-market services as construction, healthcare, insurance, import–export, government, education, telecommunications, and travel and tourism. All are vital segments of the economy which together comprise some of the nation's best opportunities for employment and economic growth.

Another important trend is the disappearance of the distinction once made between public and private sector quality standards. As both sectors strive for excellence in service quality, systems for defining and managing quality merge. In many ways, *all* organizations are becoming more "public," especially complex regulated services such as communications, education, healthcare, transportation, and public utilities (Boseman, 1987). It is equally apparent that quality and productivity management systems designed for early 20th century private large-scale manufacturing cannot simply be installed in complex service environments. Nor can modern off-the-shelf statistically based manufacturing systems be applied to services without substantial modification.

The purpose of any organization is to deliver the highest quality products, services, and product support to demanding and valued customers. Clearly, the public and private sectors have overlapping missions and purposes. The importance of integrating common elements such as customer responsiveness, empowerment, planning, process focus, marketing, system design, technology, and information management is stressed throughout this book.

ENDNOTES

1. Several professional schools within leading research universities recognize this gap and offer modules or courses, are redesigning curricula, and are even developing new programs in total quality and productivity management concepts. While the number is increasing, few institutions have yet applied quality concepts and techniques to individual courses. Engineering schools at the University of Michigan, Oregon State, and Pennsylvania State have implemented TQM programs. Several business schools have added or revised courses, developed specialized curricular material on quality management, and created programs or institutes to study quality; examples include Columbia University, Fordham University Graduate School, Rochester Institute of Technology, Samford University (Birmingham, Alabama), Sloan School at the Massachusetts Institute of Technology, Texas Agricultural and Mechanical, and the Universities of Minnesota, Miami (Florida), Pennsylvania, Tennessee, and Wisconsin-Madison. The University of Miami Institute for the Study of Quality in Coral Gables, Florida is a unique center that draws industry support as well as faculty from both the Engineering and Business Schools and focuses on services as well as manufacturing quality. For elaboration, see Karen Bemowski, "Restoring the Pillars of Higher Education," *Quality Progress*, Vol. 24, No. 10, October 1991, pp. 36–42.

2. There is no playing field between universities comparable to free markets. In addition, there few incentives to engage in genuine competition (except on the gridiron) between various institutions of higher learning. Thus, competitive rankings would accurately reflect the actual value of services received from investments in higher education only if department chairs and professors from individual academic specialties (management, marketing, economics, or political science, for example) acted more like coaches and competed with others in teams made up of the best students in their departments.

3. Christopher W.L. Hart and Paul E. Morrison, "Students Aren't Learning Quality Principles in Business Schools," *Quality Progress*, January 1992, pp. 25–27; Suzanne Axland, "A Higher Degree of Quality," *Quality Progress*, October 1992, pp. 44–61.

2

APPLYING TOTAL QUALITY SERVICE CONCEPTS

During the 1980s, U.S. manufacturers learned harsh lessons about how *not* to compete in international manufacturing markets. Many businesses experienced substantial losses and were forced to either respond to their customers' preferences or withdraw from the market altogether. There were many success stories, notably the U.S. automobile manufacturing sector, computer hardware, and telecommunications. Many large manufacturers recognized the need to improve customer service; some of the most successful U.S. manufacturing firms— quality leaders such as Ford, 3M, Motorola, Texas Instruments, and Xerox— define themselves primarily as service organizations.

It is now evident that service providers are facing the same reality that confronted manufacturers in the last decade. For nearly all organizations, failure to respond to demands for better customer service quality at lower costs means greater likelihood of extinction in competitive markets.

Customers everywhere are concerned about the continued neglect of product and service quality. Americans are especially frustrated by unacceptable delays, mistakes, rudeness, incompetent service, defective materials, and poor workmanship. If dissatisfied, more and more are able and willing to shop internationally for alternative providers. Demanding customers will not be satisfied unless they are treated as members, guests, or associates who are delighted with the service received and whose repeat business is valued. For most, the distinction between the quality of a finished product or service consumed at the point of delivery is increasingly irrelevant. Informed consumers now want both. Thus, continuously improving customer-driven service quality has become a top priority—if not an obsession—for all types of organizations.

Despite fierce competition between providers and the high frustration levels among customers, many service firms still have not accepted reality. (Some would say they "just don't get it.") Either they have not yet heard the message from their customers or they fail to redesign service quality monitoring systems to meet customer needs. Some have tried but failed to consistently apply existing systems to monitor progress toward continuous quality improvement. Regardless, the results are equally damaging.

Those service firms that have heard the message and are responding with new strategies designed to eliminate barriers to customer quality improvement are more likely to prosper in the future. For these firms, total quality service is as much a survival strategy as a means of increasing market share.

Suppliers and providers must not only deliver initial product and service quality, but must also maintain a sustained commitment to excellence in follow-up services as well. Even when purchasing non-durable goods or professional services such as legal advice, higher education, or medical care, "total quality" is judged as much by the before- and after-sale service as the initial product quality.

Improving its customer-defined quality position has emerged as a strategic opportunity for nearly all organizations, especially those competing for greater shares of expanding international markets. Not only do most people work in service industries, but over one-third of all U.S. services are now exported.[1] Stated simply, future expansion for American service industries increasingly depends on access to global markets—and success in global markets means competition on the basis of quality.

There is a gap, however, between the understanding of quality improvement (QI) theories and their application in various service industries. Although strategies for improvement differ, most service industries are now aware of the changes required to compete in a global economy. Even those services protected as monopolies or regulated by governments are increasingly accepting the need to change.

A brief retrospective view of past attempts to raise quality and productivity levels by responding to customer needs and expectations is provided in this chapter. This is followed by discussions of the changes in the definitions of quality and the elements that make up the total quality service approach.

ORIGINS AND EVOLUTION OF TOTAL QUALITY SERVICE

The evolution of the total quality service (TQS) movement is a mix of various American and Japanese philosophies and strategies. While greater numbers of Japanese firms first succeeded in applying the strategy later labeled **total quality management** (TQM) in the United States, several Americans are recognized internationally as the intellectual founders of the concept. It is vitally important to select a quality approach that matches the working culture of the organization. The importance of controlling the quality of industrial products was recognized in the early 20th century. In the 1920s, Walter Shewhart first introduced **statistical process control** (SPC) charts to monitor quality in mass production manufacturing (Shewhart, 1931). During the 1930s, SPC techniques were expanded at the Western Electric Bell Labs factory in Chicago by Shewhart and his colleagues, including a young Ph.D. in statistics from Yale—W. Edwards Deming. SPC techniques provided an efficient method for controlling the quality of mass-produced goods. These techniques were expanded, perfected, and successfully applied to the mass production of weapons and war materials during World War II. In the boom years following the war, the lessons learned from the war were largely forgotten. In the absence of competition, American industry leaders mistakenly believed that their products and management systems were superior.

In the early 1950s, Armand V. Feigenbaum (1983) coined the term **total quality control** (TQC), and W. Edwards Deming (1982, 1986) and Joseph M. Juran (1964, 1980, 1988, 1989), among others, were invited by General Douglas MacArthur to teach SPC techniques to the Japanese during the occupation after World War II. Deming and Juran both met and influenced Kaoru Ishikawa (1985), who became Japan's foremost expert in **company-wide quality control** (CWQC). Philip Crosby (1979, 1984, 1992) alerted the public to the importance of quality at a time when few skeptical American managers listened.[2] The evolution of TQS concepts during the 20th century is outlined in Figure 2.1.

Japanese manufacturing companies have used statistically based SPC since the early 1950s. These principles have evolved into a team-based management philosophy called TQC or CWQC (Ishikawa, 1985). Statistical quality control was strongly promoted by powerful political and economic forces, most notably the Union of Japanese Scientists and Engineers (JUSE). JUSE was formed in 1947 with about 60 members for the express purpose of guiding Japan's economic rebirth. Today, it selects about 2000 members, primarily university professors and business leaders, who teach and practice TQC theories and methods. No such group encouraged the quality effort in the United States until the mid-1980s.

As a consequence, quality concepts were slow to reach American firms. The theories and techniques underlying TQM/CQI were ignored in favor of traditional, top-down, hierarchical management by objectives or results-oriented approaches. Leading quality theorists directly challenged these approaches and stressed the need to change work environments in order to achieve customer-driven quality goals (Crosby, 1979; Deming, 1982, 1986; Ishikawa, 1985). Deming, Juran, and Ishikawa are today recognized by the Japanese as the intellectual "godfathers" of their economic miracle. Deming refined his teachings into Fourteen Points (see Appendix B) intended to guide American quality

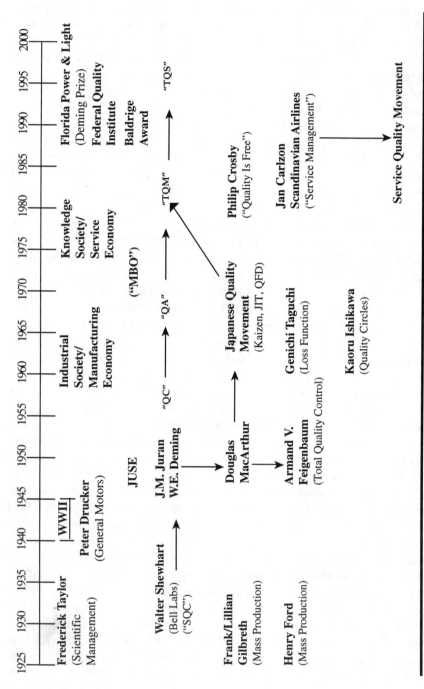

FIGURE 2.1 Evolution of Total Quality Service (Adapted from Karl Albrecht/The TQS Group)

and productivity improvement efforts. Juran's approach is less prescriptive yet emphasizes the importance of cross-functional management and achieving breakthroughs (see Figure 3.3) through teamwork and process improvements. Both Juran and Deming agree on the importance of teams and stress that at least 85 percent of an organization's quality problems are under management's control. Kaoru Ishikawa recognized the importance of self-managed work teams, statistical control, continual training, and worker participation.

When accompanied by changes in the workplace, management systems designed to continuously monitor and improve quality have achieved remarkable gains in quality, productivity, and competitive position in two to three years (Deming, 1986; Scherkenbach, 1988, 1991; Gabor, 1990; U.S. General Accounting Office, 1991). The need to transform management attitudes, change organizational structures, and alter performance appraisal and reward systems in order to obtain employee buy-in for customer service is widely recognized (Albrecht, 1992; Albrecht and Zemke, 1985; Berry, 1990; Clemmer, 1992; Gilbert, 1992; Ouchi, 1984; Peters, 1987, 1992; Rosander, 1989; Zeithaml et al., 1990; Zemke and Schaaf, 1989). Concepts such as employee empowerment and process ownership have been used more recently to describe the organizational changes required to implement TQS (Block, 1991, 1994).

While there is an emerging consensus that broad participation is needed to implement service quality, several different theories exist (and sometimes compete) to explain how best to improve an organization's work environment. Some approaches are statistically based and aimed at better process control, improving measurement capability, and reducing variation. Others stress marketing and customer satisfaction, measuring gaps between customer expectations and perceptions, and motivating employees to provide better customer service. Still others place greater value on the need to change top management behavior to direct the change effort from the top down. The latest emphasis on process reengineering to redesign business systems extends these principles by identifying critical internal processes, focusing on customer requirements, and revisioning the mission of the organization (Hammer and Champy, 1993). As knowledge and appreciation of the power of various QI theories increase, these approaches are merging into a common set of principles (listed later) that reflect successful applications in both manufacturing and service industries.

Largely as a result of the efforts of a coalition of business and public interests, TQM and continuous quality improvement principles have been rediscovered and applied primarily (but not exclusively) by large American multinational manufacturing firms. A detailed discussion of these quality leaders (Tables 3.1, and 5.1) is presented in Chapters 3 and 5. Given the ideological resistance and general disinterest of many American businesses prior to the 1980s, it is not surprising that service organizations began to experience the full impact of these changes only since the early 1990s.

CHANGING PERSPECTIVES ON QUALITY AND CONTROL

With the evolution of modern quality theories has come a change in the definitions of quality and productivity. Definitions based on the requirements of large-scale manufacturing industries are gradually being adapted to fit service delivery environments. Traditional manufacturing concepts include the appropriateness of design and specifications of a product's function and use, as well as the degree to which a finished product conforms to the design and performs according to customer specifications.

Quality of design reflects the designer's intention to include specific features (such as size, weight, or color) in a finished product. Design choices demanded by customers typically originate from marketing representatives who listen to and gather information from *external* customers. Because production resources are always limited, the end product or service usually reflects some compromise between the voices of customers and the capacity of processes to deliver results. **Quality of conformance** is to the degree to which goods and services are consistent with the intent of design. Factors that influence conformance include the capability of equipment, the training and skills of employees, process monitoring to assess conformance, worker motivation, and management commitment. **Quality of performance** encompasses the reliability of the original product and/ or service as well as the competence, integrity, and promptness of staff and support services. Different types of services can themselves be characterized by quality of design, conformance, or performance.

For some fortunate suppliers and a few well-to-do consumers, quality will always be defined in luxury terms as the best available—a Mercedes-Benz or Lexus, Russian caviar, or a five-star hotel. One of the key lessons of the Japanese manufacturing miracle is that reliable, high-quality goods can be produced at lower and lower costs. Thus, rather than being based solely on manufacturer specifications, conformance to design, or luxury features, other dimensions of quality began to be considered by American producers in the 1980s.

In 1984, Harvard Professor David A. Garvin proposed five distinct groupings of quality definitions: **transcendent** (quality is innate excellence), **product based** (quality as a measure of the quantity of some ingredient or attribute built into the product), **user based** (a reflection of the consumer's preference), **manufacturing based** (conformance to specifications), and **value based** (performance or conformance at an acceptable level of price or cost). Variations of these five definitions have since been used by academicians and practitioners in such varied services as clinical medicine, engineering, philosophy, economics, law, marketing, operations research, and construction management. These specialties define quality from the perspectives of their own professional standards and *internal* users. Different definitions have also emerged based on the unique research methods, procedures, information systems, and databases of each of these disciplines. Under all of these concepts, customer preferences are typically interpreted by professionals.

Another reason why customer-based quality concepts have been slow to reach the American service culture is that each subspecialty has its own (sometime conflicting) definition based on design, conformance, or performance requirements. Without the motivation or technical capacity to measure improvements in service processes, definitions tend to shift as information, goods, or services flow through internal processes toward the point of final delivery. This problem of entropy (the displacement of uniform standards as products flow through the production cycle) is recognized in all manufacturing and service systems.

Successful service firms recognize the complexity and multidimensional nature of quality, yet they decide in which aspects to compete and strategically focus their efforts on responding to those *customer-defined* areas. Why? The answer is because it is less expensive to respond to customer needs in the first place than to correct errors after they are made. FedEx (see Case Study 2.1) is a good example of how a successful package delivery service firm successfully balances internal and external definitions of quality yet provides employees with sufficient discretion to respond to special customer needs.

While the design, conformance, and performance approaches to defining quality have existed for some time, incorporating customer-driven or user-based perspectives on service quality is relatively new to the American service sector.[5] In 1987, David Garvin identified eight dimensions of quality as a framework for considering how *customers* define quality. This framework can be described as a multifaceted attempt to gauge quality on the basis of the following elements:

1. Performance   5. Durability
2. Features   6. Serviceability
3. Reliability   7. Aesthetics
4. Conformance   8. Perceived quality

This multidimensional, customer-focused view of quality shows how quality can be used as a competitive weapon in the struggle for international markets (see Chapter 5). Understanding how these elements interact reinforces the importance of defining quality from the perspective of customer demands and needs. It enables all participants to strategically manage quality as an "interdisciplinary" and flexible resource for initially *meeting,* then *exceeding,* and subsequently *anticipating* customer expectations. Multidimensional definitions of service quality must be customer based and measured against the extent to which a service at least fulfills, if not surpasses, customer expectations.

Case Study 2.1

FedEx

At FedEx, dedication to customer satisfaction, on-time delivery, and continuous monitoring has produced measurable results. Many lessons can be learned by benchmarking this airline, a leader in the application of customer-driven service in the aviation industry. Twenty years ago, FedEx launched the air-express industry. By constantly adhering to a management philosophy that emphasizes people, service, and profit, the company has achieved high levels of customer satisfaction and has experienced rapid sales growth. Annual revenues topped $1 billion within just ten years of the company's founding, an exceptional achievement for any new business. Past accomplishments do not ensure future success, however, which is why FedEx has set ever-higher goals for quality performance and customer satisfaction, enhanced and expanded service, invested heavily in advanced technology, and developed its human resources to establish its reputation as an excellent employer. Company leaders stress management by fact, analysis, and improvement.

FedEx began operations in 1973. At that time, a fleet of only eight small aircraft was sufficient to handle demand. Just five years later, the company employed 10,000 people, who handled a daily volume of 35,000 shipments. Today, approximately 90,000 FedEx employees, at more than 1650 sites, process 1.5 million shipments daily, all of which must be tracked in a central information system; sorted in a short time at facilities in Memphis, Indianapolis, Newark, Oakland, Los Angeles, Anchorage, and Brussels, Belgium; and delivered by a highly decentralized distribution network. The firm's air cargo fleet is now the world's largest. FedEx revenues totaled $7 billion in fiscal year 1990. Domestic overnight and second-day deliveries accounted for nearly three-fourths of the total, with the remainder coming from international deliveries. The company's share of the domestic market in 1989 was 43 percent, compared with 26 percent for its nearest competitor.

FedEx's "People-Service-Profit" philosophy guides management policies and actions. The company has a well-developed and thoroughly deployed management evaluation system called SFA (Survey/Feedback/Action), which involves a survey of employees, analysis of results by each work group's manager, and a discussion between the manager and the work group to develop written action plans in order for the manager to become more effective. The employee work groups offer solutions and monitor progress. Data from the SFA process are aggregated at all levels of the organization for use in policymaking. Training of frontline personnel is a responsibility of managers, and recurrency training is a widely used instrument for service quality improvement. Work teams regularly assess training needs, and a worldwide staff of training professionals devise programs to address those needs. To aid these efforts, FedEx has developed an interactive video system for employee instruction. An internal television network, accessible throughout the company, also serves as an important avenue for employee education.

Consistently included in listings of the best U.S. companies for which to work, FedEx has a "no layoff" philosophy, and its "guaranteed fair treatment" procedure for handling employee grievances is used as a model by firms in many industries.[3] Employees can participate in a program to qualify frontline workers for management positions. In addition, FedEx has a well-developed recognition program for team and individual contributions to company performance. Over the last five years, at least 91 percent of employees responded that they were "proud to work for FedEx."

An internationally recognized quality leader and winner of the 1990 Malcolm Baldrige Quality Award, FedEx is one of the nation's leading service quality package delivery firms.[4] FedEx stresses the 1:10:100 Rule in its employee training. If a mistake is caught at the source, it costs just $1 to correct; if the flaw is passed on to the next process, it costs $10; and if the mistake reaches the end user, it costs $100 to remedy! Every FedEx employee knows it is 100 times less costly to prevent mistakes from happening in the first place. Thus, rather than relying on inspection or customer complaints to detect errors, FedEx empowers each employee to deliver quality to the customer by preventing errors. To achieve its goal of 100 percent customer satisfaction, FedEx initiated a comprehensive Service Quality Indicator (SQI) system which describes how its performance is viewed by customers.

SQI recently replaced FedEx's old measure of quality performance—percent of on-time deliveries—with a 12-component index that comprehensively describes how its performance is viewed by customers. Each item in the SQI is weighted to reflect how significantly it affects overall customer satisfaction. Through a process that focuses on 12 SQIs (see table), FedEx sets higher standards for service and customer satisfaction and measures itself against a 100 percent service standard. Managers and employees strive to improve all aspects of the way FedEx does business.

FedEx Service Quality Indicators (SQI)

Indicator	Weight
Abandoned calls	1
Complaints reopened	5
Damaged packages	10
International	1
Invoice adjustments requested	1
Lost packages	10
Missed pickups	10
Missing proofs of delivery	1
Overgoods (lost and found)	5
Right day late deliveries	1
Traces	1
Wrong day late deliveries	5

Performance data are gathered with the company's advanced computer and tracking systems, including the SuperTracker, a hand-held computer used for scanning a shipment's bar code every time a package changes hands between pickup and delivery. Rapid analysis of data from the firm's far-flung operations yields daily SQI reports, which are transmitted to workers at all FedEx sites. Management meets daily to discuss the previous day's performance and tracks weekly, monthly, and annual trends. Analysis of data contained in the company's more than 30 major databases assists quality actions teams (QATs) in locating the root causes of problems that surface in SQI reviews. Extensive customer and internal data are used by cross-functional teams involved in the company's new product introduction process.

Recognizing multiple perspectives on quality within market- and non-market-driven (competitive and non-competitive) service organizations, a working definition of quality used here is *customer or user determined*. Measures used to evaluate quality must be based on valid service quality characteristics[6] and reliable measures of customer satisfaction to anticipate, meet, and exceed customer expectations.

High-performance service quality delivery systems seek to go beyond these definitions and provide services or products that dazzle, delight, or electrify customers. The relative quality of competing providers, under these emotionally

To reach its aggressive quality goals, the company has set up one cross-functional team for each service component in the SQI. A senior executive heads each team and assures the involvement of frontline employees, support personnel, and managers from all parts of the corporation when needed. Two of these company-wide teams have a network of over 1000 employees working on improvements. The SQI measurements are directly linked to the corporate planning process, which begins with the CEO and COO and an executive planning committee. SQIs form the basis on which corporate executives are evaluated. Individual performance objectives are established and monitored. Executive bonuses rest upon the performance of the entire corporation in meeting performance improvement goals. In the annual employee survey, if employees do not rate management leadership at least as high as the year before, no executive receives a year-end bonus.

Employees are encouraged to be innovative and to make decisions that advance quality goals. FedEx provides employees with the information and technology they need to continuously improve their performance. An example is the Digitally Assisted Dispatch System (DADS), which communicates to some 30,000 couriers through screens in their vans. The system enables quick response to pickup and delivery dispatches and allows couriers to manage their time and routes with high efficiency.

Since 1987, overall customer satisfaction with FedEx's domestic service has averaged better than 95 percent, and its international service has rated a satisfaction score of about 94 percent. In an independently conducted survey of air-express industry customers, 53 percent gave FedEx a perfect score, as compared with 39 percent for the next-best competitor. The company has received 195 awards over the last 13 years, and representatives of nearly 600 businesses and organizations have visited its facilities.

Source: Malcolm Baldrige Award, U.S. Department of Commerce, 1990

---

based definitions, can then be defined in terms of the customer's willingness to boast about the product or service. This extended network of satisfied customers then serves to market the service among friends, relatives, and co-workers. Long-term success in achieving a level of service beyond current definitions of total quality depends on the ability to positively "surprise" the customer. In addition, high-performance firms develop the capacity to foresee or anticipate customer needs. This is obviously a more challenging, but no less important, dimension of TQS.

To improve the delivery of services, it is also critical to develop flexible use criteria for ultimately anticipating customer needs. Because services are less tangible than manufactured products, their production and consumption are often closely linked. For some services, customers must wait months or years to evaluate quality and reliability. Common examples include higher education, healthcare, and life insurance policies. Understanding how customers form expectations and perceptions is essential to improving service quality. In addition to the previously listed criteria, quality of services can be judged by the competence, courtesy, credibility, responsiveness, sense of security, and accessibility communicated by all employees providing the service. This underscores the importance of horizontal or *cross-functional integration* of organizational branches, departments, or divisions (see Point 1 in the next section, in which the importance of this critical TQS element is described). Thus, the subjective perceptions and expectations of customers must be considered when selecting a strategy for monitoring QI (Zeithaml et al., 1990).

At first glance, it would appear to be unrealistic to apply the same standard to public or non-profit agencies, especially where services are not purchased on the open market or where regulatory, law enforcement, evaluative, or authority relationships exist. Customer-driven quality definitions, however, need not assume a competitive market and multiple providers of goods or services. Delivery of healthcare services, education, law enforcement, revenue collection, environmental protection, and building and zoning inspections are but a few examples of services where delighting the customers may seem to be an unattainable goal. On the contrary, it is precisely in non-voluntary compliance agencies such as state and local police departments, state bureaus, and the Internal Revenue Service where extraordinary progress is being made in the application of service quality principles (Galloway, 1992; Kravchuk and Leighton, 1993; Presidential Award for Quality, 1992; New York State Police, 1993; West et al., 1994).

Thus, for all types of service organizations (public, private, competitive, or market driven) as well as voluntary non-profits, quality characteristics must be carefully selected, applied, and validated in order to determine customer preferences. Here, process and performance techniques such as customer surveys, focus groups, and internal monitoring systems can be used to establish baseline data and validate customer quality characteristics (see Chapter 6). In addition, advanced systems and techniques are available to listen more carefully to the many voices of customers, measure results, and motivate employees. To maintain quality gains, many service firms are applying advanced methods such as benchmarking, gainsharing, and quality function deployment. **Benchmarking** consists of examining those firms that are the best at performing a certain process or group of processes (for example, preparing a payroll), studying that process or group of processes, and then transplanting the methods into one's own organization. **Gainsharing** is a variation of profit sharing in which team members share equally in any gains or savings from successes. **Quality function deployment** is a comparison of the voice of the customer with the capability of the system to deliver specific customer requirements. Customer preferences are identified, structured, and deployed throughout manufacturing and service delivery processes.[7]

TOTAL QUALITY SERVICE: A WORKING DEFINITION

TQS is a continuous, cross-functional, interdisciplinary, and horizontally integrated approach that is applicable to all types of organizations. TQS is not an end in itself, but rather a *carefully designed and executed strategy for improving processes, products, and services through continual improvements in quality, reliability, systems, and performance.* Successfully applying TQS requires an unwavering commitment to rethinking existing production and delivery systems, not only from an internal systems perspective, but from the perspectives of their many users as well. By definition and in practice, TQS must be multidisciplinary, customer driven, and organization-wide.

TQS is a powerful yet simple method of process improvement for achieving valid customer quality requirements and productivity goals without the long-term need for substantial additional resources. TQS streamlines internal processes and merges process measurement characteristics with customer satisfaction data. In the short term, additional resources may be required for retraining, but when organizational changes and simple statistical management techniques are combined, TQS reduces internal competition, fosters teamwork, improves decision-making processes, and lowers costs.

Developing a Total Quality Service Culture

Key elements in developing a TQS culture are identified here and amplified in subsequent chapters. At a minimum, they include training everyone to apply the following concepts:

1. Integrating cross-functional management through teamwork and flattening the hierarchy

2. Strengthening customer–supplier relationships

3. Increasing employee empowerment and participation

4. Monitoring results and customer feedback

5. Understanding systemic interrelationships

6. Implementing continuous quality improvement or *kaizen*

7. Reducing poor quality cost practices

Cross-Functional Management, Teamwork, and Delayering

All organizations must make a visible *company-wide* commitment to customer-driven QI. The importance of continually improving internal processes to better serve customers must be communicated to everyone. There is more, however, to implementing TQS, especially in non-market or regulated services: all internal management activities must be carefully integrated and aimed at *anticipating* customer demands for higher quality service and *individualized* treatment, often within preset budget limits or at costs suited to the prevailing market. Such system integration is difficult for all organizations but is especially challenging for non-market-driven services. Unlike the for-profit sector, budgets are less likely to increase as a result of greater demand for services. In fact, the opposite is true, because operating revenues are typically set by charities, elected legislatures, regulatory agencies, or local government boards and not by the customers who directly receive the service. *Without incentive systems to reward employees for better service, customers are often thought of and treated as recipients of services paid for by others.*

The service quality revolution in government, healthcare, and education (detailed in Chapters 7 to 9) is rapidly changing this dependency relationship. Public agencies increasingly receive a greater share of their operating revenues from direct charges, tolls, federal aid, or user fees. Sources include direct and indirect revenues for airline landing fees, water and sewer charges, trash collection, highway access, special district assessments, and designated taxes. These types of assessments are the largest growing sources of revenue for states and local governments.

We have entered an era of "no excuses" management in the market-driven as well as the non-competitive segments of the economy. While board policies are set by others, operating parameters or actual revenues of regulated utilities, special districts, or general-purpose governments are increasingly responsive to customers. Because operating revenues are much less "elastic" (expandable), there are fewer incentives to reduce costs by improving internal processes and acting on customer preferences. *Clearly, when services are paid for directly, customers of public services demand and deserve the same level of quality provided by the private sector.*

High-performance service firms have also discovered that individual customer needs differ and that systems must be designed to accommodate those preferences. Whether a service is provided by the competitive or regulated sector of the economy, **cross-functional teams** such as those employed at FedEx (see Case Study 2.1) and AT&T Universal Card Services (see Case Study 2.2) are the most effective means to achieve the vital goal of customizing service requirements for each valued customer (Parker, 1994).

Service quality leaders are flattening their hierarchies, training employees to respond to customers, and achieving improvements in response time and productivity. Organizations still operating under vertically controlled hierarchical and patriarchal systems are doomed. Organizational structures must be flattened and thinned; all employees, not just customer service representatives, must be trained to respond courteously, flexibly, and promptly to valid customer requirements. Training must be more than just "charm school" for employees, because the manner in which all employees are trained to respond to customer needs often makes the difference between survival and extinction (training strategies are described in Chapter 4). To better manage *across* an organization and respond to customers, barriers to internal communication between departments, divisions, and bureaus must at least be reduced if not totally eliminated. Attention should be focused on creating better *horizontal* integration between groups or divisions, thus enhancing **teamwork** and reducing the distance between customer and supplier. Traditional top-down (vertically managed) or tall "pyramid" structures foster leadership styles that limit the ability of employees to act effectively to serve customers. Hierarchies further reinforce fear-based, top-down, non-participatory management patterns. Moreover, they inhibit genuine **empowerment** of employees and increase the distance between senior management, employees, suppliers, and customers.

Leaders of all organizations are applying TQS principles to enhance their long-term strategic market position as well as improve internal management processes. The perceived benefits of an *organization-wide* cross-functional quality management strategy are better communication between departments, reduced rework, greater productivity, lower unit cost, improved competitive position, and greater long-term job security for the entire work force. Teams, committees, work groups, community councils, and quality control circles can be used to create this seamless structure of cross-functional, horizontally integrated unity among the work force. Achieving this goal has become easier with the publication of several excellent books on how to teach teamwork (Katzenbach and Smith, 1992; Parker, 1994; Sholtes, 1988; Shonk, 1992). With proper training and top management support, the service organization work force can be empowered to respond to customer demands and needs.

The need for delayering or flattening the hierarchy in successful service organizations was demonstrated by Columbia University Business Professor John Whitney, who analyzed insurance companies and food service providers and found in one case that there were 17! layers of bureaucracy between the customer and top management (Whitney, 1989). In organizations such as these, even if senior management wanted to implement TQS, it would be highly unlikely that the multiple layers of middle managers would facilitate internal communication or be able to respond effectively to customer needs. The need to reduce the distance between customers and senior management is increasingly apparent in all service delivery environments.

Cross-functional management of internal processes is both necessary and difficult to achieve within a vertical hierarchical structure. To implement TQS, managers require a broader horizontally based system which emphasizes prevention, promotes new service innovations, and encourages all those involved in the redesign of service delivery processes to make suggestions for improvement. Frontline workers, supervisors, and middle managers often lack the sense of mission to respond to the many "moments of truth" which contribute positively to an organization's reputation and increase market share (Carlzon, 1987). To achieve closer customer–supplier relationships, many states and local governments (the most rigid of bureaucracies) are successfully applying total quality concepts, delayering hierarchical pyramids of unnecessary authority, training and empowering employees, and redesigning systems to better serve customer needs (Kravchuk and Leighton, 1993; West et al., 1994; Berman and West, 1995).

One of the basic tenets (values) of most strategies for QI is the need to transform existing vertical hierarchical structures. This involves everyone in process improvements and efforts to delayer and eliminate internal barriers between departments, sometimes referred to as vertical "chimneys" or "missile silos." These functional departments, and the efforts expended to defend them, violate TQS principles and limit communication and empowerment. Commitment to QI also means changing the relationships between departments, eliminating non-value-added costs, increasing teamwork among different branches, and reducing internal competition by recognizing fellow employees as lifelong customers with valid needs.

Strengthen Customer–Supplier Relationships

Whether to earn a profit for stockholders, carry out its role as a voluntary non-profit association, or serve the broader public interest, **the primary mission of any organization is to identify, nurture, and maintain the customer**. The best way to keep current customers happy and increase the number of new ones is to offer quality services at lower costs to greater numbers of people faster than the competition. This has always been a wise strategy for competitive service because it is *five times* more expensive to acquire a new customer than it is to retain a current one.

In a quality-driven service culture, the concept of the customer or user as the final arbiter of quality standards must be extended to include the *internal* customers (employees in departments, divisions, or bureaus) and *external* customers (buyers, vendors, or regulators) of a firm's products and services. Valid customer requirements thus become the essential linchpin that binds the provider or supplier of services with the internal and external customers in an extended process. Together, supplier and customer can streamline processes to eliminate non-value-added steps or activities. This results in substantial internal efficiencies and cost savings; it can be achieved without substantial additional resources through better training and improved procedures. (See Chapter 4 for a discussion of training and Chapter 6 for procedures to add value to internal processes.)

The Japanese, who have perfected these methods in manufacturing for over 40 years, often say that "the next process is your customer." This alerts all internal employees to be more sensitive and responsive to customer–supplier relationships within the extended process (Ishikawa, 1985). The general model of process improvement is shown in Figure 2.2. (An extended definition of this relationship in a healthcare service environment is given in Figure 8.1.)

Getting everyone to recognize the importance of listening to the customer is one of top management's initial and continuing challenges. Once customer–supplier relationships are established or "mapped" for all users, processes improve, costs decline (because fewer mistakes are made), there are fewer complaints, and market share increases.[8] Continuously monitoring feedback in order to detect critical service quality and reliability problems before they become more serious (the 1:10:100 Rule) is challenging. Often, the internal "voices of the process," such as personnel records, financial reports, and annual evaluations tend to be biased indicators of performance. Moreover, they often conflict

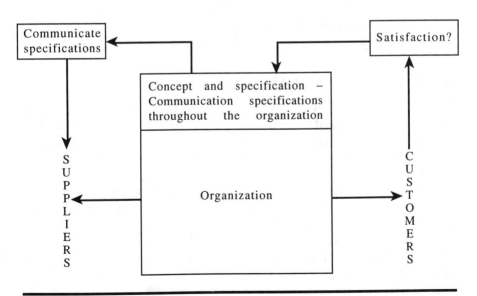

FIGURE 2.2 The Extended Process

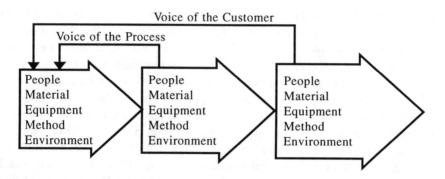

FIGURE 2.3   Sources of Organizational Feedback (*Source:* Adapted from William W. Scherkenbach, *The Deming Route to Quality and Productivity: Road Maps and Roadblocks,* Washington, D.C.: CEEP Press, 1988, pp. 35–39)

with external "voice of the customer" data (Scherkenbach, 1988, 1991). Therefore, it is critical that data accurately reflect external as well as internal customer feedback and reach top management. All voices, but especially the voices of dissatisfied customers, should be heard—loudly and clearly. As indicated in Figure 2.3, bringing the "voice of the process" in line with the "voice of the customer" strengthens customer–supplier relations, helps reduce process variation, and eliminates non-value-added expenses. Achieving this in the absence of new resources is especially challenging for public and private service organizations. Significant differences exist among public sector agencies in the definitions of citizens, customers, recipients of services, and taxpayers.

Empower Employees to Meet Customer Quality Requirements

Empowering work groups requires a fundamental change in the way an organization is managed. It begins with breaking down internal barriers to communication, as noted earlier. Training everyone to listen carefully and respond appropriately to the needs of all customers—internal and external as well as individuals whose roles are changing—is an important requirement for TQS. It is also an area of intense controversy in some organizations.

Rather than a set of rigid rules, policies, positions, or practices, **empowerment** is a state of mind or attitude shared by all the members of an organization. Employees are empowered when they have the training, knowledge, and experience necessary to identify and respond to the needs of all customers. Empowerment is the delegation of authority and resources, within preset limits, to those who serve the customers. As process owners, they are expected to make decisions and act on the customer's behalf in their work areas. It is the confidence, mutually reinforced by trust and experience, among all members of a quality-focused service organization that customer interests will be served. Concomitant with empowerment is the requirement to monitor results from the perspective of those being served (see below).

While senior managers may have to give up some control, line managers, supervisors, and workers will assume more responsibility for achieving customer satisfaction. The boundaries of individual decision making are not unlimited. They can be established with the help of external customer-focused groups, internally focused teams, and process redesign work groups. This can and does include critical decisions regarding work redesign, as well as the selection and retention of individuals as team members. Not all senior executives are equally enthusiastic about the potential (perceived) loss of power which might accompany genuine empowerment.

Similar to the concept of bounded rationality in organizational theory (Thompson, 1967), empowerment is a participatory management strategy that encourages employees to continuously analyze and redesign their jobs. Because first-line employees best know customer needs, they must be the ones who are empowered to act. Management must recognize this critical linkage and listen to employees before making decisions that affect customers or work groups. When accurate customer definitions of quality are added to an organization's repertoire of strategic planning skills, the determination of quality standards or outcomes becomes part of regular operations. The questions then become: Just who are the customers? What are their quality requirements? How are they defined? How can they be met?

A set of five simple questions can be used at the beginning to address the quality requirements at each customer–supplier linkage within an integrated quality managed organization. Once these requirements have been established for all customers, then top management can proceed with the reduction of poor quality costs by integrating financial, customer service, and quality measurement systems.

1. What is your major product or service?

2. Who are your major users/customers?

3. What are the quality requirements demanded by your users/customers?

4. What is the most respected product or service offered by your competitors?

5. What kinds of comparative studies do you conduct to compare your service with your competitors' for the quality requirements of your customers? (Kano and Gitlow, 1988–89)

Serving customers directly and effectively in turn requires training to perform each subtask that is necessary to satisfy customers. This implies an in-depth understanding of the systems or processes, the capacity to exercise independent judgment in the interest of the customer, and familiarity with the mission of the organization. Understanding systems relationships, combined with human resource training and teamwork, are the keys to unlocking the potential for an empowered and self-managed work force. In exchange for the authority delegated to control processes and respond directly to customers, everyone is expected to achieve results that meet or exceed customer expectations.

Carefully Monitor Results

Customer satisfaction is a critical step in the journey toward consistently delivering TQS. Measuring how customers respond is equally important. Only employees who have direct contact can delight customers. Even world-class service companies tend to neglect the training and support needs of first-line customer contact employees (Fromm and Schlesinger, 1994). As described in Case Study 2.2, Baldrige Award winner AT&T Universal Card Services (UCS) has succeeded in achieving this goal by empowering line employees to act in behalf of customer interests. UCS carefully measures customer satisfaction with elaborate surveys, including 8 primary, 18 secondary, and 125 key measurement indicators which are monitored and analyzed daily. These results are shared with customer-contact "associates" to provide error-free service.

All organizations receive feedback from customers and employees. Some listen to these voices more carefully than others. Feedback can be in the form of informal communication, complaints, surveys, suggestion boxes, or more formal written comments. Not all organizations deploy measurement systems as comprehensive as AT&T's (described in Case Study 2.2), but most now use customer surveys and other forms of direct customer-to-management evaluations to systematically collect data on both employee and customer satisfaction. It is especially important to listen and respond to internal as well as external customers, and some companies have found it advantageous to set up formal channels for employees to express complaints.

These "safe harbors" for venting frustration (without fear of punishment or reprisal) are important for establishing genuine empowerment in the work force. Such internal communication, especially if it is negative, may be as important as external feedback from customers. In order to be consistent in their service to all customers, employees must be capable of enjoying their work in a positive environment. Increased power or control over work responsibilities enhances feelings of empowerment and, in most instances, results in higher customer satisfaction. The opportunity to express frustrations freely, without fear, is central to improving daily work.

Case Study 2.2

AT&T Universal Card

Customer focused—That's what AT&T Universal Card Services (UCS) believes it must continue to be if it is to maintain the rapid ascent that made its Universal Card the second largest in the credit card industry in just 30 months. Indeed, the young business was designed around the use of the quality principle to "delight the customer." A comprehensive data and tracking system helps the AT&T subsidiary chart a well-marked course for continuous improvement in its customer relationships, internal operations, supplier partnerships, and business performance. For example, determinants of customer satisfaction—the starting point for all quality planning—are studied in layers of detail.

UCS's eight broad categories of "satisfiers," including price and customer service, are used to define the company's quality focus. In turn, these prioritized determinants of how customers perceive the value of credit card services are underpinned by 125 satisfiers, each of which is also weighted to reflect its relative importance.

One practical product of this increasing specificity is an exhaustive set of concrete performance measures that link internal operations and customer satisfaction. Another is a clear picture of what UCS must do to better its services, performance, and market share. Management knows what improvements are likely to yield the greatest gains in quality. Each part of the business, from UCS as a whole to individual work units, has a list of "10 most wanted" quality improvements. UCS reports that it leads the credit card industry in such areas as speed and accuracy of application processing and customer satisfaction. UCS also cites its industry leadership position in all eight primary customer satisfiers.

UCS: A Snapshot

Since AT&T established UCS in March 1990, the AT&T Universal Card (a combination general-purpose credit and long-distance calling card) has attracted 16 million cardholders. UCS now employs 2500 people, or ten times more that its initial payroll. Nearly 90 percent work at UCS's main facility and headquarters in Jacksonville, Florida. The collections operation in Houston and the payment processing center in Columbus, Georgia employ the remainder. Two-thirds of all employees are in customer-contact positions.

AT&T views its Universal Card as a strategic tool for protecting and bolstering its long-distance customer base. In 1991, UCS's first full year, AT&T documented a 40 percent annual increase in calling card revenues from UCS customers. UCS competes against some 6000 national, regional, and local issuers of general-purpose credit cards.

Delight Customers

UCS began with a straightforward strategy: Offer a credit card with a comprehensive set of competitive services. Then, through a carefully conceived and executed strategic plan, continuously improve internal performance and continuously pursue enhancements in product and service offerings. The twofold aim was delighting customer and distancing the Universal Card from competitors' products.

Fundamental to the strategy was the need to listen to customers. This resulted in, for example, 8 customer-related databases and 11 monthly surveys that track overall satisfaction and the quality of specific services. Also fundamental was an organizational structure that would respond quickly to changing customer requirements and competitive conditions by efficiently carrying out quality improvement initiatives.

From the outset, quality has been a top concern of UCS President and Chief Executive Officer Paul Kahn and the other 11 members of the business team. The team crafted a long-term incentive plan that rewards members for accomplishing quality objectives. In addition, executives and managers "own" specific short- and long-term quality goals (numbering more than 100 in 1991), each with a predetermined target date.

Although the business team develops UCS's annual and long-term strategic plans, mechanisms that go beyond evaluating all relevant trend data provide other avenues for customer and employee input in establishing quality and business goals. For example, during 1992, all employees met with a senior executive to exchange ideas in gatherings of no more than ten people. Employee suggestions also feed into the planning process. In 1992, UCS personnel submitted more than 6200 suggestions, compared with 1727 in 1990. Nearly half of all suggestions were accepted and acted on by management.

All business team members are required to devote some of their time to meeting with customers. Several also serve on the Customer Listening Post Team, which evaluates the effectiveness of UCS procedures for gathering, responding to, and evaluating customer comments and survey results.

The business team translates goals into key initiatives. At the top of the list are the business team's "10 most wanted" quality improvements. All key initiatives are assigned to teams composed of representatives from various UCS units. In support of each initiative, these cross-functional teams develop specific programs as well as the associated performance measures that link programs to UCS's strategic goals.

Another tier of cross-functional teams, which include supplier representatives, implements the programs. If the goal of the program is to develop a new service, customer focus groups also participate in the process. If the goal is improving an existing process or service, a company-wide quality assurance group helps the team establish measures for assessing how changes affect levels of customer satisfaction.

Employees Are Key

UCS exhibits a strong culture of concern for its people. Associates are made to feel that they are the key to delighting the customer. This is made real by empowering line employees. In an effort to move beyond project-focused quality teams, the company has begun a pilot program to introduce self-directed work teams responsible for all day-to-day activities and decisions. Customer-contact employees already have considerable authority to act on their own. For example, they can grant credit line increases and adjust customers' bills without management approval.

Training opportunities are numerous and range from traditional classroom sessions to computer-based instruction. In 1991, hourly employees underwent an average of 84 hours of training, in addition to the eight-week orientation for new customer service employees. Monthly surveys track employee satisfaction. UCS has developed a list of employee "satisfiers" that guide improvements in training, recognition programs, and other human resource activities. Widespread use of advanced information technology undergirds important components of quality improvement efforts. A Strategic Systems Plan, now in its final phase of development, will provide the company with world-class on-line processing and analysis capabilities. In 1991, UCS spent $20 million on computer workstations to provide customer support personnel with easy access to detailed card-member information.

In may key areas of performance and customer satisfaction, UCS ranks as best in its class; for example, speed in processing telephone applications is three days versus ten days for the nearest competitor. In setting ever-higher standards for itself, the company is nurturing customer loyalty and reports that over 98 percent of its customers rate overall service as better than the competition.

Source: Malcolm Baldrige Award, U.S. Department of Commerce, 1992

Measuring the quality of service provided to customers involves more than assessing outputs, productivity ratios, or aggregate financial expenditures. Customer perceptions are equally important and often include the manner in which the service is delivered as well as its costs. Useful techniques to analyze the differences between expectations and perceptions are gap analysis and the SERVQUAL survey (Zeithaml et al., 1990). Various gaps include discrepancies between top management and consumer expectations, internal barriers in meeting consumer expectations, employee delivery vs. perceptions, communication, and the difference between expected and perceived service. The magnitude of the last gap equals the sum of the first four. The use of SERVQUAL behavioral measures encourages consistency between employees performance and customer expectations of quality service.

With greater freedom to act as an empowered work team comes enhanced responsibility for better measurement of group results. Managers must focus on processes rather than individual performance, narrow tasks, or reinforcing hierarchies. Performance measures reflect customer satisfaction rather than traditional profits or losses. Employees are rewarded for team performance as well as individual performance. Specialists are trained to measure results and communicate process improvement opportunities to all staff members. A few companies have gone as far as having subordinates rate their supervisors on team skills. Current efforts to improve government performance focus on monitoring results as well (DiIulio et al., 1993). Whatever monitoring system is selected, empowerment, performance measures, and better understanding of systems relationships are required.

Understand Systemic Relationships

Once the vision of the organization and the mission of internal work groups have been defined and communicated, applying TQS requires understanding and application of problem identification, problem-solving, and process improvement cycles. Peter Senge describes this aspect as "systems thinking," or the importance of understanding the behavior of non-linear systems in a learning organization (Senge, 1990). Techniques can be taught as simple methods to identify problems and implement solutions (see Chapter 6). The approach is an applied variation of the scientific method or problem-solving process (Figure 2.4) variously known as Planning-Activation-Control-Evaluation (PACE), Focus-Analyze-Develop-Execute (FADE) (Figure 2.5), and the Shewhart Cycle or Plan-Do-Study-Act Wheel (PDSA) (Figure 2.6).

The Shewhart Cycle consists of four steps which form the basic systemic analytical approach to quality improvement:

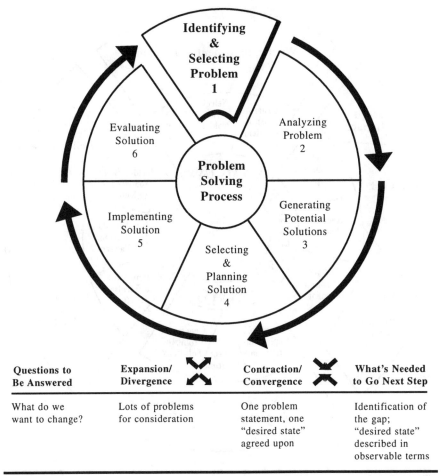

FIGURE 2.4   Step 1: Identifying and Selecting a Problem

■ **Step 1: Plan.**   The initial step in an effort to accomplish a goal is to recognize an improvement opportunity. The problem or problems are defined and possible causes are diagnosed. Planning recommends changes in areas that need improvement.

■ **Step 2: Do.**   Test the theory, recommend action, and execute or implement the planned change, initially on a small scale. Establish measures and collect data.

■ **Step 3: Study.**   Observe the results, summarize data, identify root causes, analyze, evaluate, and compare the effects of the actual change with expected or planned outcomes.

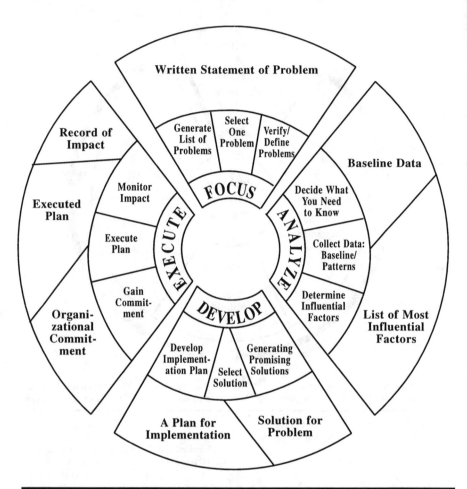

FIGURE 2.5   The FADE Process (*Source:* Ryder Corporation, Miami, Florida)

■ **Step 4: Act.**   Take action on the results. Make changes in the "plan" where expectations were not met. Improve, test, monitor results and improve. Hold the gain and repeat the process to achieve breakthroughs to higher performance levels.

The underlying purpose of these analytical cycles is to visualize and better understand the systemic relationships inherent in the critical systems of all types of organizations. As such, they are a process-oriented way of thinking about problems which emphasize eliminating non-value-added costs and achieving higher levels of performance (see Figure 2.7). Systemic thinking involves seeing relationships in a non-linear fashion, that is, with no beginning, middle, or end.

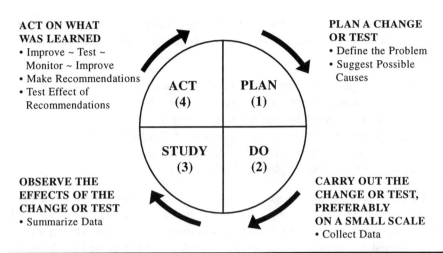

ACT ON WHAT WAS LEARNED
- Improve ~ Test ~ Monitor ~ Improve
- Make Recommendations
- Test Effect of Recommendations

PLAN A CHANGE OR TEST
- Define the Problem
- Suggest Possible Causes

OBSERVE THE EFFECTS OF THE CHANGE OR TEST
- Summarize Data

CARRY OUT THE CHANGE OR TEST, PREFERABLY ON A SMALL SCALE
- Collect Data

FIGURE 2.6   The Plan-Do-Study-Act Cycle (*Source:* Michael E. Milakovich, "Creating a Total Quality Healthcare Environment," *Healthcare Management Review,* Vol. 16, No. 2, Spring 1991, p. 16)

Many problems can be analyzed by utilizing basic problem identification and problem-solving techniques discussed by others.[9] More complicated interactions within organizations may require the discipline of a FADE or PDSA cycle. Finding a permanent solution may require a combination of these techniques with a more comprehensive team approach to identify sources and eliminate the causes of variation (see Chapter 6).

Successfully implementing TQS requires a process focus, systems thinking, teamwork, cross-functional management, and an understanding of how and why the output or result of one's work impacts the next process. That means coordination and communication across, as well as up and down, the organization. Combining cross-functional management, teamwork, and systems thinking assists in the redesign of internal management systems to break down horizontal barriers between departments. Everyone's attention can then be focused on meeting valid customer service requirements. When this is achieved, managers become less preoccupied with control, inspection, and supervision and become more concerned with improving systems and continuously meeting customer-defined quality requirements.

Implement Continuous Quality Improvements

Underlying all QI theories is the concept of **continuous quality improvement** (CQI), known to the Japanese as *kaizen*. The term was coined by Masaaki Imai and is used to describe organized attempts to achieve "constant improvement through efforts of the entire work force." According to Imai (1986), a *kaizen* strategy:

> maintains and improves the working standards through small, gradual improvements. A successful *kaizen* strategy clearly delineates responsibility for maintaining standards to the worker with management role being the improvement of standards....In process-oriented management, a manager must support and stimulate efforts to improve the way employees do their jobs.

CQI instills in the work force an attitude of mutual support between management and labor which encourages gradual improvements in work processes and rewards employees for their efforts to reduce process variation. The goal is to achieve breakthroughs to higher levels of work performance and productivity (Imai, 1986; Juran, 1988). In other words, CQI recognizes that there are always processes that can be improved and provides statistical analytical tools to achieve the improvements. (Training should be based on CQI theories to improve internal work processes and organizational behavior within service providers. Various strategies are discussed in Chapter 4, and an overview of the techniques used to monitor progress is provided in Chapter 6.)

The diffusion of a quality consciousness and a commitment to CQI are clearly linked to increasing competitiveness in world markets (Chapter 5). Japan's success in applying CQI principles to continuously raise product quality at lower costs further strengthens the concept's appeal as a tool for international economic competition. How the concept of CQI can be combined with systems thinking (the PDSA cycle) to reduce variation and raise the level of quality within an organization is illustrated in Figure 2.7.

CQI can also be used to reduce the costs of poor quality by eliminating non-value-added costs. Statistical tools and techniques are available to manage systems, flatten existing hierarchies, eliminate the need for performance appraisals, empower employees, and minimize external control systems. All participants can analyze problems and base decisions on facts, data, and information. *As a result, processes become more "visible," costs of poor quality practices are discovered and eliminated, and empowered teams can be held accountable for results.*

Reduce the Costs of Poor Quality

The general condition of the economy as well as the specific condition of one's business influence the need to uncover and eliminate the costs of poor

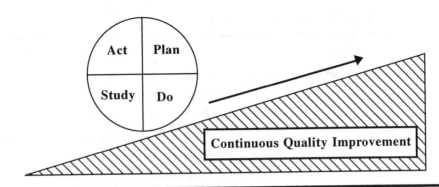

FIGURE 2.7   The Shewhart Cycle and *Kaizen* Breakthroughs to Higher Levels

quality. In an expanding market, there are fewer incentives to measure the costs of poor quality and to take actions to reduce rework, correct defective systems, and minimize returns. Thus, hidden losses attributable to poor underlying quality processes are routinely covered by expanding revenues. The prevailing attitude becomes: When you are making money, who cares how? Just make more! In the short run, it may appear to be a less costly alternative to bury causes of poor quality processes in obscure accounting systems or to ignore quality problems altogether by denying that they exist. Without systematic attention to the causes of poor quality, however, cost reductions will be superficial and short-lived.

Philip Crosby highlighted the importance of understanding the costs of poor quality with the Eternally Successful Organizational Grid (Appendix A). Using a healthcare analogy, Crosby classified organizations (or work units within them) as being at one of five stages of quality management, from comatose to wellness (Crosby, 1979, p. 31). Dimensions of organizational performance such as quality, growth, customer orientation, change (flexibility), and employee morale were evaluated against the health of an organization. The progressive, healing, or wellness organizations understand and minimize both the visible and hidden costs of poor quality practices.[10]

The journey toward a healthier organization begins when everyone is capable of managing across functions, expresses pride in working for their employer, has accurate feedback from customers, is willing to objectively examine customer–supplier relationships, and understands systems relationships. When these elements are applied by a critical mass of individuals working together toward a common set of goals, then organizations can learn and change to reflect the new values outlined in Table 2.1.

TABLE 2.1   Changing Organizational Values

Old	New
Hierarchical "Theory X" top-down organizational structure	Flatter, leaner "Theory Y or Z" participatory organizational structure
Centralized command and control structure	Decentralized and empowered work force
Productivity vs. quality	Productivity gains are achieved through quality
Separate data systems	Integrated data systems
Blame workers for poor quality	Management is responsible
Quality achieved through inspection	Quality is built into systems and processes
Supplier relationships are short term and cost oriented	Supplier relationships are long term and quality oriented
People are viewed as variable costs and replaceable	People are viewed as assets for their contributions to the organization
Training is external to the mission of the organization	Training is integrated with quality and productivity goals
External definition of quality standards	Quality is measured by customer needs and process improvement
Quality is measured by degree of conformance to standards	Quality reflects continuous improvement and user satisfaction

SUMMARY AND CONCLUSIONS

The modern quality revolution began in Japan during the early 1950s. Its concepts and theories were exported, along with Toyotas, Hondas, cameras, and VCRs, to the United States during the 1980s. It has forever changed how corporations, hospitals, governments, schools, colleges, and small businesses are managed. Customers are demanding more and better service satisfaction and are willing to shop worldwide to obtain it. The sheer size of the U.S. service sector (two-thirds of the American economy), the competing demands on scarce public resources, and the poor reputation of American products require national leaders to seriously consider the consequences of not improving service quality. This is especially true in vital "non-market" areas such as education, healthcare, public assistance, and law enforcement.

Educational institutions, for example, increasingly recognize the need to redesign curricula to teach quality and productivity in order to prepare students for productive careers in the new competitive global market economy (Seymour, 1992). The connection between improving classroom education and competition in world markets has become the focus of many conferences. In 1993 alone, over 50 conferences focused on improving quality at the elementary, secondary, and higher education level. Pinellas County, Florida has been recognized as a leader in this rapidly expanding movement (see Case Study 7.1). Corporate leaders recognize the need for educational quality, and greater numbers of school districts are applying quality theories to improve educational services at all levels (Finn and Rebarber, 1992; McCormick, 1993; Murgatroyd and Morgan, 1993).

Without empowerment, motivation, and training, the changes required to achieve this transformation can be very threatening to the work force, especially middle managers already experiencing on-the-job pressures for increased productivity. Resistance or even paralysis can result. Such reforms must be supported by resources and, above all, a commitment to active leadership and training for advanced knowledge of the importance of quality as a means to respond to customers and expand future markets.

A more detailed description of the theoretical basis for major quality strategies is provided in Chapter 3. No one approach is favored. In practice, most organizations adopt a hybrid approach, borrowing elements from each of the major quality theorists. It is important to understand how each component interacts to strengthen the others. These interrelationships have been illustrated in the figures included in this chapter. Only when the basic principles described here are understood and incorporated as part of the TQS effort can the journey to apply them begin.

ENDNOTES

1. Source: "The Final Frontier," *The Economist,* Vol. 326, No. 7799, February 20, 1993, p. 63.
2. The theoretical work of these and other world leaders in the field of quality improvement paved the way for service professionals to apply these principles to their organizations. The details of their contributions are described more fully in Chapter 3.
3. Robert Levering and Milton Moskowitz, *The 100 Best Companies to Work for in America,* New York: Doubleday, 1993, p. 121.
4. Other Baldrige winners are listed in Table 5.1.
5. Reflecting W. Edwards Deming's influence, University of Miami statistician Howard S. Gitlow defines quality as "...a judgment by customers or users of a product or service;

[quality] is the extent to which the customers or users feel the product or service surpasses their needs and expectations." Howard S. Gitlow, *Planning for Quality, Productivity, and Competitive Position,* Homewood, Ill.: Dow Jones-Irwin, 1990, p. 7.

6. How to develop these characteristics is a critical element in the application of TQS to services. Methodology is described further in Chapter 6.

7. Advanced quality approaches are just now being applied to services. These approaches include benchmarking (Camp, 1989), gainsharing (Gartman and Fargher, 1988; Masternak, 1993), and quality function deployment (Day, 1993; King, 1987; Hauser and Clausing, 1988; Griffin and Hauser, 1993).

8. An excellent technique for "mapping" customer–supplier processes is flow charting.

9. For additional information, see James E. Anderson, *Public Policy Making,* 3rd ed., New York: Holt, Rinehart and Winston, 1984; Thomas R. Dye, *Understanding Public Policy,* 8th ed., Englewood Cliffs, N.J.: Prentice-Hall, 1995; Dennis V. Palumbo, *Public Policy in America,* 2nd ed., Orlando, Fla.: Harcourt, Brace, 1994; Guy B. Peters, *American Public Policy: Promise and Performance,* Chatham, N.J.: Chatham House, 1993.

10. See Figure 6.2 for a description of the cost of poor quality iceberg, which shows how neglecting hidden poor quality costs further impacts service delivery systems.

3

FROM QUALITY CONTROL TO CONTINUOUS IMPROVEMENT

In complex service delivery environments, issues such as cultural change, diversity, customer relations, and work redesign often frustrate permanent quality improvements. Suppliers of goods and services to all types of markets must be capable of anticipating customer needs, monitoring progress, and showing results to current and potential customers. Equally important, however, are changes in the way services are delivered at the point of customer contact.

Most service organizations realize the importance of meeting or exceeding valid customer needs but lack consistent strategies or theories to guide the internal organizational change process. Employees not only ask what is required, but seek opportunities to actively participate as well. They want to assist in the achievement of the total quality service (TQS) transformation. Most books on the subject are written by consultants and are little more than rehashes of someone else's instant method for quality salvation (This book will save your company!). Obviously, if it were that easy, more customers would express delight rather than disgust with the services they receive.

All experienced managers know just how difficult it can be to convince others to implement any type of change. Defining and maintaining a long-term commitment to deliver high-performance services can be even more demanding. For those firms that have mastered the means to achieve success, results are rewarding. For others contemplating the adoption of TQS, reflecting on the various theories of recognized experts may provide inspiration and direction. Despite the occasional (and inevitable) misuse of the term *quality* to sell books and create unrealistic expectations, several prominent world-class quality masters have positively influenced the direction of modern (post-1950) efforts. Their theories and strategies provide the basis for a more informed choice of available alternatives. First, however, a brief look at the evolution of quality control will provide a framework for the discussion of how modern service quality improvement (QI) concepts developed.

EVOLUTION OF QUALITY CONTROL CONCEPTS

Modern concepts of quality, productivity, and quality control evolved rapidly as major quality and productivity management theorists advanced the knowledge base of the field (see Figure 2.1). Quality control concepts were significantly influenced by the aforementioned inspection and product liability principles as well as (1) mass production, division of labor, and interchangeability of parts; (2) changes in management–labor relations and behavioral expectations within organizations; (3) the emergence of global markets; and (4) changes in prevailing social values, economies, and political conditions in different cultures.

Societal concern with the productivity of workers and quality of products and services can be traced back to ancient civilizations. Documents such as the Code of Hammurabi (2150 B.C.) show that society was willing to impose severe penalties to deter those who practiced unsafe production and service techniques. Under the code, if an unsafe dwelling collapsed and killed the occupants, the builder would forfeit his life.[1] The principle of retribution ("an eye for an eye") has been codified and substantially modified by modern liability insurance requirements. However, holding those who produce poor quality goods or services, which may cause injury, responsible for errors in the production or delivery process remains a powerful deterrent to assure the quality of residential and commercial construction.

Apprenticeships, guilds, and trade associations developed in the Middle Ages as early efforts to assure the quality of goods. The definition of quality standards was personal and individual—a contract between the artisan who produced the good and the consumer who purchased it. During the Industrial Revolution in the late 19th century, quality became bureaucratized, as government agencies began setting standards and inspecting the quality of mass-produced goods. Inspection of agricultural products and services, such as meat and poultry processing, followed in the early 20th century.

The need to improve productivity was recognized in the United States at the founding of the republic. Political economist Adam Smith advocated division and specialization of labor in his classic treatise *The Wealth of Nations,* first published in 1776. Eli Whitney made a significant contribution to U.S. productivity in the late 1700s with the interchangeability of musket parts, built in the same factory which first used Smith's specialization of labor concepts.[2]

Frederick Winslow Taylor's *Principles of Scientific Management* was published in 1911, about the same time Henry Ford applied Scientific Management concepts to the automobile assembly line. Under this approach, complex tasks were broken down into simple operations that could be performed by semi-skilled laborers. Highly technical products could be mass produced at lower costs, while inspection maintained quality standards. Management did the thinking, while labor did the work. Scientific Management rested on four underlying values which further reinforced the hierarchy: (1) efficiency in production: obtaining the maximum possible from a given investment of resources, (2) rationality in work procedures: the arrangement of work in the most direct relationship to objectives sought, (3) maintaining the highest levels of productivity possible, and (4) profit, which Taylor conceived (and Henry Ford enjoyed) as the ultimate objective of everyone within the organization (Gordon and Milakovich, 1995). Quality control was further depersonalized as a necessary part of the end-product inspection process.

Organizational management concepts were based on military and religious principles dating from ancient civilizations. Max Weber's seminal work on *The Theory of Social and Economic Organization* was written in 1922 but was not translated and published in English until 1947. The central themes of the Weberian model are discipline and control of behavior within organizations. Preoccupation with control lay at the heart of virtually every element of this formalized, closed system of organization. Rules, procedures, personnel files, and exercise of authority through a hierarchy reinforced the need for organizations to be "effectively" managed, i.e., for managers to tightly control behavior. Control over all organizational activities had to be exercised from the top down. Many organizations continue to use Weberian principles such as span of control, hierarchy, professionalism, and specialization of functions to maintain control and establish accountability. These closed systems were not designed to respond to customer needs but rather to "defeat" outsiders, enemies, and non-believers. The use of strict internal command and control structures required absolute discipline; independent judgment or empowerment in response to customer needs was explicitly forbidden.

Matrix organization was introduced in the late 1950s. Under a matrix structure, employees report to multiple superiors in separate control structures. For example, a construction engineer in the South American division of a large multinational firm would be simultaneously accountable to the head of the geographic division, the construction division, and the engineering division. All of these theories of organization implied a closed, formal structure dominated by a hierarchical superior–inferior relationship between management and the work force. Not only did these models actively discourage participation and customer responsiveness, but they also failed to encourage workers to interact with other employees or managers. Pleasing one's superiors, by any means, to advance one's own position in the hierarchy became the road to success.

Participatory or Theory Z management systems developed in response to the low productivity rates generated by the inspection-based hierarchical and matrix systems. Japan's post-war success with less control-dominated quality circles, team problem solving, and worker participation accelerated the movement toward the participatory organizational model (Ouchi, 1984). Since the 1960s, many American firms have applied a human relations approach to organizational behavior (MacGregor, 1960). By the late 1970s, as international competitors challenged U.S. manufacturers, concern with inspection-based quality assurance and production control re-emerged.

Historically, **quality assurance** (QA) was based on the need to carefully inspect end products to assure that they met predetermined standards and specifications. Preventing defective products from reaching the market protected manufacturers against liability. Since the early 1950s, W. Edwards Deming and others have criticized inspection-based quality control systems as costly and ineffective (Deming, 1982). Inspection can identify defective products only *after* they have been manufactured. The only action that can then be taken is to either rework the defective products or discard them. In either case, inspection-based quality control wastes resources and decreases productivity.

In service industries, where "output" is generally consumed at the point of delivery, end process inspection is even more wasteful and ineffective. Without a system to monitor performance at each point of customer contact, analysis of errors that lead to complications or dissatisfaction with the service encounter can be very costly, as well as ineffectual. In many instances, the documentation required to audit or reconstruct errors in service delivery processes exceeds the cost of the service. (Consider medical malpractice suits or any errors that result in litigation, for example.) How can the quality of the advice given by a physician to his or her patient be assured? The reason most often cited by plaintiffs (those bringing suit) for actions against physicians or hospitals is not lack of technical competence, but the *attitude* or treatment of the service provider, most of whom are licensed and therefore assumed to be competent to practice.

Inspection will always be one of the central concepts of quality control. It is increasingly obvious, however, that continuous quality improvement (CQI), especially in complex service delivery environments that require intense human contact, cannot be achieved by inspection alone. The shortcomings of inspection-based QA led to the development of concepts that emphasize the continual improvement of internal systems and processes to prevent the need for inspection.

CQI is achieved by training everyone, particularly customer contact workers, and building quality features into each step of service delivery processes. Therefore, *the CQI approach requires widespread employee participation.* While QA is based exclusively in the inspection division, process-control–oriented CQI requires the involvement of several divisions of an organization (for example, admissions, purchasing, customer service, and marketing), as well as the cooperation of all suppliers. The Japanese refer to this type of comprehensive system as **total quality control** (TQC) or **company-wide quality control** (CWQC). Company-wide participation is required because each division—as an internal customer—must participate in quality control activities. Moreover, CWQC includes employee-friendly aspects such as employee assistance plans, flextime, organizational restructuring, interorganizational agreements (in both the private and public sectors), and retraining employees for new responsibilities. In contrast to the Weberian "tall" hierarchical or more contemporary matrix approaches, CWQC emphasizes "flat" organizations, independent judgment, education for self-directed quality control, peer review, worker participation, and multilevel managerial leadership. The entire system is redefined to support those who assume responsibility for quality at each step in the process.[3]

In summary, QA is inspection based and aimed at minimizing defects in a product or service before delivery to an end user. Quality control uses sampling techniques to achieve the same end after the product or service is produced. Both TQC and CWQC seek to minimize defects during the production process, in order to achieve CQI. TQC, CWQC, and CQI are widely practiced in Japan. Understanding the theoretical basis for CQI as distinct from QA and quality control is important in making the transition from traditional to more advanced QI practices.

SELECTING QUALITY IMPROVEMENT STRATEGIES

U.S. business executives (in both large and small firms) now view quality or total quality management or QI as an important means to respond to customers. Definitions of these concepts vary considerably, however, depending upon their application. These terms are sometimes misused as hollow advertising slogans to demonstrate a commitment to end users or as a consultant's siren for generating higher profits.

Without a management system capable of monitoring quality control efforts, such a commitment represents little more than false advertising. When asked to show results with comparative statistics (facts and data that compare performance against the competition), many pseudo-quality efforts disintegrate. In time, companies practicing "cosmetic" quality soon fall behind the competition. Submitting quality management systems to rigorous neutral evaluations, such as that required for the Malcolm Baldrige Quality Award (MBQA), provides an objective basis for comparison between quality providers. (See the discussion in Chapter 5 and Appendix D for a description of the criteria used by MBQA examiners.)

Advocates of various approaches can point to success stories primarily, but not exclusively, in manufacturing. While service managers have used various productivity improvement methods such as profit sharing, work redesign, and suggestion boxes, the most revealing research on the application of these techniques is still based on manufacturing systems.[4] Although less frequent, service quality success stories are increasing as breakthroughs occur in various sectors formerly isolated from competitive quality considerations.

One insurance and financial services company that has been nationally recognized for its customer quality systems and use of benchmarking to identify improvement opportunities is United Services Automobile Association (USAA). USAA is the fifth largest provider of auto and homeowners insurance in the United States. Formed in 1922 by a group of Army officers who could not get private insurance on their automobiles, USAA serves military officers and their dependents and has grown to over 2 million members. USAA Federal Savings Bank has become the second largest Master Card provider in the nation (Gass, 1992; Spechler, 1993).

More than ever, service firms must demonstrate improvement efforts with statistically valid data, not necessarily based on one of the recognized quality awards, but at least from an independent and reliable source (for example, J.D. Power for automobile service, A.M. Best for insurance, or *Condé Nast Traveler* for hotels, travel, and tourism). Having a comparative basis to judge quality is especially important for services, because there are fewer examples to benchmark for successful applications. In addition, variations in internal processes tend to be greater. The lack of a tangible product (such as a car, radio, or TV) and consumption of the service at the time of delivery further complicates efforts to compare and evaluate performance over time. Nonetheless, methodologies are available, and service firms are increasingly willing to submit to the same rigorous examination standards as manufacturers.

Thousands of companies use various principles espoused by quality masters such as Philip Crosby, W. Edwards Deming, Maasaki Imai, Joseph M. Juran, Kaoru Ishikawa, and Shigeo Shingo. The major product or service, date(s) of origin, and theoretical basis used by several world-class U.S. corporations are provided in Table 3.1. The list is by no means exhaustive. These quality leaders

TABLE 3.1   American Quality Management Leaders

Organization[a]	Major product/service	Basis for quality[b]	Origin
AT&T Universal Card (MBQA)	Utility/communications	In-house*	1985
Corning Glass Works	Large manuf. high-tech	In-house***	1984
Eastman Kodak	Large manuf.	Crosby	1984
Federal Express (MBQA)	Package delivery	In-house	1987
Florida Power & Light (D)	Utility/electric power	In-house****	1981–89
Ford Motor Company	Large manuf. automobile	Deming	1979
General Motors (MBQA) X	Large manuf. automobile	Deming	1980
Globe Metallurgical (MBQA, S)	Small manuf. high-tech	In-house, SPC	1985
Milliken & Company (MBQA)	Large manuf. textile	In-house	1981
Motorola (MBQA)	Large manuf. high-tech	Juran–Crosby	1981
Nashua Corporation	Large manuf. high-tech	Deming	1980
NUMMI (GM/Toyota)	Large manuf. high-tech	In-house	1984
Ritz-Carlton (MBQA)	Leisure services/hotels	In-house	1991
3M	Large manuf. high-tech	In-house*	1979
United Service (USAA)	Insurance/financial services	In-house	1989
Xerox (MBQA)	Large manuf. high-tech	In-house***	1984

[a] D = Deming Prize winner, MBQA = Malcolm Baldrige Quality Award winner, S = Shingo Prize, X = Cadillac Motor Car Division won MBQA in 1990.

[b] * = dominated by Deming, ** = dominated by Juran, *** = dominated by Crosby, **** = dominated by Ishikawa–Juran. SPC = statistical process control.

have drawn from different theories to produce in-house strategies (as noted in the table). Many have been recognized as recipients of Japan's Deming Prize, the MBQA, or the Shingo Prize for Excellence in American Manufacturing. The origin and purpose of these prizes are described in greater detail in Chapter 5.

MASTERS OF TOTAL QUALITY IMPROVEMENT

Commitment to QI is rooted in the teaching, research, and consulting of five pioneering leaders of the quality movement: W. Edwards Deming, Joseph M. Juran, Armand V. Feigenbaum, Kaoru Ishikawa, and Philip B. Crosby. Their philosophies are not limited to the statistical management of quality alone. They are all leaders and teachers who encourage company-wide integration of purpose (vision), recognize the importance of process variation on job performance, and possess a genuine respect for people. All recommend a systems approach to improving quality, from the design, procurement, production, and delivery stages to service after the sale and consumer education. The remainder of this chapter provides an overview of the theories of these American and Japanese experts who advocate both statistical and behavioral (non-quantitative) approaches to motivate employees and respond to customers.

W. Edwards Deming (1900–1993)

An American raised at the turn of the century in Wyoming, W. Edwards Deming has been a hero to the Japanese for more than 40 years. Deming gained wide-spread recognition in the United States in June 1980, when NBC first broadcast the documentary "If Japan Can…Why Can't We?"

The Deming philosophy stresses that production processes and equipment must be designed to meet customer quality objectives. Blaming employees for producing poor quality products or services does no good unless all system causes of poor productivity have been eliminated. According to Deming, the management system (94 percent of the time), and not the worker, causes productivity problems, defective products, and poor quality service. Most workers are judged by performance figures which contain both common and special variation (detailed in Chapter 6), over which they have no direct control. It is top management's responsibility to provide employees with the proper training and tools to meet or exceed customer requirements. Top management is responsible for working *on* and continuously improving the system, while workers work *in* the system.

Deming further advocates the use of the plan-do-study-act cycle, a systems approach, cross-functional management, and the use of self-managed work teams

(Chapter 2). Not surprisingly, his theoretical formulations were considered too radical and were largely ignored by American business leaders until the 1980s.

Often using blunt and caustic language, Deming chided North American managers to (1) continually improve internal processes, (2) identify and meet the *valid* requirements of internal and external customers, and (3) minimize the influence of external processes unrelated to the extended process (see Figure 2.2) upon which the quality of the product or service is based. Resistance to his management philosophy (prior to the 1980s) provides a plausible explanation for the weak status of U.S. exports and the poor quality of services at home. Reasons for this ignorance differ, but include such explanations as:

1. Most U.S. corporate leaders were trained in accounting and finance, disciplines not generally recognized for valuing human assets, flexibility, and innovative thinking.

2. From the post-World War II era until the late 1970s, the United States had little if any competition from the recovering European and Asian economies, and therefore there was little incentive to change management systems.

3. Consequently, there was no need to systematically address customer-driven quality requirements, since any products manufactured by U.S. firms were assumed to be of high quality.

The dramatic loss of U.S. share of global markets for goods and services during the 1980s shows just how accurate Deming was in his predictions. One graphic and disturbing reason for the attitude change is the increasing loss of market share of basic U.S. industries, including automobile manufacturing, which was once dominated by U.S. producers (Figure 3.1). While U.S. automobile firms have become more competitive since the early 1990s, similar losses in market share have occurred in consumer electronics, computer chips, steel production, and a wide range of manufactured goods once dominated by U.S. producers. Under current economic forecasts, it will be very challenging for U.S. manufacturers to regain their dominance in many of these markets.

The Chain Reaction of Quality

The emphasis on quality as an *integrative* management function is based on Deming's **chain reaction of quality improvement**, a theoretical relationship first proposed in the late 1940s. Before Deming's theories were accepted in the United States, a common belief was that quality and productivity were inversely related. That is, if one is increased, the other must be decreased. The chain reaction of quality shows how improved quality reduces waste and rework and

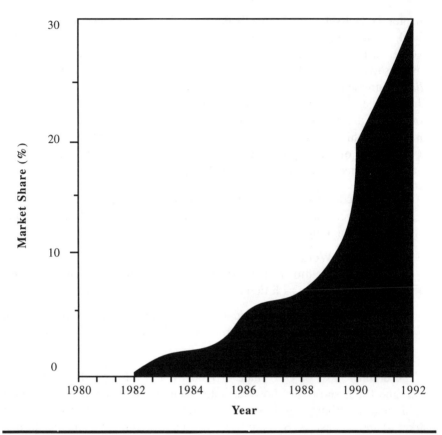

FIGURE 3.1   The Growing Japanese Share of North American Auto Production

increases efficiency with better use of people, time, materials, and equipment. Commitment reduces losses due to poor quality, pleases customers, increases productivity, expands market share, and secures jobs. Another result is increased sales through word-of-mouth advertising (Figure 3.2). Once a theory, the chain reaction of quality has become a reality in thousands of service organizations throughout the world (Groocock, 1986).

Deadly Diseases and Obstacles to Transformation

In his book *Out of the Crisis* (1986), Dr. Deming identified several "deadly diseases" of American management and prescribed his Fourteen-Point remedy to correct them (see Appendix B). Removing the causes of these diseases

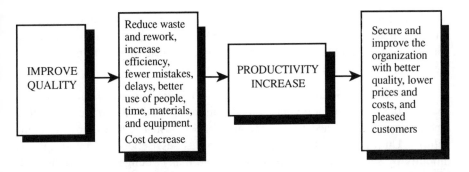

FIGURE 3.2   The Chain Reaction for Quality Improvement (*Source:* W. Edwards Deming, *Out of the Crisis,* Cambridge, Mass.: MIT Center for Advanced Engineering Study, 1986, p. 3)

can have profoundly positive effects because of the lingering "past sins" and current practices which diminish the quality of services, lower productivity, and distract employees from serving customers. The deadly diseases are as follows.

1. Lack of Constancy of Purpose.   This disease results from a failure to plan for services that will be needed in the future, provide leadership for change, and guarantee productive and rewarding future employment opportunities. One reason American firms lack direction is because management treats employees as replaceable assets, not unlike the physical plant or equipment. Under-investment in training further reinforces lack of employee motivation and poor service quality.

2. Short-Term Thinking.   Decisions are made on a short-term, often crisis-to-crisis, basis that reflects annual budget cycles and pressures for immediate profits. Predictably, continual improvement of processes, training of employees, and upgrading of services are ignored. Unless companies are on the verge of bankruptcy, senior managers have no incentives to guide the transformation to a quality-oriented work environment. Because they enjoy greater job security, it is in the best interest of management to support TQS as a means of enhancing job satisfaction and security.

3. Individual Performance Appraisal.   As commonly used, evaluations are a means to control and discipline the work force rather than improve performance. They rob management *and* labor of motivation, foster mediocrity, instill fear, prevent teamwork, and remove the intrinsic joy of work. Annual performance reviews and other internally competitive punishment–reward systems which lack methods for accomplishing objectives distract everyone from their primary mission of service to the customer. Often, those who conduct the performance reviews lack incentives to change because they were promoted to their current positions under the same system.

4. Mobility of Senior Management. Although less significant in recent years as the world economy has stalled, failure to "make the grade" in annual (short-term) performance ratings encourages senior managers to move to competitors. Until recently, the emphasis within business schools on rapid upward mobility by showing quick results encouraged many younger managers to "job hop" without becoming familiar with the critical functions in their current positions.[5] In the public sector, turnover of elected officials limits service quality and productivity efforts.

5. Managing by Numbers Alone. This practice is endemic to all types of service organizations, especially governments. Like the tip of an iceberg, numbers give only a superficial picture of the organization. Rather than relying on visible numbers (weekly worksheets, bank statements, hospital patient censuses, audits), managers must carefully study underlying processes to uncover the causes of losses from poor quality cost practices (see Figure 6.2). Substantial empirical research supports this assertion, and Deming's points 10 and 11 call for the elimination of numerical goals and quotas (see Appendix B).

6, 7. Excessive Medical and Liability Costs, Swelled by Lawyers Who Work on Contingency Fees.[6] Losses from unnecessary procedures, fraud, waste, and inefficiency in the health service delivery area alone equal nearly one out of every four dollars. With the national healthcare bill now consuming 15 percent of the gross national product and exceeding $1 trillion, losses from poor quality practices approach $250 billion! For most businesses, employee benefit costs alone exceed 50 percent of total net revenues. Worse yet, costs for employee health insurance in the early 1990s rose at the astronomical rate of 25 to 30 percent per year, in effect doubling every 30 months! The rate of increase has declined somewhat due to the threat of federal intervention, but malpractice fees and health insurance costs still consume a large share of business and government resources.

Compounding the problem is not only the legal profession's greed, but also the disregard for the patient's view of quality by many in the medical profession. Healthcare organizational cultures are often driven by the paternalistic notion that "management knows best." The self-serving attitude among many physicians—that only they can define the parameters of quality in healthcare—further limits customer-driven service quality. Healthcare service delivery is a complex mix of public and private sector resources, roles, and responsibilities. Efforts made by the public sector to reallocate resources are often resisted by the special interests that control those resources. The federal government subsidizes over one-half of the total dollars in Medicare, Medicaid, Veterans Hospitals, and other tax-supported healthcare programs. The Clinton administration's attempts to act in this vital area by implementing health security for all Americans has encountered resistance from many of those who benefit from these subsidies (see Chapter 8 for details).

The hope of applying industrial formula solutions to obtain sudden results, reliance on technology to solve problems, and inadequate testing of prototypes are all common barriers. Acceptance of Deming's methods is further limited by false starts, poor quality practices ("it's okay as long as it's within specifications"), blaming employees ("our trouble lies entirely in the work force"), excuses ("our problems are different"), and negative attitudes ("we installed quality control").

Applying the Deming Management Method

Leadership for change and knowledge of quality are viewed as critical responses to competition in world markets. Without greater knowledge of how to strategically manage quality, productivity will suffer, costs will rise, employee morale will plunge, and market position will decline. For those who listen, Deming offers an alternative.

In contrast to other QI strategies, the Deming method is a statistically based system that identifies process variation as a major problem. Various analytical tools such as run charts, histograms, cause-and-effect diagrams, and statistical control charts are used to identify the causes of and reduce variation. In what has become a classic statement of goals for an aspiring quality organization, Deming has summarized his recommendations for change into Fourteen Principles intended as a philosophy to transform American managerial thinking. He also asserted that service organizations can remedy the ills they face by implementing both statistical process control as well as behavioral management techniques to improve quality. Both are equally important, since it is "the synergistic implementation of all the [14] points that improves quality in a never-ending fashion".[7] In other words, knowing *what* to do is as important as knowing *how* to do it.

Deming's statistical methods show how variations are endemic to all systems and processes. In the Funnel Experiment, he demonstrated how adjusting a stable process by compensating for each observation results in greater variation than if no mid-process adjustments are made.[8] To further illustrate the random nature of process variation, Deming also devised the Red Bead Experiment, which is still used in his seminars. Each of six "workers" (seminar participants selected at random) stirs a mixture of 3200 white beads and 800 red beads and then removes 50 beads. Because red beads simulate defects, the object is to produce as many white beads as possible. The results in a typical experiment are:

	White	Red
Marsha	35	15
Bill	41	9
Barney	40	10
Michelle	46	4
David	43	7
George	41	9
TOTAL	**246**	**54**

Under traditional hierarchical management theory, if the number of white beads were to represent daily or monthly performance, Michelle (with 46) would be recognized as "Employee of the Month." Marsha, on the other hand (with only 35), would probably be demoted or fired. In fact, a simple statistical analysis of variation shows it was just luck that Michelle drew the high score.[9] Next month it could just as easily be David, George, or Barney. As long as flaws remain in the process, Michelle did nothing special to be emulated.

The Red Bead Experiment demonstrates statistically that about 85 percent of problems traditionally blamed on individual workers are the fault of the system in which the workers operate.[10] Deming's message is simple and clear: people should not be punished or rewarded for performance over which they have no control. All system causes of variation must be eliminated before individuals are blamed for poor performance.

In a TQS organization, teams of workers are fully trained as participants who aspire to become *owners* of work processes. As owners, they are empowered to anticipate and prevent errors from happening in the first place. Incentives and reward systems may be adjusted to enhance a work team's ability to eliminate causes of system problems.

Joseph M. Juran (1904–)

Statistical quality control expert, popular author, lecturer, and consultant Joseph M. Juran is another well-known leader of the quality movement. As editor-in-chief of the established quality control guide for industrial engineers,[11] Juran stresses that productivity gains will only be achieved through emphasis on quality. His pragmatic and mechanistic approach emphasizes rationality, analysis, diagnosis, and management processes to achieve what he calls quality "breakthroughs" to higher levels of performance (represented in Figure 2.7).

Unlike Deming, Juran offers few recommendations for changing organizational structures to accomplish quality goals. He is far less prescriptive than Deming in his recommendations for managerial change and defines quality as

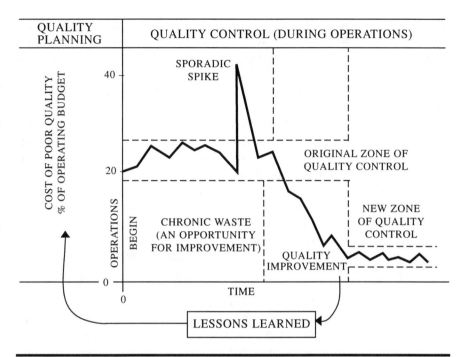

FIGURE 3.3   The Juran Trilogy (*Source:* Joseph M. Juran, *Juran on Planning for Quality,* New York: The Free Press, 1988, p. 12)

customer-based "fitness for use." Juran advocates translating this criterion into a language that is easily understood by the technicians who are responsible for detecting problems and monitoring and improving a process. In his classic definition (first mentioned in Chapter 2), he further divides quality into three components: design, conformance, and performance. The theoretical basis of Juranian quality control is the **Juran Trilogy**: planning, control, and break-through (Figure 3.3), which together form a cycle interlocked with a second cycle: the old standard, breakthrough, and the new standard. The Juran Trilogy is repeated in a never-ending cycle of continuous improvement. Proper quality planning yields processes that reduce the costs of poor quality by meeting quality control goals. This, in turn, leads to a new zone of quality control. Unlike Deming, Juran encourages organizations to manage by objectives and work toward defined goals. On this last point, as well as the need for performance appraisal, he and Deming strongly disagree.

The key to Juran's approach is that management can and must seek continual improvement in quality. He shares Deming's belief in the Pareto principle: at least 85 percent of a firm's quality problems are management controllable.

Management, therefore, is most in need of change that results from breakthroughs, which emerge from the following sequence: (1) convince others that a breakthrough is needed; (2) separate the vital few from the necessary many problems, activities, variables, and characteristics;[12] (3) organize for breakthroughs in knowledge; (4) conduct an analysis to discover the cause(s) of the problem; (5) determine the effect of the proposed changes on the people involved, and find ways to overcome resistance to these changes; (6) take action to institute changes, including training of all personnel involved; and (7) institute appropriate controls to hold new improved quality levels but not to restrict continued improvement, perhaps through another breakthrough sequence.

In services, breakthroughs involve evaluating actual performance, comparing it with a standard, and adjusting the difference. Planning deficiencies contribute to chronic waste, and stricter control processes would reduce this waste. Similar to the Japanese *kaizen* (CQI) approach, this approach goes beyond quality control by breaking through to higher levels of performance. The basic sequence involves breakthroughs in attitude, knowledge, culture, and results.

Breakthrough in Attitude. Rather than reacting to a crisis, Juran believes that changes in quality attitude must be based on fire prevention rather than fire fighting. Attitudes should reflect a willingness to innovate, to enlist change agents within the organization, and to encourage leadership and creative solutions to problems.

Breakthrough in Knowledge: Diagnosis. This step includes problem identification and problem solution techniques (Figures 2.4 to 2.6) as well as flattening the hierarchy. Non-hierarchical participation is essential to diagnosing the cause of system problems. Clearly, those closest to the customers are best able to diagnose and respond to customer needs.

Breakthrough in Cultural Patterns. This breakthrough includes seven steps: (1) planning, including participation by advocates, those affected, and third parties (for balance and objectivity); (2) eliminating technical and cultural baggage not needed for change; (3) working with recognized leadership of corporate culture; (4) treating everyone with dignity; (5) reducing the impact of changes by weaving them into an existing pattern of behavior or acceptable other change; (6) using empathy by putting yourself in the other person's place; and (7) making use of a wide variety of methods to deal with resistance to change.

Breakthrough in Results. This breakthrough includes six steps: (1) set up a steering group to organize the drive; (2) convince people of the importance of safety, cost, and quality; (3) show everyone how to contribute to safety, cost, and quality; (4) solicit ideas from everyone; (5) establish goals for improvement and a scoreboard to follow progress; and (6) incorporate new techniques into standard operating procedures.

During each of the "standard" periods, a manager should encourage activities aimed at eliminating the root causes of **special variation,** when any observation falls above a preset upper control limit or below the lower control limit of a process control chart.[9] When special variation is eliminated, a process is said to be in statistical control. The next step is identifying the root causes of special variation. To prevent a recurrence of the problem, statistical tools, especially Pareto analysis, are required.

Detecting a problem is the first step toward greater process control and reduction of variation. Some mechanism is needed to scan performance and to convert the data monitored into communicable language. This is referred to as a "sensor," or detecting device which recognizes certain stimuli and converts the data into information (useful knowledge). In service organizations, where contact with customers is often direct, human beings act as sensors. The sensor should use a system of measurement to compare actual performance with a preset standard. The comparison becomes the basis for decision making. The **feedback loop** is an excellent technique for improving participation and establishing team standards. Organizational feedback consists of components such as a **sensing device**, which detects what is occurring; a **control center**, which compares data collected with the **nominal** value of a quality characteristic; and a **motor device**, which adjusts a process as necessary to bring results in line with standards. A **monitor** determines whether or not a stable process exists, and a **steering arm** directs "the discovery, dissemination, and subsequent use of new knowledge." Feedback is provided by a **diagnostic arm**, which is responsible for the design of experiments, collection and analysis of data, and interpretation of data (Juran, 1988, pp. 85–100). In services, these tasks are especially important to monitor because they are typically performed by line-level customer service employees and by supervisors who monitor interactions with customers.

Juran and his associates also advocate **statistical process control** (SPC), **statistical quality control** (SQC), and **management by self-control** (MSC), where employees and managers establish and monitor performance objectives. SPC uses statistically valid methods for the collection of statistics and provides feedback. SQC is the use of scientific quality management to perform quality control instead of QA. **Scientific quality management** is the philosophy that everything about any task necessary to meet valid customer requirements can be measured. This is not the same as Frederick Winslow Taylor's **Scientific Management,** according to which there is one "best" way to do any task (Taylor, 1911). MSC, which was the original idea behind Peter Drucker's **management**

by objectives, occurs when managers negotiate quantitative objectives and performance measurement criteria with superiors and then receive the autonomy to execute (Sedell, 1991).

While less prescriptive than other quality gurus in ultimate goals, Joseph Juran offers very specific suggestions for managers to create a stimulating environment:

> (1) never ask an employee to do something without explaining what and why first, (2) never tell how to do something without first asking the employee how he/she thinks it should be done, and (3) either tell the employee what result you want and leave the method to him/her, or explain what you want to be done and assume responsibility for the result (Juran, 1989, pp. 272–273).

Armand V. Feigenbaum (1920–)

In 1951, decades ahead of its application in either manufacturing or services, A.V. Feigenbaum defined total quality control (TQC) as the "composite product and service characteristics of marketing, engineering, manufacture, and maintenance through which the product and service in use will meet the expectations of the customer" (Feigenbaum, 1983, p. 7). Feigenbaum is a mathematician best known for originating the concept of TQC, which he explains as follows:

> The underlying principle of the total quality view, and its basic difference from all other concepts, is that to provide genuine effectiveness, control must start with identification of customer quality requirements and end only when the product has been placed in the hands of a customer who remains satisfied. Total quality control guides the coordinated actions of people and information to achieve this goal (Feigenbaum, 1983, p. 11).

As a harbinger of today's intensive customer-friendly services, Feigenbaum recognized that significant gains would be made only when quality control systems were applied to white-collar services. In contrast to Juran and Deming, Feigenbaum initially placed the responsibility for quality control with the makers of the part or the providers of the service rather than top management of the organization. In recent years, he, like Deming and Juran, has become increasingly critical of top management's reluctance to initiate QI systems.

Feigenbaum was an early proponent of the idea that doing it right the first time is cheaper in the long run than inspecting for defects. His rationale for such breadth of scope is his view that quality is influenced at all stages of what he calls the "industrial cycle." The cycle's stages are marketing, engineering (design), purchasing, manufacturing engineering, manufacturing supervision, shop operations, inspection and testing, shipping, installation, and service. Like Deming and Juran, Feigenbaum also recommends the use of statistical methods such as histograms, control charts, sampling tables, linear and multiple regression analysis (including t-tests and F-tests), cumulative curve probability graphs, Taguchi experiments, and design of experiments to better control processes. He further suggests that a feedback cycle should be applied to each of the above eight steps of the industrial cycle.[13]

The hidden plant and under-capacity scheduling are two other important concepts developed by Feigenbaum which apply equally well to services. The **hidden plant** is the proportion of plant capacity that exists in order to rework unsatisfactory parts. **Under-capacity scheduling** refers to providing enough time to do the job right instead of maximizing output without concern for the quality of the output. Feigenbaum clarified quality costs and with his example of the hidden plant estimated that the proportion of total capacity that exists in order to rework unsatisfactory parts (the hidden plant) ranges from 15 to 50 percent. This estimate is likely to be higher for most service organizations.

Kaoru Ishikawa (1915–1989)

Kaoru Ishikawa was a highly respected Japanese authority who acknowledged the influence of Deming, Feigenbaum, and Juran on his thinking. Ishikawa made several original contributions toward understanding processes and implementing change. He proposed the **quality control circle** (QCC) in both concept and practice to encourage participation and attention to detail by all workers ranked at or below the level of foreman. A QCC is a small work unit (seven to ten members optimum), with a facilitator, that meets to identify actual problems, potential problems, and solutions. A QCC addresses problems using an eight-step process:

1. Determine the problem.

2. Select the subject for discussion.

3. Fix a time limit.

4. Study the present situation (using the basic tools).

5. Analyze the factors.

6. Work out a policy (using brainstorming, scenario writing, etc.).

7. Implement a policy.

8. Confirm the result.

The idea behind the QCC is that there is no one in the organization who knows a production or service task better than the individual worker who actually performs that task. A similar approach, aimed at shifting the burden of quality from the inspector to the worker, is the *saratov* system, used in the former Soviet Union. Other approaches are the Polish *debra robota* (good work) and the German *ohne fehler* (without defects) systems. All of these systems are variations on the theme of worker self-management, a suspect ideology during much of the Cold War and, therefore, resisted in the United States.

The formation of a quality circle starts by providing training in SQC and opportunities for the work force to participate. The quality circle is strictly a *voluntary* group which meets on company time at scheduled intervals to discuss possible projects that could lead to improvements in quality. Once these projects are selected, the circle as a group sets priorities and implements solutions through the use of the quality story technique. (See Chapter 5 for a description of the quality story technique applied to an American public utility.)

Although the QCC has developed a bad reputation with some U.S. firms, there has been a resurgence of interest in it and a realization that it was not the concept but rather its execution as a fad during the 1970s that was faulty (Bowman, 1989).

In the first decade of their use in Japan, the number of QCCs exceeded five million. Because the average saving per group was thousands of dollars, the effect of quality circles has been widely felt in Japan. (Case Study 3.1 offers insight into the strengths and weaknesses of the QCC.)

Kaoru Ishikawa, Maasaki Imai, Shigeo Shingo, and Genichi Taguchi are well-known advocates of the Japanese school of CWQC. When it comes to cost–benefit analysis (in terms of both the organization and society as a whole) applied to productivity, procurement, and materials testing issues, the work by Genichi Taguchi is recognized worldwide. Taguchi defines quality in terms of maximizing the net benefit to society in cost–benefit terms (Taguchi and Clausing, 1990). The basics of Taguchi methodology are taught to every industrial engineer in the free world, and the methodology is spreading to newly democratized Russia and Eastern Europe. Advanced Taguchi methods have been used in both the private and public sectors in Europe and Japan by engineers and statisticians trained in TQC and/or CWQC. Similar in methodology to the Deming method, CWQC seeks to set the nominal, eliminate special variation, and reduce common variation. Once a process is under statistical control, it is possible to reduce variation even further by locating and eliminating causes of common variation.

Case Study 3.1

Quality Control Circles: They Work and Don't Work

Quality control circles, so spectacularly successful in Japan in recent years, hold little promise of short-term gains. They take generations to bear fruit and cannot be expected to succeed if they are ordered by edict. Moreover, the scope of their achievement, though impressive over time, is limited.

A QC circle is a group of about ten relatively autonomous workers from the same division of a company who volunteer to meet for an hour or so once or twice a month. After work (usually they are paid overtime), they discuss ways to improve the quality of their products, the production process in their part of the plant, and the working environment. Their long-term objective is to build a sense of responsibility for improving quality, but the immediate goal is to exchange ideas in a setting uninhibited by barriers of age, sex, or company rank.

Japan's experience has revealed several preconditions for the success of QC circles. Some may be indigenous.

First, the work force must be intelligent and reasonably well-educated. Members of the circles must be able to use statistical and industrial engineering analysis. They must know what it takes to make things work on a nuts and bolts level, and they must be able to brainstorm together. It is no coincidence that the Japanese companies that have been most successful with these circles and other participatory methods for improving productivity (Hitachi, Teijin, Asahi Glass, and Nippon Kokan) are also well-known for their fine recruiting and internal training programs.

Second, management must be willing to trust workers with cost data and important information and to give them the authority to implement their ideas. At Japanese companies with successful QC programs, managers have tended to work their way up through the ranks. They really believe in their work force. It is no surprise to them that groups of workers, if given information and authority to experiment by trial and error, will be able to reduce downtime, waste, or reworking the sorts of questions that the circles are most effective in addressing.

Third, workers must be willing and eager to cooperate with each other. Unlike the suggestion box and other worker incentive programs that reward individuals, QC programs reward groups. A genuine "team spirit" is therefore necessary. Workers must be willing to express themselves and find fulfillment by reaching an agreement. Moreover, if authority in production decisions is to be decentralized down to the level of these circles, then the circles have to be able to cooperate with each other lest they work at cross-purposes. Unless there is a spirit of cooperation within the work force, an attitude that talking a problem through with peers is more rewarding than taking it up to management, a company is better off using individual carrots instead of the circles. Otherwise, it may find night shifts undoing the improvements of day shifts.

One of the most important features of QC circles in Japan is that they did not originate with senior management. They spring rather from a voluntary, grass-roots movement of workers and middle managers from across the nation.

The spearhead has been the Union of Japanese Scientists and Engineers, or Nikka-Giren. In 1962 it began publishing a magazine, later named *FQC*, which called for QC circles among factory workers and foremen and helped precipitate a change from the Western concept of QC as the prerogative of technical experts. The magazine circulated widely among industrial workers, who bought it themselves (it cost them about the same as a pack of cigarettes), rather than receiving it through their employers, and read it together—in a circle. The magazine, together with a generation of supervisors familiar with QC concepts from the 1950s, helped initiate massive training for non-supervisors.

The Nikka-Giren Union continues to have great influence. It publishes case histories of successful QC circles and sponsors regional and national conferences, where circle participants from different companies share their experiences.

Since most Japanese companies are very secretive with each other, this openness seems a paradox. But the movement was initially popular in the steel and ship-building industries, where there was a tradition of letting other companies freely inspect production methods and facilities. Had the movement started in the Japanese camera or auto industry, it is doubtful whether the current openness and cross-fertilization would have developed. Today, cross-fertilization is one of the keys to the success of the circles in Japan—the exchanges not only encourage but also keep workers interested in the process.

QC circles don't run themselves. They must be revitalized. Most important is the specific set of goals they are given and a strong manager who coordinates QC circle changes with corporate objectives. In companies that use both the suggestion box and QC circle, management can gather directly from workers ideas that may require significant capital expenditures and at the same time use suggestion box successes to encourage QC circle efforts.

Management spends more time today on sustaining existing circles than starting new ones, understanding that their effects are incremental and cumulative. In 1951 Toyota received 700 proposals from its new worker participation program. Today it gets 500,000 per year, which saves a reported $230 million.

But there are limits to what the circles can do. The abrupt quantum leaps in cost reduction that the Japanese have achieved in industries as diverse as steel and consumer electronics do not result from QC circles. Instead, they come from major strategic decisions about new technologies and plants and entirely new ways of producing and delivering a product.

At Ricoh, for example, it wasn't a circle that figured out how to redesign the business system by changing the technology manufacturing and marketing to completely change the game in plain paper copiers. Nor was it the circles that led to the elimination of inventory and the Just-in-Time "Kanban" System at Toyota. QC circles, composed of workers from a single division, can't come up with these bold strokes.

A Single-Minded Focus

Nor can they replace strategy. Indeed, in many industries a single-minded focus on productivity improvements and concomitant QC activities may be less important for success than focused R&D and targeted marketing.

QC circles work best when they are part of what the Japanese call total quality control, which embraces concerns about the entire spectrum of a business. And they are one of a number of productivity improvement techniques that work best when put together. As the Japanese would say, it's like collecting dust to make a mountain. But somebody has to envision the mountain and know which way the wind is blowing.

Source: Kenichi Ohmae, *Wall Street Journal,* March 29, 1982, cited in Malcolm Golden, "Quality Concepts, Statistical Analysis and Modern Techniques of Quality Improvement," unpublished paper, Management Science Department, University of Miami, June 1990

Following Ishikawa's death in 1989, Noriaki Kano of Tokyo University has become increasingly recognized as a leader of this school (Lillrank and Kano, 1989; Kano, 1993). Genichi Taguchi (1986) defines quality in terms of maximizing the net benefit to society in cost–benefit analysis terms. CWQC uses SPC, SQC, and the **total care concept (TCC)** for both quality assurance and quality control.[14] Maasaki Imai (1986) advocates teaching all workers an attitude of *kaizen* to achieve CQI at the level of the individual employee. The late Dr. Shigeo Shingo (1986, 1989) served as president of Japan's Institute of Management Improvement and created many of the internationally know features of Toyota's just-in-time production system. Shingo is also credited with developing the concept of *poka-yoke,* which allows manufacturing companies to fail-safe their processes from human error (Shingo, 1986).

While crediting Feigenbaum for his development of the TQC concept, Ishikawa favors an extension beyond the quality profession. Feigenbaum includes all company divisions in his call for TQC, while Ishikawa argues that there is not enough reliance on contributions to quality from non-specialists. In 1968, Ishikawa began using the term CWQC to differentiate the Japanese approach to TQC from the more specialized and hierarchical view attributed to Feigenbaum. The exchange of views has caused both to evolve, and today the terms TQC and CWQC are used almost interchangeably. Feigenbaum, Ishikawa, and Deming favor a total, company-wide involvement in the commitment to quality.

In his revealing book entitled *What Is Total Quality Control? The Japanese Way* (1985), Ishikawa reflects philosophically on why the Japanese were more successful than Western industry in applying QI concepts. He suggests that quality control in the West was delegated to a few staff specialists or consultants, and then only when a crisis forced Western leaders to consider options.[15] In most U.S. organizations, crisis resolution fire-fighting is the basis for promoting and rewarding managers. In contrast, the commitment to quality in Japan has been total and lasts throughout the company's life. Fire prevention is encouraged and rewarded as well.

Philip Crosby (1926–)

The youngest and least statistically driven of the quality masters, Philip Crosby was corporate vice-president of ITT for 14 years. He is presently a consultant, lecturer, and author of several popular books, including *Quality Is Free* (1979). The concept of this book, which explains his overall approach, is that:

> Quality is free. It is not a gift, but it is free. What costs money are the unquality things—all the actions that involve not doing jobs right the

first time. Quality is not only free, it is an honest-to-everything profit maker. Every penny you don't spend on doing things wrong, over, or instead becomes half a penny right on the bottom line" (Crosby, 1979, p. 2).

Crosby's philosophy is based on four primary ideas which he calls absolutes:

1. **The definition of quality is conformance to requirements.** The output must conform to design, and the design and price must conform to customer requirements.

2. **The system of quality is prevention.** Do it right the first time. Use fire prevention instead of fire fighting.

3. **The performance standard is zero defects.** Eliminate the practice of issuing waivers and variances. Do not use sampling tables or the acceptable quality level.

4. **The measurement of quality is the price of non-conformance,** or the cost of poor quality, which Crosby estimates as "20 percent or more of sales in manufacturing companies and 35 percent of operating costs in service companies" (Crosby, 1984, pp. 85–86).

His approach to quality, which he simply calls **quality management,** is guided by 14 steps (see Appendix C) and stresses individual and organizational changes rather than SQC. His method involves three primary management tasks: (1) establish the requirements that employees are to meet, (2) supply the wherewithal that the employees need in order to meet those requirements, and (3) spend time encouraging and helping the employees to meet those requirements.

Crosby's approach represents a very different concept of quality management. Like Deming, he emphasizes that organizations must be committed to building quality into the culture of the company rather than relying on inspection to minimize defects. In contrast to the numbers- and variation-based approaches of Deming, Juran, and Ishikawa, Crosby's method is based on individual attitude, awareness, and a more behavioral–managerial orientation. Crosby stresses that quality means "conformance to requirements" and proposes "zero defects" as a goal. He criticizes one often-used figure, the **acceptable quality level** (AQL), which originated in manufacturing and is widely used in services. He says that an AQL is not really a standard or target, but instead a commitment to produce a certain amount of imperfect material—before delivery or production is even started. It is simply acceptance of the status quo and is inconsistent with the commitment to continuous improvement. Taking the consumer's view, Crosby makes his point quite clearly:

Consider the AQL you would establish on the product you buy. Would you accept an automobile that you knew in advance was 15 percent defective? 5 percent? 1 percent? One half of 1 percent? How about the nurses that care for newborn babies? Would an AQL of 3 percent on mishandling newborns be too rigid? (Crosby, 1979, p. 146)

Too many service organizations continue to accept a certain percentage of errors or defects. The acceptable range is usually from 1 to 5 percent, depending on the type of business. Even 99.9 percent is not good enough, especially if you are among the unlucky one-tenth of one percent whom the error affects. When it comes to critical processes, less than 100 percent simply is not good enough. If other vital services accepted the 99.9 percent AQL standard:

- 22,000 checks would be deducted from the wrong bank accounts in the next 60 minutes
- 18,000 pieces of mail would be lost or delivered to the wrong address every hour
- 2 unsafe aircraft landings would occur at major airports every day
- 25,000 prescriptions for drugs would be incorrectly filled each year
- 500 defective medical procedures would be performed by surgeons each week
- 2 million documents would be lost by the IRS this year

The quest for zero defects is endless, especially in critical services such as healthcare, government, and education, where the continued use of AQLs results in low performance standards.

SUMMARY AND CONCLUSIONS

Following their exportation to the United States in the early 1980s, quality management principles spread rapidly, if unevenly, in American firms. Different theories competed for the attention of service organizations seeking to improve their quality. Rarely consistent in their definitions, some are strongly associated with a single theorist, while others are based on hybrid theories that reflect several approaches.

From the early 1950s to the late 1970s, the quality ideal was nurtured by visionaries in the field of quality management. While the specifics of their philosophies differ, pioneers such as W. Edwards Deming, Joseph Juran, A.V.

Feigenbaum, Kaoru Ishikawa, Philip Crosby, and their students have positively impacted businesses and consumers alike. They preached the quality gospel at a time when few American leaders listened. Ironically, while most of the early work in SQC was done by Americans, U.S. industry leaders were unwilling to initiate the management changes required to implement customer-driven QI until Asian and European competitors gained market share. For many markets, this change was too little too late to save American jobs.

Direct Japanese investment and the spread of Japanese companies worldwide boosted the movement to raise total product and service quality in the United States.[16] The Japanese shrewdly avoided the criticism that buying foreign products is un-American by constructing manufacturing plants and hiring workers in the United States. The cars and auto parts produced at these "transplants" meet the same quality standards as those produced in Japan. This is further evidence that QI concepts and techniques, when properly applied, will succeed with any well-trained, motivated, and empowered work force. The Japanese deserve credit for the application, implementation, and subsequent refinement of quality management techniques. Without their competitive challenge to American industry, it is unlikely that the current push toward TQS would have occurred as soon as it did—if at all.

Each quality master has contributed important insights, ideas, and terminology to the discipline of service quality improvement. Those organizations that understand the strengths and weaknesses of various QI strategies are better able to customize their TQS applications. Approaches that merely admonish the work force to adopt the 8 or 10 or 14 commandments of quality without changing the underlying organizational culture in which they must be implemented tend to be frustrating, short-lived, and unsuccessful.

In practice, most organizations "shop" for an approach that best suits their needs or "mix and match" elements from various schools, often creating new hybrid schools in the process. In the end, it is less what is *said* and more what is *done* to achieve internal process changes that allow trained and committed employees to act in the interest of customers. Having outlined the basics, we now turn to the organizational changes and training needed for service organizations to reach high-performance status.

ENDNOTES

1. Kostas G. Zografos, "Integrating Total Control and Quality Assurance Concepts in Construction Project Planning," unpublished research paper, Department of Civil Engineering, University of Miami, June 1990.

2. Samuel T. Coleridge first documented use of the term "productivity" in the early 1800s. Toward the end of the 19th century, modern industrial systems emerged. J.B. Clarke first used the concept of productivity to refer to a ratio of outputs to inputs in 1899.

3. Toyota has a system in which 98 percent of its employees submit suggestions, with a 95 percent acceptance rate; the ratio of suggestions to total employees was 360 to 1 in 1990. Globe Metallurgical, a 1988 MBQA winner, and Saturn Automotive have employed similar systems with positive results. Such a cooperative work optimization procedure allowed 1988 MBQA winner Motorola and its suppliers to reduce the time required to fill a phone order for a cellular telephone from an average of 40 days to an average of 2 hours! While the results in service applications may be less spectacular, significant successes can be achieved with greater employee participation.

4. There is clear evidence from the automotive manufacturing sector that the "quality gap" between American and Japanese products may be closing. Ford Motor Company and Cadillac Division of General Motors have been recognized for their quality successes (Table 3.1). The joint GM/Toyota New United Motor Manufacturing Industry (NUMMI) plant in Fremont, California and the General Motors Saturn automobile assembly plant in Spring Hill, Tennessee have received extensive media attention as well. In the 1992 J.D. Power automotive owner satisfaction survey, Saturn ranked third behind the Japanese luxury cars Lexus and Infiniti. Other widely cited examples of successful quality companies in the United States are AT&T, Corning Glass, Federal Express, Milliken, 3M, Ritz-Carlton, and Xerox.

5. This contrasts sharply with the traditional Japanese practice of lifelong employment and loyalty to one's primary employer. Economic recession in Japan has ironically required employers to modify this promise in recent years.

6. The United States is the only advanced industrialized nation that does not offer universal healthcare to all its citizens. The lack of a healthy work force has been associated with the lack of competitiveness in many American industries. A more detailed analysis of the significance of this problem for U.S. service quality and productivity is presented in Chapter 8.

7. Howard S. Gitlow, Shelly Gitlow, Alan Oppenheim, and Rosa Oppenheim, *Tools and Methods for the Improvement of Quality,* Homewood, Ill.: Irwin, 1989, p. 15.

8. This can be accomplished by first making a target by marking an "X" on a convenient surface. Then place a funnel in a holder so that the end points towards the X. Drop a marble through the funnel and place a dot where it rests. Repeat as many times as desired. There are many possible combinations for adjusting the funnel between drops, but it can be shown mathematically that the best results will be obtained by not adjusting the funnel at all. This experiment demonstrates the danger of overcontrol and shows that only the most carefully reasoned changes in a stable system can improve quality. Repeatedly tampering with the system only makes thing worse.

9. Consider the following statistical analysis. The average number of red beads (defects) per worker is $546 \div 9$. The overall percentage of red beads to total beads extracted is $54 \div 300 = 18\%$. The upper control limit is (average number of defects) + $3\sqrt{}$(average number of defects) × (1 − percentage of defects), or $9 + 3\sqrt{9} \times (1 - 0.18) = 9 + 3\sqrt{7.38} \approx 17.15$. The lower control limit is $9 - 3\sqrt{9} \times (1 - 0.18) = 9 - 3\sqrt{7.38} \approx 0.85$. Thus, someone would do exceptionally well if he or she drew 50 white beads. Someone would do exceptionally poorly if he or she drew less than 33 (50 − 17) white beads. The range from 33 to 49 white beads represents common variation. Calculations are drawn from an

unpublished research paper by Ken Sedell, Department of Political Science, University of Miami Public Administration Program, revised Summer 1990.

10. For details of the Red Bead Experiment, see Deming (1986), pp. 110–112, 346–350, and 459–464.

11. *Juran's Quality Control Handbook,* 4th edition, Frank M. Guyna (Assoc. Ed.), New York: McGraw-Hill, 1988.

12. The vital few are the causes that generate a majority of the problems. Typically, the vital few constitute 20 percent or less of the items on a Pareto diagram yet account for 80 percent or more of the problems. The necessary many constitute the remaining problems.

13. The feedback cycle is a never-ending cycle that includes the following steps: (1) planning what should be done, (2) measuring whether it is being done, and (3) analyzing how to improve the plan.

14. Under the Japanese TCC, employees are divided by seniority into permanent status and those on probation. Permanent employees receive full company benefits and services, including the use of an in-house travel service and assistance in locating child and elderly care facilities, placing children in schools, and locating housing. Job enhancements such as dual career couple recruiting and employee assistance plans (EAPs) are also used as incentives under TCC. The spouse in a dual career couple is assisted in finding employment either within or outside the organization, and in some cases both are offered jobs as a package deal. Under most EAPs, employee files are inaccessible to supervisors. Employees with problems (stress, alcohol, drugs, etc.) are entitled to receive appropriate counseling and treatment (Sedell, 1991).

15. This opinion is not shared by Americans, who recognize the value of CQI and accept the costs of training the entire work force in teamwork and the basic statistical methods necessary to apply concepts to complex service organizations.

16. Discussions with Professor Duane Kujawa, Miami, Florida, October 1989. For elaboration, see Duane Kujawa, *Japanese Multinationals in the United States: Case Studies,* New York: Praeger, 1986 and Duane Kujawa and Daniel Bob, *American Public Opinion on Japanese Direct Investment,* Survey Report of the Japan Society, July 1988.

4

ENCOURAGING TOTAL QUALITY HUMAN RESOURCES: PARTICIPATION AND TRAINING[1]

High-performance service leaders successfully practice total quality service (TQS) by anticipating customer needs and continuously responding to their environments. As a result, leading firms in various service sectors reap such benefits as increased market share, cost savings, higher customer satisfaction, and reductions in complaint rates. Some of these firms (and sectors) include AT&T (communications); Disney (entertainment); FedEx (delivery); Knight-Ridder (publishing, information systems); L.L. Bean (mail order); Metlife, New York Life, Paul Revere, and United Services Automobile Association (diversified finance and insurance); and Hyatt, Marriott, and Ritz-Carlton (hotels) (Spechler, 1993).

Within any organization, the interaction of employees and customers with equipment, surroundings, policies, procedures, and technology influences how quality is delivered. To allow for system-wide improvement, training in TQS must be participatory and process oriented, as opposed to the more traditional control-based and results-oriented approaches such as management by objectives (MBO), planning-programming-budgeting-system, and, when outputs fall short of goals, management by exception. Training in this new way of thinking (Table 2.1) about customer, employee, manager, and supplier relationships is critical to the success of organizational change strategies.

The implications of TQS for human resource management, organizational behavior, and training to encourage participation and overcome resistance within internal work cultures are explored in this chapter. The purpose of training is described as an interactive model that links the leadership, teamwork, customer orientation, and statistical management capability of an organization (see Figure 4.1). This conceptual model represents an alternative to traditional results-oriented, fear-based, numbers- and control-driven systems which emphasize reinforcement of authority, centralization, hierarchy, performance appraisal, ranking employees, and MBO.

CHARACTERISTICS OF TOTAL QUALITY HUMAN RESOURCE MANAGEMENT

Some still mistakenly assume that service quality improvement cannot be accurately measured because it is composed primarily of human resources (people) and human behavior is inherently too difficult to change. In the past, that may have been an excuse (or the truth) in some businesses. Service processes are often more complex, less tangible, and more difficult to measure. Nonetheless, quality improvement (QI) in services increasingly depends on participation and training.

Organizations frequently rotate their employees through training seminars to learn techniques for customer service QI. Many also maintain schools or training centers to orient new and existing employees in corporate policies, standard operating procedures, and working culture. Because behavioral change is explicitly or implicitly a goal of TQS, modifications of attitudes, behaviors, perceptions, and authority systems are part of any training exercise. The TQS training goals, guidelines, and their implications for organizational development and training are discussed here. These guidelines could be incorporated into any training exercise for service organizations interested in the critical human and behavioral change aspects of TQS (the seven elements of TQS described in Chapter 2).

TQS is a comprehensive approach which includes a wide range of subsystems referred to as hardware, software, and humanware (Kano and Gitlow, 1989). The level of service experienced by a customer results not only from the human interactions between customer and provider, but from the combination of three sources as well, each of which provides legitimate areas to measure and improve. TQS reflects customer satisfaction with:

1. **Physical surroundings:**   Furnishings, structures, and equipment are tangible factors that can be measured as any manufactured product would be. For example, a broken bed in a hotel room, the cleanliness of a rental car, a bus or aircraft in need of maintenance, and a faulty transformer all impact service quality. When customers report the need for maintenance improvements, the system must respond. The time it takes from reporting the need to making the repair is as valid and reliable an indicator as the customer's satisfaction with the person sent to make the repair.

2. **System processes:**   Procedures, policies, and software are less visible but no less important as valid sources of satisfaction or dissatisfaction with services. The software for a computer information system, check-in and check-out policies at a hotel, police procedures for responding to citizen complaints, and airline reservation systems are all examples of various measurable system processes. These elements are more difficult to measure, but they may be the most important factors in terms of overall customer satisfaction.

3. **Human resources:**   People, personnel, and training are perhaps the most variable but nonetheless important components in responding to customer preferences. The actual service provided by an employee, such as repairing a car or aircraft, filling out a claim form, booking a reservation, or correctly reading a utility meter, often determines customer satisfaction. Training for performing tasks required to exceed customer expectations is essential. *Without adequate systems, tools, and the knowledge to perform the task, even the best intentioned and most motivated employee will fall short of customer (and probably employer) expectations.*

When measured against valid customer needs, the success of nearly all service organizations begins and ends with its people. Regardless of how well a system of quality and productivity improvement is designed, it is the responsiveness of an organization's human resources in applying the technology, distributing resources, interpreting rules, serving customers, and producing value-added processes that ultimately determines the level of performance. Continuously improving quality systems without the active participation and full cooperation of everyone who is affected virtually guarantees failure. This is why the top-down "do-it-or-else" approach may succeed initially but fails in the long run to change underlying organizational behavior.

TQS can be understood in terms of its priorities, nature, and orientation. Perhaps the most striking feature of TQS is that it makes the *needs of the customers* and the *quality of work life for employees* its priorities (Romero-Simpson, 1990). Leadership, planning, and policies must reach beyond the traditional short-term immediate profit-making approach geared solely toward a limited number of interested parties (usually boards of directors and stockholders) and aim instead at changing the organizational subculture to reward customer-directed service QI.

The human resource training necessary to understand and apply TQS principles requires active participation in **cross-functional teams** or **task forces** aimed at overcoming traditional barriers to participation and cooperation (Milakovich, 1991). The purpose of such teams is to identify and solve problems that cut across different staff areas by forming work groups with representatives from each responsible work unit. Groups are led by a **facilitator** or lead team member who is trained in organizational behavior, statistics, and group dynamics and chairs team meetings and interacts with other lead team members.[2] Employee participation, cooperation, and cross-functional teams are clearly as important to management in the 1990s as MBO, quality control circles, and performance appraisals were to administration in the 1980s.

In summary, achieving TQS involves training and development in dynamically interrelated human and technical subsystems through a closely knit organizational value structure oriented toward constantly improving customer service processes and systems. This integrated approach is a significant departure from the more specialized compartmentalized management systems used by most organizations. Thus, TQS requires a different style of training based on total quality improvement guidelines.

TOTAL QUALITY IMPROVEMENT GUIDELINES

The following guidelines were chosen on the basis of values and principles discussed in previous chapters:

1. Unwavering commitment to the customer

2. Recognition by management of quality and a willingness to accept responsibility for the well-being and improvement of the system

3. Accepting the crucial role of education and self-improvement in accomplishing the change

4. Teaching the spirit of *kaizen* or constant improvement through the efforts of the entire work force

5. Adopting a process orientation (as opposed to a results orientation)

6. Developing and emphasizing the importance of a stimulating environment which is free of fear

7. Implementing a team-based approach to cross-functional management and breaking down internal barriers to cooperation

8. Using communication channels rather than relying on regulation or inspection to overcome obstacles, improve the system, and achieve quality

9. Thinking systemically and using appropriate statistical tools to measure and control variation

10. Personal commitment to the diffusion of TQS based on a conviction of its value by each employee (Romero-Simpson, 1990)

It is clearly beyond the scope of this book to describe the full extent of quality training required to implement TQS within a particular service organization. The preceding ten principles of TQS form the basis for the teaching philosophy in any training course on human resource development. In this chapter, these principles are posed as questions to be answered by the members of any organization seeking to gain a commitment (Guideline #10) to implement TQS.

In most training activities (short-courses or workshops), students, instructor(s), classrooms, and available resources comprise a learning systems environment which consists of several interconnected processes. The main purpose is to constantly improve learning processes through the joint efforts of the participants and the instructor. *The ultimate goal is to empower each employee with the confidence and knowledge to meet or exceed customer requirements.* In the learning environment, all participants are expected to maximize self-improvement opportunities as well as contribute to the development of improved versions of similar training courses in the future.

Guideline #1:
Is the organization committed to its customers?

As noted earlier, the term *quality* has many different definitions, dimensions, and interpretations (Garvin, 1984, 1988). Throughout this chapter, quality is defined as a pervasive concern with developing the human resources of an organization or work unit. This concept reflects the continuous commitment to improving the environment in which work takes place, sometimes known as **quality in daily work**. This is one component of a TQS strategy aimed at increasing the productivity of a service work force by improving the quality of working conditions.

TQS practitioners must perceive the customer as the center of their activities, and other employees, policies, and systems must be responsive to customer needs. This is a fundamental premise. In discussing this assumption, Peter Scholtes (1988), one of the best-known quality practitioners, who also once served as a city manager, writes, "…an organization's goal is to meet and exceed customer needs by giving lasting value to the customer. The return will follow as customers boast of the company's quality and service." In essence, the goal is to create satisfied employees and customers who then become an extension of the marketing and advertising efforts of the organization.

Implications of Guideline #1

Everyone with whom the organization has contact is viewed as a current or potential customer whose needs must be anticipated, met, or exceeded. Those who undergo training play the role of internal customers who are eventually responsible for process improvement and external customer satisfaction. This approach reflects the extended process of suppliers and customers (see Figure 2.2) and illustrates how all voices of the process are linked together as part of an integrated service delivery system (see Figure 2.3). Communicating how the seemingly isolated decisions of individual internal customers (employees) add or detract value as "moments of truth" when serving external customers is another key to successful TQS transformation (Carlzon, 1987; Liswood, 1990).

This lesson is important not only for training, but for customer retention as well. Not only does it cost five times less to keep a current customer than to acquire a new one, but complaints from customers reflect only a small fraction (less than 10 percent) of the estimated number of dissatisfied customers. This means that for every vocally dissatisfied customer, there are at least ten others who, for various reasons, do not register complaints about the offending service. Many who do not bother to complain just disappear. Others complain to their friends, neighbors, and business associates, who often repeat the negative comments. This informal, word-of-mouth marketing network can result in significant loss of business, especially for small or medium-sized service firms. For non-profits and public agencies, negative interactions often generate mountains of paperwork in the form of complaints, appeals, investigations, grievances, and unnecessarily duplicative efforts.

The reverse is also true. Satisfied customers generate new customers by making positive comments about the service received. Accurate data are difficult to obtain, but a single satisfied customer can positively influence the buying decisions of many other potential customers.

Customer responsiveness training should be designed to satisfy the learning needs of all participants, which hopefully will extend beyond obtaining a certification, positive evaluation, or higher ranking. If employee learning needs are understood and met, then the learners/workers will change their behavior in relation to those they must satisfy. They will internalize the principles, behave in a manner consistent with them, and recommend them to others (both fellow employees and prospective customers). Thus, instructors are encouraged to perfect their learning systems (workshops or courses) as examples to fulfill the present and future needs of other internal and external customers.

Guideline #2:
Is management committed in word and in deed
to quality and willing to accept responsibility
for the well-being and improvement of the system?

As more service industries develop their high-performance skills, leadership efforts consume a greater share of senior management's time and effort, perhaps as much as one-quarter in initial start-up phases. Awareness, knowledge, and understanding of basic TQS principles and concepts is no longer optional; it is required of most senior executives. The ultimate payoffs from commitment to service QI can be substantial. Without top-level involvement, valuable training and implementation resources are wasted.

At the Ritz-Carlton Hotel Company, winner of the 1992 Malcolm Baldrige National Quality Award, employee commitment to total customer satisfaction requires not only executive support, but adherence to customer service standards, detailed planning, and quality data as well. As described in Case study 4.1, once these "Gold Standards" were achieved, the hotel chain received widespread recognition as a quality provider in an extremely competitive industry.

In order to initiate, learn, and sustain a quality transformation, visible commitment from top management is absolutely crucial. This principle is perhaps the most important one for change agents to keep in mind when pursuing organizational transformation (Bennis and Nanus, 1986). Once there is commitment from top management, *maintaining credibility* with employees is the single largest problem for management; management can never underestimate how often its commitment needs to be reinforced. If employees detect inconsistencies or perceive mixed messages in terms of the company's commitment to quality or if management fails to meet established requirements, then management's credibility suffers.

Implications of Guideline #2

In any learning environment where new skills and work habits are being taught, the instructor represents management. Thus, consistency and commitment in this role are crucial as well. Instructors must be well versed in company quality policy and able to communicate clearly and effectively. Like any good teacher, the course instructor should lead by example, "walk the talk," and become a role model to his or her students. It is extremely important for the instructor's behavior to be consistent with the principles taught in class. The instructor should constantly operate under a TQS framework throughout the duration of the training. In several companies, senior executives have taken the lead and taught others. This becomes a vehicle for understanding TQS as well as a tangible example of company-wide commitment.

Case Study 4.1

1992 National Quality Award Winner: The Ritz-Carlton Hotel Company

The Ritz-Carlton Hotel Company aims to succeed in one of the world's most logistically complex and competitive service businesses. Targeting primarily industry executives, meeting and corporate travel planners, and affluent travelers, the Atlanta-based company manages 25 luxury hotels that pursue the distinction of being the very best in each market they serve. It does so on the strength of a comprehensive total service quality program that is integrated into marketing and business objectives.

Hallmarks of the program include participatory executive leadership, thorough information gathering, coordinated planning and execution, and a trained work force that is empowered "to move heaven and earth" to satisfy customers. Committed employees rank as the most essential of these elements. All employees are trained in the company's "Gold Standards," which set out Ritz-Carlton's service credo and basics of premium service.

The Ritz-Carlton: A Snapshot

The Ritz-Carlton Hotel Company is a management company that develops and operates luxury hotels for W.B. Johnson Properties, also based in Atlanta. In 1983, W.B. Johnson acquired exclusive U.S. rights to the Ritz-Carlton trademark, the name associated with luxury hotels for 100 years. The Ritz-Carlton Hotel Company operates 23 business and resort hotels in the United States and two hotels in Australia. It also has nine international sales offices and employs 11,500 people. Two subsidiary products, restaurants and banquets, are marketed heavily to local residents. The company claims distinctive facilities and environments, highly personalized services, and exceptional food and beverages.

"Gold Standards"

Quality planning begins with President and Chief Operating Officer Horst Schulze and the other 13 senior executives who make up the corporate steering committee. This group, which doubles as the senior quality management team, meets weekly to review the quality of products and services, guest satisfaction, market growth and development, organizational indicators, profits, and competitive status. Each year, executives devote about one-fourth of their time to quality-related matters.

The company's business plan demonstrates the value it places on goals for quality products and services. Quality goals draw heavily on consumer requirements derived from extensive research by the travel industry and the company's customer reaction data, focus groups, and surveys. The plan relies upon a management system designed to avoid the variability of service delivery traditionally associated with hotels. Uniform processes are well defined and documented at all levels of the company.

Key product and service requirements of the travel consumer have been translated into Ritz-Carlton "Gold Standards," which include a credo, motto, three steps of service, and 20 "Ritz-Carlton Basics." Each employee is expected to understand and adhere to these standards, which describe processes for solving problems guests may have as well as detailed grooming, housekeeping, and safety and efficiency standards. Company studies prove that this emphasis pays dividends to customers and, ultimately, to Ritz-Carlton.

The corporate motto is "ladies and gentlemen serving ladies and gentlemen." To provide superior service, Ritz-Carlton trains employees with a thorough orientation, followed by on-the-job training, and then job certification. Ritz-Carlton values are reinforced continuously by daily "line-ups," frequent recognition for extraordinary achievement, and performance appraisal based on expectations explained during the orientation, training, and certification processes. "To ensure problems are resolved quickly, workers are required to act at first notice—regardless of the type of problem or customer complaint. All employees are empowered to do whatever it takes to provide "instant pacification." No matter what their normal duties are, other employees must assist if aid is requested by a fellow worker who is responding to a guest's complaint or wish. Much of the responsibility for ensuring high-quality guest services and accommodations rests with employees. Surveyed annually to ascertain their levels of satisfaction and understanding of quality standards, workers are keenly aware that excellence in guest services is a top hotel and personal priority. A full 96 percent of all employees surveyed in 1991 singled out this priority, even though the company had added 3000 new employees in the previous three years.

Detailed Planning

At each level of the company—from corporate leaders to managers and employees in individual work areas—teams are charged with setting objectives and devising action plans, which are reviewed by the corporate steering committee. In addition, each hotel has a "quality leader," who serves as a resource and advocate as teams and workers develop and implement their quality plans. Teams and other mechanisms cultivate employee commitment. For example, each work area is covered by three teams that are responsible for setting quality certification standards for each position, problem solving, and strategic planning.

The benefits of detailed planning and the hands-on involvement of executives are evident during the seven days leading up to the opening of a new hotel. Rather than opening a hotel in phases, as is the practice in the industry, Ritz-Carlton aims to have everything right when the door opens to the first customer. A "7-day countdown control plan" synchronizes all steps leading to the opening. The company president and other senior leaders personally instruct new employees on the "Gold Standards" and quality management during a two-day orientation, and a specially selected start-up team composed of staff from other hotels around the country ensures that all work areas, processes, and equipment are ready.

Guideline #3:
Are education and self-improvement recognized as means to accomplish change?

Education is defined in *Webster's New World Dictionary* as "the process of training and developing the knowledge, skill, mind, and character, especially by formal schooling; teaching; training." Self-improvement is defined as "improvement of one's status, mind, abilities, etc. by one's own efforts." Change denotes a making or "becoming distinctly different and implies either a radical transmutation of character or replacement with something else."

Education for self-improvement requires the acquisition of specific technical knowledge as well as learning new attitudes, behaviors, and skills to build mind

Quality Data

Daily quality production reports, derived from data submitted from each of the 720 work areas in the hotel system, serve as an early warning system for identifying problems that can impede progress toward meeting quality and customer satisfaction goals. Coupled with quarterly summaries of guest and meeting planner reactions, the combined data are compared with predetermined customer expectations to improve services. Among the data gathered and tracked over time are guest room preventive maintenance cycles per year, percentage of check-ins with no queuing, time spent to achieve industry-best clean room appearance, and time to service an occupied guest room.

From automated building and safety systems to computerized reservation systems, Ritz-Carlton uses advanced technology to its full advantage. For example, each employee is trained to note guest likes and dislikes. These data are entered in a computerized guest history profile that provides information on the preferences of 240,000 repeat Ritz-Carlton guests, which results in more personalized service.

The aim of these and other customer-focused measures is not simply to meet the expectations of guests, but to provide them with a "memorable visit." According to surveys conducted for Ritz-Carlton by an independent research firm, 92 to 97 percent of the company's guests leave with that impression. Evidence of the effectiveness of the company's efforts also includes the 121 quality-related awards it received in 1991 and industry-best rankings by all three major hotel rating organizations.

Source: Malcolm Baldrige Award, U.S. Department of Commerce, 1992

and character. This cannot be a passive experience; a display of personal effort is required. Some have compared this to a religious experience or metamorphosis. Education helps smooth the transformation process, and training is seen as a means to fit people with jobs and responsibilities for which they are best suited. In addition, a personal commitment to advance these principles is required from those who undergo training.

Employee training is the essence of effective QI. Questions every U.S. manager should ask himself or herself are:

■   Was I ever trained for my job?

■   Who trained me?

■ When was I last trained for my current position?

■ Were my subordinates or staff ever trained for their jobs?

■ Who trained them?

■ Do I really know what the jobs of my subordinates entail and are their duties accurately reflected in their job descriptions?

■ Do I even know where their job descriptions are?

■ When did I last revise *my* job description?

■ Does my boss know what I do?

■ Do I agree with my job description and job classification?

Efforts to increase participation such as labor–management committees, labor–management task forces, and quality control circles are all part of, and originated from, the quality movement. Without TQS to support team efforts, the tendency is for group efforts to become diffuse and unfocused. At the same time, too much control can stifle creative solutions to problems presented to empowered teams of employees. Reflecting a longer-term view of the importance of the human resources needed to increase productivity, a Japanese factory has negligible output the first 6 to 12 months after it would be considered operational by U.S. standards. That additional time is spent training workers in all aspects of company-wide quality control. Every employee is trained to do her or his job; learn who his or her customers, subordinates, superiors, and suppliers are; and understand fellow employees' jobs (Imai, 1986).

Implications of Guideline #3

In a time of drastic change,
it is the Learners who inherit the future.
The Learned find themselves equipped
to live in a world that no long exists.

Eric Hoffer

An established technique, known as **experiential learning**, is particularly well suited for TQS training. Experiential learning is defined as "the process whereby knowledge is created through the transformation of experience" (Kolb et al., 1984), and it is appropriate for QI training because it (1) is geared toward continuous change, (2) requires the learner to take an active rather than a passive role in his or her learning, and (3) goes beyond the immediate classroom environment yet can be enhanced in the classroom. Several critical elements of the learning process can be enhanced by the experiential perspective.

The first aspect of experiential learning is emphasis on the process of adaptation and learning as opposed to the content or outcome of the learning process. Knowledge is viewed as a transformational process which is continuously created and recreated rather than an independent entity to be acquired or transmitted. The second aspect is that learning transforms experience in both its objective and subjective forms. Finally, in order to understand learning, the nature of knowledge itself must be understood. Rather than being passive recipients of information, everyone assumes an active role in transforming the educational process itself. This is often difficult for American workers who have been trained since elementary school to be passive recipients of knowledge in a non-participatory learning environment.

Guidelines #4 and 5:
Does the organization practice *kaizen*
and continuous process-oriented learning?

Although each concept has its own separate definition and identity, *kaizen* and process improvement go hand in hand. Together, they help focus the entire organization toward customer-driven QI. *Kaizen* is a process rather than a results-oriented concept, with a "people" as opposed to a budgetary or financial orientation. Teaching everyone to be aware of process improvement opportunities requires changing organizational as well as individual behavior. To reiterate, familiarity with problem identification and process control tools is also necessary. The extent to which those tools and techniques are data- or statistics-driven depends upon the nature of the service offered and the complexity of the processes being improved.

Organizational behavior has been defined as "the study of the behavior, attitudes and performance of workers in an organizational setting; how the organization and subgroup impact the worker's perceptions, feelings, and actions; the environment's effect on the organization and its human resources and goals; and the effect of the workers on the organization and its effectiveness" (Cohen et al., 1992; Szilagyi and Wallace, 1990). Thus, changing organizational behavior(s) must be viewed within a broader context of factors that dynamically interact with each other.

The basic unit of analysis is the individual worker who deals with his or her own expectations and those of the organization. Perhaps the most complex unit is the organization's dynamic interaction with its environment. The field also contains units of intermediate complexity such as interpersonal communication, formal and informal groups, teamwork, organizational change, and work redesign. In quality-managed service environments, all these elements must be integrated within a systems perspective (see Figure 2.6) as leadership focuses on strategy, planning, redesign, and implementation.

This open systems model of organizational behavior and change represents a dynamic rather than a static vision of the organization as it interacts with its environment (Thompson, 1967). Throughout the process of developing new and better quality-related solutions to team-defined problems, creative efforts should be focused not only on producing completely new knowledge, but on combining traditional knowledge with new knowledge in small steps that gradually improve processes.

Implications of Guidelines #4 and 5

During training, instructors must constantly improve the learning systems (training sessions and workshops) for which they are responsible, just as operations managers are responsible for constantly improving the systems under their control. Also, the learner/student is responsible for maintaining standards and taking the initiative to suggest positive changes to improve the system. This forms the basis of team-based problem identification and reduces the need for external control and evaluation.

An important objective of any training exercise is to encourage participants to "learn how to learn" within realistic, work-related situations. The focus of a TQS-oriented course should be to constantly perfect processes that lead to system learning. This may be accomplished through the joint efforts of the different student teams and the instructor (i.e., simulating the entire work force). Everyone must convey an attitude of respect toward each other as fellow customers and suppliers. The instructor must deliver each topic enthusiastically and maintain a strong belief in QI along with the learning process. If such an attitude prevails, the spirit of *kaizen* will be translated into observable behavioral changes. Once this spirit has been conveyed, it should be nourished so that it transcends the training sessions and permeates the organization.

Guideline #6:
Is the work environment stimulating and free of fear?

After having been exposed to the basics of TQS, it is difficult to believe that anyone, regardless of his or her position, would question the benefits of a non-stressful, stimulating, and secure work environment. It is not uncommon, however, to experience high stress levels and non-stimulating environments in many different organizational settings. This reality, combined with personal and family pressures, results in increased absenteeism, family breakdown, drug and alcohol dependencies, disability claims, and excessive healthcare expenses. Training efforts must not only promote the spirit of continuous improvement, but also address and eliminate the underlying causes of stressful work environments (Ryan and Oestreich, 1991).

Among the most important research in organizational behavior is that of Abraham Maslow, who wrote of **self-actualizing** workers achieving the highest degree of self-fulfillment on the job through maximum use of their creative capacities and individual independence (Maslow, 1954). Maslow viewed workers as having a hierarchy of needs and suggested that each level has to be satisfied before a worker can go on to the next one.

The first level is physiological needs: food, shelter—the basic means for survival. Next is minimum job security, or a reasonable assurance (but not necessarily a guarantee) of continued employment. Following these essentials come social needs: group acceptance on and off the job and interpersonal relationships that are positive and supportive. Ego satisfaction and independence needs represent the fourth step in Maslow's hierarchy; these are derived from accomplishments in one's work and public recognition of one's accomplishments. Finally, Maslow's highest level is self-actualization, or feelings of personal fulfillment that result from independent, creative, and responsible job performance.

As the worker satisfies the needs of one level, he or she is seen as being further motivated to work toward satisfying the needs of the next higher level. Thus, Maslow emphasizes interactions among the essential needs of the employee on and off the job, the work being done, the attitude of both management and the employee toward work performance, and the relationship among employees in the work situation. The hierarchy of needs, like other theoretical formulations in the application of approaches referred to as organizational humanism, assumes that worker satisfaction can be affected by many factors in the organization, both close to the work situation itself and more distant from it; the theory does not assume that all workers will be motivated by the same set of needs (Gordon and Milakovich, 1995, p. 134).

Frederick Herzberg, another influential organizational theorist, proposed the Dual Factor Theory, in which two independent sets of factors account for worker dissatisfaction and satisfaction (Herzberg, 1966). The first set of external factors are basics: minimum conditions which include adequate hygienic facilities in the workplace and proper illumination, ventilation, and space. The second set of internal (or motivational) factors are more important to individuals. If external factors are properly managed, there should be no cause for dissatisfaction among the workers. However, external factors are related to basic needs such as fringe benefits, salary, security, group identity, and social needs. Internal or motivating factors are related to the higher-level self-actualizing needs that contribute to worker satisfaction. One such factor is the comfort experienced by a worker when there is compatibility between skills, preferences, and the specific nature of work. Recognition for achievement, responsibility, and pride stemming from a service rendered are more significant motivating factors for most workers.

According to Herzberg, because these intangibles are the more satisfying aspects of one's job, they are far better motivators than more tangible behavioral rewards such as pay for performance, bonuses, or additional fringe benefits. Alfie Cohen (1993) suggests that rewards actually punish workers by destroying the intrinsic value of the work itself. He suggests that growth and individual development are derived from the job itself and that most people not only work to live, but live to work. External factors should be carefully controlled to prevent dissatisfaction at work, and internal factors should be properly managed to promote job satisfaction. High-performance service organizations go one step further.

Because training should be aimed at improving worker identification with the primary mission of the organization, any kind of system improvement related to either external or internal factors should trigger positive feelings in the entire work force. These feelings would originate from the commitment to an organization that has a value-related mission and thus takes on some of the characteristics of a political cause or social movement. Thus, internal work-related stress is minimized when management and employees communicate openly, humor rather than fear is encouraged, jobs are well-defined, compensation is adequate for the tasks expected, and workers can relax or exercise during the day.

Managing Fear in the Workplace

Never tell people how to do things.
Tell them what you want to achieve
and they will surprise you with their ingenuity.

General George S. Patton, 1944

To some extent, all employees are apprehensive about some elements of the workplace. Merely trying to do one's best creates some degree of anxiety. This is a natural, physiologically based concern about the quality of one's work. Protracted anxiety, defensiveness, and negative fear caused by overcontrol and unnecessary command structures is (or should be) of more concern to quality managers. To reduce the consequences of this latter type of fear, management must establish "long term goals that are consistent with the new philosophy" (Gitlow and Gitlow, 1987). Reflecting Deming's management method, workers are not blamed for faults inherent in the system. Rather, their opinions and suggestions are valued by management as a way to improve the system. Only when employees sense that management can be trusted do they become less defensive and more honest and open in discussing barriers that hinder job performance. Only after elements of fear are removed can workers be properly trained and treated with dignity and respect. They are then more likely to treat customers with the same degree of respect and courtesy.

Implications of Guideline #6

The following factors contribute to a more stimulating learning environment and to effective training:

1. A *clear specification of objectives* must be offered at the beginning. All participants should have an opportunity to ask questions, resolve any doubts they may have, and contribute their suggestions. It is important that the nature of the training is understood and procedures consistently followed. It is also important that all participants are involved during the entire instructional process; this can be accomplished by requesting and offering immediate feedback throughout the course.

2. Training should be designed so that everyone can realize the advantage of immediate feedback as measured by the level of mastery of the subject matter. Because of their previous experience as students, some may place a greater emphasis on grades. It is important that participants shift that emphasis to a *sense of pride and accomplishment in learning how to learn*. This is accomplished to a great extent via **personal application assignments** (PAAs), which are written goal statements designed to reflect learning from a specific exercise, knowledge of the readings, application to real situations, and self-knowledge. They become the basis for workshop participants to express problems in such a way that they can be addressed by other team members (Romero-Simpson, 1990).

3. An *atmosphere of openness* to questions and suggestions from the participants and *enthusiasm toward learning* should be strongly encouraged from the beginning of the course. This should enhance commitment to achieve course goals, to the objectives, and to the procedures being followed.

4. *Learning should stem from experiences* (structured situations and simulations) to which individuals can relate. Work groups should be encouraged to develop problem-solving and process improvement exercises from their own unit's daily work experiences. (If the training is held on campus in the work facility, then the opposite problem may occur. Too many daily work problems could interfere with the workshop.)

5. Participants should be given an opportunity to *discuss the experiences* related to a specific topic as team members and in the light of different theoretical models (Deming, Juran, and Crosby, as described in Chapter 3).

6. Everyone should be given an opportunity to state the *practical implications and limitations* of the subject matter in the light of his or her present and future supervisory or managerial experience.

Although some anxiety can enhance learning, dysfunctional levels of fear can inhibit constructive learning. Fear in a learning environment, as in the workplace, can actually hinder a person's capacity to realize that there is a need for improvement, to discern its real nature, and to generate possible solutions. Past educational experience may precondition some when entering an on-the-job learning environment. Many are fearful of getting a low grade or being criticized by the instructor if they say the wrong thing. In a competitive environment, some may also fear their own associates. They may also be afraid of themselves and how they perform under pressure. This reflects upon the interactions they might engage in within an organization. They do not know their own strengths and weaknesses.

Many have also been taught by past educational experiences to be passive recipients of the instructor's knowledge. Few attended classes with the conviction that they will actually learn useful concepts. Thus, they merely take notes and prepare for quizzes and exams. In any TQS course or training activity, a special effort is made to link the material to be learned to the actual needs and expectations of the learners, taking into account their specific problem-solving styles. Interactive learning and team-based evaluations result. Grading or ranking of participants, if done at all, should reflect quality management principles and interactive learning environments.

Suggested Strategy

Training should be as relevant and interesting as possible in light of the objectives to be accomplished. Although not all employees are self-starters, special efforts should be made to encourage intrinsic motivation and thoroughly enjoying the process as well as the results of learning. In order to accomplish this, the following are suggested: (1) the terminology should be geared toward the learner's level of experience, (2) concepts should be explored within situations familiar to the learners, (3) participants should take active responsibility for their own learning and problem solving (PAAs are useful for this purpose), and (4) the classroom should become a stimulating environment in which transactions among students and between students and the instructor are the rule rather than the exception (Romero-Simpson, 1990). In an organization committed to TQS, this could involve "creative backtalk" between workers and managers at all levels. Indeed, the freedom to express concerns about necessary process improvements cannot take place in a work environment where there is fear of reprisal for comments that may at first be considered to be negative. (Recall the preceding discussion of safe channels for complaints to relieve worker frustrations with workplace conditions.)

Guideline #7:
Is teamwork used to determine
how to meet or exceed customer expectations?

Breakthroughs to higher levels of organizational performance are most likely to be achieved by team effort. Some of the other benefits that can be attributed to the team approach are meeting social needs, fulfillment of ego needs, and self-fulfillment. Self-motivated and properly trained teams eventually increase organizational responsiveness to all customers, both internal or external.

Peter Scholtes (1988) expresses the rationale for teamwork as follows:

> Where once there may have been barriers, rivalries, and distrust, the quality company fosters teamwork and partnerships with the work force and their representatives. This partnership is not a pretense, a new look at an old battle. It is a common struggle for the customers, not separate struggles for power....The notion of a common struggle for quality also applies to relationships with suppliers, regulating agencies, and local communities (Scholtes, 1988, pp. 1–13).

Implications of Guideline #7

Workshop participants should be organized in teams according to their specific learning needs and problem-solving styles. This should be done very early in the training session. Every topic is approached within a team and among teams. The careful matching of teams by problem-solving style may reduce variations attributable to differences in style and minimize the homogeneous outcomes that are prone to emerge from each team. This is a useful strategy to reduce common causes of variation attributed to individual differences in work styles and varying ability to work with others.

Guideline #8:
Are communication channels other than
inspection used to overcome obstacles,
improve the system, and achieve quality?

TQS involves the entire work force in a never-ending process improvement. It inherently requires leadership, mutual trust, and open communication. Mass inspection, on the other hand, according to W. Edwards Deming "...is an attitude born out of mistrust, misunderstanding and failure to monitor and improve the process." Mass inspection must be modified because it fosters fear and distrust. What is the alternative, then, to achieve goals and maintain standards? As mentioned earlier, using teams as human sensors to develop feedback loops within the work team is one feasible alternative.

Implications of Guideline #8

The traditional grading system in schools is comparable to organizational inspection policies (checking at the end to determine whether the student has in fact memorized the material) as well as performance appraisals. Gitlow et al. (1989) use Deming's classic Funnel Experiment (see Chapter 3) to illustrate the absurdity of such procedures to improve organizational quality. They show how performance appraisals are a form of *overcontrol* based on common or random system variation. Performance appraisals can artificially increase system variation in a significant way. Alternatives to traditional performance appraisal are now available to organizations concerned about the destructive competition fostered by individual performance review. Under a quality evaluation system, the entire organization is considered a system of interlocking processes. The institution rather than the individual employee becomes the object of performance improvement (Bowman, 1994).

Another point is that inspection and performance appraisal, like grading, do not reflect learning if learning is equated with problem solving. Typically, those being tested are reinforced for recalling the right response or for recognizing the correct response among several multiple-choice answers. Concept memorization and concept recognition, however, are just two of many components that are present in the learning process.

Inspection devices such as quizzes, exams, and ranking workshop participants should be minimized in light of the above arguments, among others. It is important, however, to realize that many of those in training will have been conditioned by the present educational system, which relies heavily on individual grading procedures. Many participants may find it difficult to understand learning without quizzes, exams, and grades. Thus, the complete absence of these devices could generate a great deal of confusion and possibly lead to dysfunctional effects. Quizzes may be used during the early stages to benchmark acquisition of technical information and to gauge retention of critical skills needed to solve problems. However, they should account for only a small proportion of the final evaluation (less than 25 percent). There should be a gradual transition from quizzes, to problem-solving exercises, to the use of PAAs. Also, the emphasis of the evaluation should shift from individual performance to team performance assessed via a feedback loop similar to that described above.

Detecting Devices, Pinches, Measurement, and Information Lines

Using Juran's terminology, each service worker becomes a "detecting device" to recognize possible "pinches," or situations which the Japanese call *warusa-kagen* (things that are not yet problems but are still not quite right). Left untended, they may develop into serious problems. *Warusa-kagen* are often the starting point for improvement activities identified by team members. Communication or feedback between management and the employees must encourage immediate action to deal with any problems that may emerge. (Recall Ritz-Carlton's efforts to "move heaven and earth" for customers.) In the instructional setting, all participants should be encouraged to bring forward their concerns and questions in order to clarify any issue related to the content of readings, classroom procedures, and expectations *before* the learning experience begins. Thus, each team plays the role of a "measuring and analysis station" by processing information and critically evaluating it.

Establishing a non-threatening atmosphere in the workshop allows participants to bring their concerns, doubts, and frustrations out into the open. Such "pinches" should be dealt with as soon as possible by the instructor and fellow students as a team. Team-focused activities become useful as "control centers" by comparing and contrasting actual behavior with ideal or stipulated behavior.

Finally, the PAA is a highly useful tool and is quite compatible with the TQS process orientation. PAAs become the *information lines* between the participants (workers) and the instructor (management). The assigned PAA evaluation should reflect the balance between the different stages of the learning process (feeling, observing, thinking, and acting). PAAs are ideal for such a purpose. They also promote participation and may include such criteria as discipline, time management, skill development, participation, involvement, and communication (Imai, 1986). The final stage, active experimentation, is particularly useful as a "motor device." In this stage, the student describes the specific steps he or she intends to take as a result of his or her experience pertaining to the specific topic of concern. The PAAs then become "learning contracts" and a basis for measuring and evaluating future progress.

Guideline #9:
Is systems thinking used to measure and eliminate variation?

In a quality-managed service organization, management's key mission is to lead in the direction of never-ending and continuous improvement, pursued by continual reduction of variation in an organization's processes. By closely monitoring the process using statistical methods, management can determine if its various subsystems exhibit common or special variations. Failing to deal with the system in statistical terms can actually increase process variation and reduce management's ability to strategically control, lead, and direct. Thus, even if a team is process oriented, lack of leadership in directing the change process can result in failure.

Management without TQS makes it more difficult to establish policies, conduct performance appraisals, or set goals. Failure to differentiate common from special causes of variation means that rewards and punishments are assigned arbitrarily (the Red Bead Experiment). Even though performance is system focused rather than worker related, decisions arbitrarily made reinforce and penalize individual behavior. This could lead to low morale and resentment among the work force. The lack of a connection between effort, performance, and rewards can be extremely detrimental, particularly for those workers who are penalized. In light of learning and imitation theory, workers are expected to engage in behaviors that seem conducive to future rewards. When rewards and punishments are awarded without an understanding of variation and its impact on the work force, results can be quite dysfunctional for the entire organization.

Implications of Guideline #9

There are two different implications for Guideline #9, both of which relate to participation. One touches upon the manager/instructor's role and the other upon the participant/worker's role as a future manager. The instructor who plays the role of management in the classroom should be technically competent to differentiate common from special causes of variation. This will prevent him or her from rewarding or punishing in an arbitrary way and from making other mistakes. Equally important, participants must learn to think statistically if they want to become efficient managers. They must learn "mapping" processes, learn to identify critical problems, and learn to constantly reduce variation in a specific process under their control. Learning to think systemically as well as statistically can present an obstacle to new learning.

Past instructional experience may have conditioned students/workers to view statistics as a highly abstract and unrelated discipline. They may fail to see the connection between statistics and job performance. This result is partially attributable to the fact that instructors do not always clearly establish such connections in the classroom. Instructors, regardless of their topic, should teach their subject matter using the most appropriate statistical tools to illustrate their points with task-related examples.

Guideline #10:
Is everyone in the organization personally committed to the achievement of TQS, based on personal conviction of its value? (If not, begin again at step #1!)

The word *committed* implies active involvement in process improvements—doing more than just planning and directing. Commitment is not only a willingness to learn, but also a pledge or promise to *do* something with the acquired knowledge. Although it carries certain emotional overtones, the word *conviction* implies a strong *belief* and is more reflective in nature. It is possible for a strong conviction to evolve into a commitment, eventually triggering a specific behavior. Those who really believe in TQS seldom remain passive. They are eager to share its advantages with others. Thus, the diffusion of TQS becomes a natural "next step."

Implications of Guideline #10

I hear and I forget
I see and I remember
I do and I understand.

Confucius

TQS principles will not be fully understood by participants if they are merely asked to study them. Rather, the instructor should "walk the talk" as an active participant and role model who is familiar with the organization's QI strategy. He or she should consciously transmit it, talk about it, discuss it, and take advantage of any opportunity to analyze situations within this framework. Stated simply, the instructor (who represents management) should take on leadership for change and encourage workers as students to do the same thing. This is perhaps the most difficult element of TQS, because the slightest deviation from top management's commitment and conviction will be viewed by workers as a signal that they should withhold participation.

HUMAN RESOURCE TOPICS OFFERED UNDER A TOTAL QUALITY SERVICE PERSPECTIVE

Some examples of the topics typically included in quality-oriented training are provided here. Such topics are relevant to the need to institute change and are consistent with the ten TQS guidelines mentioned earlier.

1. **Worker–organization bonding** (organizational socialization): Learning through the gradual interchange of expectations, norms, and *values*, among others. Workshop participants will be exposed to the organization's quality philosophy and introduced to the need to be responsive to reducing the costs of poor quality.

2. **Leadership and communication:** Leadership is exercised at all levels in a common effort to reduce special and common causes of variation via interpersonal skills, statistical thinking, and learning to apply appropriate statistical tools. Leadership principles can be taught like any other cognitive skill. One technique to instill multilevel leadership skills is the use of audiovisual equipment. Videotaping leadership exercises allows individuals or team members to view and critique their own performance. It also rewards participants for teamwork and mutual support. The exercise offers an excellent opportunity for a team or supervisors and workers to exhibit leadership and learn from each other. The videotape, which is an objective measure, offers the opportunity to discuss what happened and decide what needs to be changed to improve the system. (A detailed discussion of leadership required to achieve high-performance status is provided in Chapter 9.)

3. **Teamwork:** While working toward the improvement of work processes, members learn to assess their own strengths and weaknesses and those of their fellow team members. The literature on quality learning recognizes the importance of individual differences when referring to employee work skills. The concept of problem-solving style is extremely useful and could be included in the TQS approach. It recognizes the differences among human learners in the way they adapt to their environment and act upon it. This concept is particularly important when analyzed within a problem-solving team perspective. Each team can be assembled in terms of problem-solving styles. Each participant's style is determined by the Learning Style Inventory (Kolb et al., 1984).

4. **The organization as an open system:** Co-workers and team members learn how to deal effectively with other workers and organizational units, divisions, and departments. This emphasizes the value of exceeding the needs of external customers as an organization's ultimate goal. Techniques for opening channels of communication to obtain feedback and thus improve existing processes and systems are taught.

The purpose of the training is to deal with the different areas of human behavior within organizations from a quality perspective. Effective organizational socialization implies giving up old values and assuming new ones (see Table 2.1). This socialization issue becomes particularly crucial when someone joins a "quality" organization. The new worker goes through the typical anxieties and apprehensions related to facing the unknown. Moreover, he or she is joining an organization with a different way of perceiving, thinking, and acting. Since socialization is the first unit taught, it offers an ideal opportunity to expose recruits to a different philosophy. Such a philosophy also calls for a different instructional strategy and for different roles for both managers and workers.

The learning strategy applied throughout a training session is horizontally interactive and process oriented, with the following required from the learners: (1) study of the specific topic as well as problem-solving exercises to be covered in class; (2) participation on a team, based on problem-solving styles (a special effort must be made to achieve a balance in styles); (3) participation in a topic-related experience which could be a case study or a simulation; (4) team discussion and interaction; (5) team reports by representatives who share the team's decisions in public; (6) discussions that involve all the members in developing specific conclusions pertaining to the subject matter; and (7) presentation of PAAs containing the above points, presented at a later date (Kolb, 1984).

The course must convey TQS concepts, particularly during the worker–organization bonding unit, designed to expose learners to quality, processes, and systems thinking. The process-oriented nature of the course focuses on learning how to learn, combined with the instructor's specific instructional philosophy, and thus eases the inclusion of quality-oriented concepts in other technical and non-technical courses. The worker–organization bonding and leadership units are very useful in acquainting learners with the most relevant concepts and tools of QI. It is important to stress that the feedback given by the customers (employees/students) is the result of their efforts to evaluate the course from both an individual and a team perspective.

Going one step further, the principles of TQS (i.e., teamwork, closer customer–supplier relationships, empowerment, systems thinking, continuous quality improvement, and cost reduction) should be presented as a way of thinking, regardless of the field of training. Under this perspective, the instructor's role is geared toward pulling together the efforts of different teams. Team members take active responsibility for their own experiential and conceptual learning and for that of their fellow members. They all work together toward a common goal: an improved system.

CRITICAL ELEMENTS IN TOTAL QUALITY SERVICE TRAINING

To summarize, several interrelated elements must in included in successful organizational change training. In addition to worker–organizational bonding, other general topics should include customer orientation, leadership, teamwork,

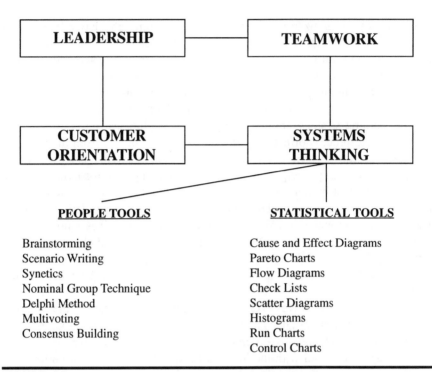

FIGURE 4.1   An Interactive Model for Total Quality Service

and thinking systemically. As a teaching philosophy, TQS is attractive because it recognizes the importance of treating individuals fairly, yet it incorporates a "hard data" approach for better results management. Human resource training must be integrated with job performance expectations and emphasize the soft and hard thinking and a systems interface unique to a TQS culture.

The interaction of each of these elements is critical to the development of a high-performance work force. Once these conceptual principles have been learned, training in specific job-related statistical skills and tools can proceed. The relationship between human resource and statistical training is diagrammed in an interactive model in Figure 4.1.

ENDNOTES

1. Portions of this chapter are adapted with permission from the creative work of Jose Eulogio Romero-Simpson, "Management: Introducing Quality Concepts in Advanced Organizational Behavior," unpublished paper, Department of Management, University of Miami. June 1990.

2. The theoretical basis of this cooperative team-based approach is derived from three sources: Deming's Points 5 and 9, which call for management to continually work to improve systems by optimizing the efforts of teams, groups, and staff areas toward the aims and purposes of the organization; Ishikawa's observation of the need to establish a structure for cross-functional management in order to achieve company-wide quality control; and Juran's emphasis on fitness for use criteria used to identify and achieve customer-defined expectations.

5

INCREASING QUALITY AND COMPETITIVENESS

The emergence of a global economy coupled with customer pressures for improved domestic service quality reinforces the need for internal organizational change. As we have seen, however, this does not happen overnight or without employee cooperation, training, strategic management, and leadership. Resources must be invested to change organizational cultures to offer incentives to adopt total quality service (TQS) principles and guidelines.

The integrated and interdisciplinary model presented in the preceding chapters can be used effectively as a powerful weapon for global as well as domestic economic competition. Organizations that invest the time and resources necessary to master and deploy TQS principles enjoy cost reductions, lower employee healthcare expenses, and greater productivity. This is accomplished by enlisting customers, employees, and suppliers in the continuous improvement of processes, services, and products. Everyone benefits.

Despite the evidence of success, the concepts underlying TQS are still underutilized in America outside of a select group of large multinational corporations (see Table 3.1). Anecdotal evidence is widely available from consultants, but application within the United States is still uneven, especially in publicly regulated services. Consequently, there is often more rhetoric about the need to improve quality than actual efforts to change organizational cultures to allow TQS to flourish. Previously mentioned barriers to implementation include maintaining individual reward systems, rigid vertical hierarchies, lack of genuine empowerment, performance appraisal systems, and outmoded management practices (such as management by objectives and merit pay), which impede the acceptance of team-based problem solving, process ownership, and customer responsiveness (Milakovich, 1991a).

For some sectors of the economy, it is more challenging to mobilize the resources and leadership necessary to make these changes. *TQS represents a long-term investment in competitiveness that many companies in the private sector may fail to make unless pushed and challenged by the public sector.* Public sector efforts to improve the internal efficiency of their own systems as well as those of other organizations are introduced in this chapter and expanded in Chapter 7. The dilemmas faced by those desiring to change are examined, and a discussion of how government policies are being used to promote the diffusion of TQS in both the public and private sectors is presented. Recognition is an important motivator as well. Various internationally recognized prizes for quality efforts, and a Florida public utility's breakthrough attempts to apply Japanese-style total quality control (TQC), are also discussed.

The Florida Power & Light case study is important because it shows just how vulnerable a service quality transformation can be in terms of internal dissension and outside political influences. The mixed experience of this public utility shows how quality control principles and techniques were introduced (from 1981 to 1989) in a (then) 15,000-person, publicly regulated, heavily unionized service organization. The Florida Power & Light experience provides important positive and negative generalizations for other services embarking on the quality improvement (QI) journey.

Despite these retrospective examples, it must be noted that no U.S. service company received the Malcolm Baldrige National Quality Award until 1990 (see FedEx, Case Study 2.1). Impressive gains have been made in some sectors since then, but far less attention has been paid to promoting TQS in smaller (under 150 employees) service organizations and medium-sized (under 1500 employees) manufacturing and service companies. These firms comprise 85 percent of the American service economy and 75 percent of new growth and employment opportunities. Further efforts to stimulate TQS may be warranted by the public sector in education, research, procurement, and small businesses in particular.

RECOGNIZING QUALITY IMPROVEMENT IN JAPAN: THE DEMING PRIZE

Since the early 1950s, the Japanese have symbolically honored the Americans who taught them how to manage quality and improve productivity by presenting the Deming Prize. The annual event is broadcast live on television, with the same size audience, level of interest, and prestige as the Academy Awards and the Nobel Prize in the West. The prize was established at a time when the Japanese economy still had not recovered from World War II. Deming used some of his own consulting fees as seed money to fund the award and served as honorary chairman since the award's inception in 1950. Ironically, Deming's primary message to post-war Japan was not competition, but world peace through free trade, open borders and reduction of trade barriers between nations. The prize is widely coveted in Japan's private sector because it symbolizes world-class high-performance status.

Prizes are awarded to those companies and individuals who improve the competitive position of Japanese products in world markets and enhance services at home. Among the Japanese companies that have won the prize are such world-class competitors as Hitachi, Fuji-Xerox, Nissan, Nippon Steel, and Toyota. The first service company to win the Deming Prize was Kansai Electric Company, a Japanese public utility, in 1984. Texas Instruments became the first non-Japanese manufacturing company to win the prize in 1985. Established and supported by the Union of Japanese Scientists and Engineers (JUSE), the Deming Prize has become the internationally recognized symbol of business excellence.

The actual award consists of a bronze medal with an accompanying certificate, but it is the honor of winning rather than the prize itself that stimulates interest and encourages companies to compete. The categories of the Deming Prize for Japanese companies are:

1. The Deming Prize for individual achievement is given to Japanese who have made outstanding contributions to the development and application of statistical quality control theory.

2. The Deming Application Prize is awarded to Japanese organizations (including service organizations) that achieve the most distinctive improvement in performance through the application of TQC based on statistical quality control methods. Separate awards are administered for small enterprises and corporate divisions.

The Deming Prize has not only become a great honor for the Japanese, but a goal for some joint Japanese–American and a select few American firms as well, although the latter must compete in a separate category. Realization of the need for QI in all sectors of the world economy prompted JUSE to establish a prize for overseas companies in 1986. The prize can be awarded to non-Japanese companies that have demonstrated distinctive improvement in performance through the application of TQC methods.[1]

Criteria for the Deming Prize

To be considered for a Deming award, an applicant must already have a quality program in operation. The first hurdle to overcome is to read and understand a 1000-page document that specifically outlines the steps that will be taken in improving and implementing quality. Then, the company(s) or individual(s) selected to compete for the prize must undergo a rigorous exam. The objective of this examination is to ensure that TQC is actually the way a company manages itself and not just a means to gain recognition or profit. The examination process is thorough, all-inclusive, and rigid. It is conducted by JUSE counsellors, who are experts in TQC applications as well as functional business areas such as accounting, engineering, and marketing. Several areas are examined in detail, including methods used to maintain effective control over costs, profits, appointed dates of deliveries, safety, inventories, manufacturing processes, equipment maintenance, instrumentation, personnel and labor relations, education and training, new product development, research, relationships with subcontractors and material suppliers, relationships with sales companies, handling of complaints, utilization of customer opinions, quality assurance and after-sale services to customers, and the relationship with companies to which products are delivered. The examination focuses on the following issues:

1. Company policy and planning: How is management policy determined, and by whom?

2. Organization and management: Are responsibility and authority clearly defined?

3. Quality control education and dissemination: How is quality control taught and how are employees trained?

4. Collection, transmission, and utilization of information on quality

5. Analysis of critical problems regarding quality

6. Establishment of standards

7. Review of the procedures used for the maintenance and improvement of quality

8. Review of quality assurance systems

9. Effects of procedures on the quality of products or services

10. Review of future plans: How will weak points be dealt with and strengthened?

In addition, on-site inspection of the following units within the company is conducted during the review: chief executive officer, head and regional offices, corporate divisions, branches, works and factories, laboratories, and sales and local offices. The inspection is done in three parts:

1. Schedule A: Presentation of important points and the inspection of operations sites

2. Schedule B: On-site investigation and general interrogation of officials (see above)

3. Interviews with the chief executive officer

All applicants are evaluated in terms of a weighted scoring system. The CEO's area can receive 70 points or more. All areas, minus that of the CEO, can receive 70 points or more. The minimum for any inspected unit is 50 points.[2] Reflecting the team approach to Japanese management, if any unit receives less that 50 points, then the entire organization fails the examination (Milakovich and Dan, 1990).

FLORIDA POWER & LIGHT COMPANY AND THE DEMING PRIZE

Not until the mid-1980s did a few large service organizations even consider implementing total service quality improvements. Florida Power & Light Company (FPL) of Juno Beach, Florida, began its notorious **Quality Improvement Program** (QIP) in 1981. FPL was recognized internationally for its company-wide quality improvement efforts in 1989 as the first American service firm to successfully compete for the prestigious Deming Prize in Japan. After receiving the prize and following a change in top management, FPL largely dismantled its effort due to financial exigencies unrelated to the success of the QIP. The positive and negative lessons learned from the FPL experience are particularly significant, as efforts were initiated at a time when few U.S. services emphasized total quality.

The following case study briefly describes how the QIP was designed, implemented, and eventually dismantled. It highlights lessons learned from the intensive and controversial effort to compete for the Deming Prize. It is important to understand the corporate history and recognize the business environment in which FPL operated in the early 1980s.[3] Not unlike other utilities, FPL found itself in the midst of a hostile business environment as inflation skyrocketed and fuel and oil prices showed no signs of decreasing. Worldwide shortages of fossil fuel, anti-nuclear power activists, deregulation, and cogeneration of electric power all threatened to reduce the company's long-term market share. In addition, there was a great need for heavy capital expenditures, and several aspects of the company's operations had grown cumbersome and overly bureaucratic. In the words of one senior manager, organizational growth at FPL had "created a rigid bureaucracy capable of acting in a set fashion...but unable to react to new and changing circumstances."[4] It became evident that a new management strategy was needed to deal with these mounting problems and successfully guide FPL into the future.

Senior FPL executives had visited Kansai Electric in the late 1970s and were impressed by the low-cost, highly efficient generating capacity of the Japanese public utility. In their minds, supply-oriented thinking had to be replaced with customer-oriented thinking in order to meet the changing demands of both the environment and the customers. This new strategy had to evolve from "just a new way of doing business" into a completely new mindset that would dominate every aspect of FPL. FPL imported not only the Japanese TQC management structure, but also the complex and time-consuming statistical methodology used to subsequently demonstrate results to the Japanese who served as Deming Prize examiners. The added quality "bureaucracy" was a poor match with FLP's predominantly blue-collar work force and sensitive political position as a publicly regulated state utility servicing central and south Florida.

Florida Power & Light's Quality Improvement Program

FPL first developed a mission statement which read: "During the next decade, we want to become the best managed electric utility in the United States and an excellent company overall, and be recognized as such." To achieve this, FPL created a three-phase QIP. In July 1981, FPL management somewhat optimistically announced that the QIP would be used to conduct business for the rest of this century and the next as well. The program promised a process for attaining QI, a chance for every worker to receive personal satisfaction for a job well done, and an opportunity to help achieve a common goal. Doing things right had always been a goal, but with the new strategy came the ideal of doing the right things right and doing so the first time. The goal was quality in everything, but the true test would be customer satisfaction.

Drawing from the expertise of quality experts such as W. Edwards Deming and Joseph Juran as well as Japan's 1984 Deming Prize-winning Kansai Electric, FPL settled on a mixed strategy and introduced the first phase of its QIP in 1982. In the process, quality was redefined as conformance to the valid requirements of the customer. Customers were redefined as well, in a way that clearly reflected Joseph M. Juran's fitness for use concept. FPL defined customers as not only the ultimate rate-paying customer, but also the person in the next department who received the product or service in the next step of the extended process (see Figure 2.2). Closer internal relationships were an explicit goal of this phase of the QIP.

Four principles of quality underlay FPL's QIP:

1. **Customer satisfaction:** Quality was defined as satisfying customers, which consists of meeting their needs and reasonable expectations.

2. **Plan-do-check-act cycle:**[5] Sometimes known as the Shewhart Cycle, this four-phase methodology (see Figure 2.6) for problem solving was embedded everywhere in FPL's QIP processes.

3. **Management by fact:** This had two meanings, not only for managers, but for all employees. First, objective data must be collected, and second, the company must be managed according to that data. This is clearly drawn from the TQC philosophy and is also known as "speaking with the facts" (Kano and Gitlow, 1988–89).

4. **Respect for people:** This principle asserted that all employees had the capacity for self-motivation and creative thought. Each employee was required to listen to and support this capacity in every other employee.

   Since it was impossible to instantly instill these principles in every employee, FPL implemented its QIP in three phases. **Quality Improvement Teams** (QITs) were started in 1982; soon over 1000 employees had been trained in team dynamics and over 100 teams were in operation company-wide. At its peak in 1989, FPL had approximately 1700 teams composed of 12,000 employees, representing an impressive 75 percent participation rate. At the same time, hundreds of employees were engaged in projects specifically designed to achieve the objectives delineated through the Policy Deployment phase.

   In 1984, **Policy Deployment** (PD) was implemented to allow management to prioritize and review problem-solving company-wide. PD was the essential *action* phase of the QIP. Its objective was to achieve breakthroughs by concentrating company efforts and resources on a few priority issues. There were many reasons for its implementation, including the improvements it generated in response to customer needs. According to the senior vice-president in charge of the effort, PD enhanced FPL's ability to focus on the most critical corporate improvement issues. It improved the linkage between the annual improvement plans and the long-term corporate vision. Finally, it increased participation in and commitment to annual and long-term plans (Woodall, 1988). PD promised greater management efficiency due to the prioritization of corporate goals. This contributed to FPL's overall attempt to achieve corporate improvement. Quality goals and quality-oriented activities at all levels supported the corporation's vision. By concentrating resources on a few priority issues, FPL was able to target breakthrough objectives in performance. Significantly, PD was not put into effect without input from all segments of the company. The process was systematic and thorough and involved everyone in planning, teamwork, and feedback. In addition to stimulating quality, PD improved communication between corporate departments and stimulated company-wide participation in the QIP.

The last phase, **Quality in Daily Work** (QDW), was introduced in 1986, and all employees began applying quality techniques to their individual tasks. It took FPL almost five years to fully introduce this program. Regardless of their involvement in the prior two phases, every FPL employee was introduced to the QDW concept. QDW was the application of the plan-do-study-act cycle to each individual job. The main purpose of QDW was to meet the needs and expectations of customers. Unlike the first two phases of the QIP, QDW was to have been a never-ending process. This phase was considered the most difficult to implement because it involved modification of the behavior of every single employee. In order to do so, a ten-step process that supposedly helped the implementation of QDW (later abandoned as overly detailed and unnecessarily complicated) was provided to every employee.

To direct the effort, a **Quality Council** composed of FPL's top officers was created and, assisted by a quality development team, guided the overall direction as well as the top-level QIP development and maintenance (Berry, 1991). FPL also charged the Quality Management Department with pushing, supporting, facilitating, and tracking quality progress for the entire organization. This centralization of authority became one of the major reasons FPL's new management subsequently used to justify dismantling the program in 1989.

Quality Improvement Teams and Stories

The purpose of the QITs was to develop the necessary skills, abilities, and attitudes, as well as to improve the quality of FPL's services. The team approach proved to be very successful.[6] Groups of workers become adept at addressing problems at their source and resolving them in accordance with company-wide policy and customer needs. Four different types of QITs were in operation at FPL:

1. **Functional teams:** Usually formed from a natural work unit, such as payroll. Members were all volunteers from a unit.

2. **Cross-functional teams:** Formed to deal with problems that cut across organizational barriers, such as travel requests, procurement, and accounts payable.

3. **Task teams:** Members were appointed from one or more organizational units to work on a specific problem, such as a cost allocation issue. When that problem was resolved, the team was disbanded and its members returned to their original work units.

4. **Lead teams:** This type of team, headed by a manager, served as a steering committee to guide the activities of other teams in the same area. The team was responsible for the selection of members and the frequency and duration of team meetings. (Some critics would later charge that these critical teams lacked sufficient direction from senior management and drifted from problem to problem without leadership.) Each of the teams would be led by a facilitator. As described in Chapter 4, a facilitator is a team leader who is specially trained in statistics and human resource skills and is appointed to help coach a team. The facilitator communicates and coordinates the efforts between cross-functional, task, and lead teams and functional units.

FPL also created an information clearinghouse, known as **Information Central**, to track team progress. IC kept files on team membership and documented their QI stories. These quality stories were an important element in the QIP and became the standard way of displaying a QIT's efforts. A story included seven steps: (1) reason for improvement, (2) current situation, (3) analysis, (4) countermeasures, (5) results, (6) standardization, and (7) future plans.[7] The QI Story format was meant to encourage participation by the work force, but its rigid methodology had the opposite effect. This seven-step process was inappropriately applied to too many processes and functions. It actually disempowered many otherwise hard-working employees who wanted to make independent decisions on the behalf of customers but were frustrated by having to apply this standard format to each decision. Moreover, this centralized approach later stigmatized the QIP as overly rigid and designed to maintain separate quality bureaucracies. Ideally, the entire organization should have implemented the QIP, but it did not. Resistance quickly set in. Many otherwise eager employees were frustrated with the amount of (uncompensated) extra effort required to learn the statistical methodology demanded of the modified TQC approach. Others felt that too much effort was devoted to winning the Deming Prize and not enough was devoted to employee empowerment and customer responsiveness.

Quality Improvement Program Results

Following other industries, FPL had begun to enlist vendors in its quality effort by the mid-1980s. The importance of vendors in the process was quite clear, in light of the fact that 60 percent of FPL's revenues are spent on the procurement of materials and services from vendors. This was a logical step to ensure that suppliers worked toward the same quality goal. To achieve that goal, FPL changed its procurement policy in November 1985 to emphasize development and maintenance of a long-term business relationship with suppliers. FPL expected that its new procurement policy would establish long-term ties with high-quality vendors, thereby extending the quality message to external customers. The communication lines established through these relationships were extremely valuable in terms of setting specifications by FPL, and vendors were allowed to contribute to the process, which resulted in better service to FPL customers.

It is always challenging to evaluate quality in the service sector. Many would look at the bottom-line ledger figures as an indication of whether or not a program is successful; however, looking at such figures alone does not necessarily reveal true successes. Increased revenues did result for FPL Group, Inc., as well as Qualtech, Inc., a software and consulting subsidiary. Qualtech is now one of the nation's largest quality management companies, with revenues of $15 million annually. Also, the $600 million saved in the construction of the St. Lucie 2 Nuclear Unit and the fact that it was completed ahead of schedule were attributed directly to the QIP efforts. A decrease in the number of customer complaints to the Florida Public Service Commission was another measurable result of the QIP. During the five years from 1984 to 1989, the number of complaints dropped by an impressive 37 percent. Also, the average length of customer service interruptions was cut to approximately 48 minutes, down from 100 minutes in 1981. In the important category of safety, lost time due to injuries decreased by 38 percent (Milakovich and Dan, 1990). These were impressive numbers, especially when compared to other utilities.

These results confirmed that the QIP was well on its way to becoming a international success story by the late 1980s. In the words of David T. Kearns, then CEO of Xerox Corporation, FPL was "the benchmark of quality in the United States." David Luther, quality director at Corning Glass, called FPL nothing less than "an extraordinary organization." A survey of *Wall Street Journal* subscribers recognized FPL Group, Inc. as the nation's "best-managed public utility." The national recognition that FPL sought arrived in 1988 when it was presented with the Edison Electric Institute Award for QI in a utility. In November 1989, FPL received international praise with the prestigious Deming Prize; it was the first non-Japanese company ever to win the award. With so much support and recognition, why was the program dismantled?

Lessons from the Application of Total Quality Control at FPL

Faced with increasing competition and an economic crisis, FPL borrowed bits and pieces from many different quality strategies but relied heavily on Japanese statistical quality control systems (Hudiberg, 1991). Top management guided implementation and gave the program strong encouragement. Although implemented gradually in several phases, the quality philosophy was kept intact and finally spread throughout the organization. Results were achieved by using a quality *control* system practiced by a successful Japanese power company (Kansai Electric). Efforts to sustain the quality focus in an American, heavily unionized, publicly regulated work force failed for the following reasons:

1. The goal of winning the Deming Prize consumed thousands of hours of extra time and fostered resentment among the workers. Morale could not be sustained following the award of the prize.

2. Serious allegations were raised concerning the misuse of ratepayers' money to support the Japanese examiners. Challenges filed with the Florida Public Service Commission over the costs of Japanese counsellors were eventually settled by a large rebate of public funds.

3. Some senior managers underestimated their own job security as well as the complexity of changing the underlying working culture in a large service organization.

4. Creating a separate Quality Management Department did not change the underlying culture of the organization, but instead bred resentment from those who were not included in the separate quality bureaucracy.

Resistance soon set in, and the process was repealed in 1990, when new leadership took over and largely dismantled the quality bureaucracy. The new chairman and CEO of FPL insisted that his decision was based on the success of the program and the fact that it had become institutionalized in the company (Broadhead, 1991). Subsequently, FPL has reduced its work force by over 20 percent through downsizing and elimination of 3000 jobs.

Despite these shortcomings, it must be noted that FPL initiated service quality improvements at a time when no other large U.S. company recognized the need or accepted the challenge. Many of the improvements were institutionalized, and the company and its customers benefited in the long term. Understanding the reasons for these mistakes will help others avoid them in the future. In addition, the positive consequences of QIP efforts can never be fully quantified or reflected in financial reports.

During the all-out mobilization to restore power to over 250,000 customers following Hurricane Andrew in the late summer of 1992, FPL crews performed almost miraculously. Within just six weeks, power was restored to all but the hardest hit areas of southwest Dade County. Contingency plans were developed during the 1980s for just such an emergency. These plans, combined with the team training in emergency response to natural disasters, served to produce the extraordinary results.

RECOGNIZING QUALITY IN THE UNITED STATES: THE MALCOLM BALDRIGE NATIONAL QUALITY AWARDS

After years of market dominance, resistance to change, and complacency, it was a crisis of foreign competition that finally motivated U.S. industries to consider recognizing quality with an award comparable to the Deming Prize. As the quality of Asian and European products began to match or exceed U.S-made products in the mid-1970s, global economic competition became a reality. By the mid-1980s, competition was stronger and the calls for an American award became louder and more numerous.

In August 1987, the U.S. Congress passed Public Law 100-107, the National Quality Improvement Act, which established the **Malcolm Baldrige Quality Award** (MBQA) for quality achievement in American manufacturing and services.[8] President Reagan made the first Baldrige presentations at a White House award ceremony in November 1988. The purpose of the award is to promote quality awareness and to publicize the successful quality strategies of large and small manufacturers and service firms. Many felt that such recognition was a major step in the right direction, but long overdue.

The Baldrige awards have received mixed reviews since their inception; some criticize them as overly bureaucratic, while others praise them as an elixir for restoring competitiveness and achieving instant quality results. The truth is somewhere in between. The awards have clearly focused public attention on the otherwise neglected area of QI in small and medium-sized companies. The task of stimulating a broad-based quality constituency is far from complete, and challenges remain, particularly in the public sector (federal, state, and local governments), educational institutions, healthcare agencies, and financial service organizations (Milakovich, 1990b). One promising consequence is that several state governments have modeled their own quality awards after the Baldrige criteria, which has broadened the base of the emerging national quality constituency (Dobson, 1993).

Early winners of the Baldrige Award include such large multinational firms as AT&T, Motorola, Texas Instruments, and Xerox Corporation, which represent the highest ideals of quality for American business and industry. All the winners since the awards were first given are listed in Table 5.1. The award is a model for public–private cooperation, privately funded yet administered in conjunction with the American Society for Quality Control, the American Productivity Center, and the U.S. Department of Commerce National Institute for Standards and Technology (NIST). To date, more than 500 firms have applied for the Baldrige Award. It has been presented to just 22 (Table 5.1). The list of winners includes a few small businesses, but consists mostly of large multinationals recognized as leaders in the international quality movement.

TABLE 5.1   Baldrige Award Winners by Year and Type of Firm

1988	**Motorola** (Schaumburg, Illinois)	Large manufacturing
	Westinghouse Commercial Nuclear Fuel Division (Pittsburgh, Pennsylvania)	Large manufacturing
1989	**Globe Metallurgical** (Cleveland, Ohio)	Small manufacturing
	Milliken & Co. (Spartanburg, South Carolina)	Large manufacturing
	Xerox Business Products and Systems (Stamford, Connecticut)	Large manufacturing
1990	**Cadillac Motor Car Division** (Detroit, Michigan)	Large manufacturing
	IBM Rochester (Rochester, New York)	Large manufacturing
	FedEx (Memphis, Tennessee)	Service
	Wallace Co. (Houston, Texas)	Small manufacturing
1991	**Solectron** (San Jose, California)	Manufacturing
	Zytec Corp. (Eden Prairie, Minnesota)	Manufacturing
	Marlow Industries (Dallas, Texas)	Small business
1992	**Texas Instruments** (Dallas, Texas)	Large manufacturing
	AT&T Universal Card (Jacksonville, Florida)	Service
	AT&T Bell Transmission Systems (Morristown, New Jersey)	Manufacturing
	Ritz-Carlton (Atlanta, Georgia)	Service
	Granite Rock Company (Watsonville, California)	Small business
1993	**Eastman Chemical Company** (Kingsport, Tennessee)	Large manufacturing
	Ames Rubber Corp. (Hamburg, New Jersey)	Small manufacturing\
1994	**AT&T Consumer Communications Division** (Basking Ridge, New Jersey)	Service
	GTE Directories Corp. (Dallas, Texas)	Service
	Wainwright Industries, Inc. (St. Peters, Missouri)	Small business

While the total number of winners has been smaller than the number of Deming Prize recipients, the "demonstration effect" of the self-assessment effort required to apply for the award has contributed to the spread of quality consciousness among U.S. public and private manufacturers and services. According to the

NIST, Baldrige winners have made more than 10,000 presentations, reaching an audience of more that 3 million (Hodgetts, 1993). The Baldrige Award criteria offer a framework of core values for QI which focus attention on seven critical areas: (1) leadership, (2) information and analysis, (3) strategic quality planning, (4) human resource development, (5) process management, (6) operational results, and (7) customer focus and satisfaction. Details and relative values of each of these criteria are presented in Appendix D.

Perhaps as important as the awards themselves is the discipline required by the examination process. All companies that apply and qualify as finalists are visited by volunteer experts and receive a full report documenting their status based on the 1000-point examination criteria. The application and examination process itself has provided many firms with objective and valuable feedback.

According to a 1991 U.S. Government Accounting Office report, in the 20 U.S. companies that had ranked highest in the Baldrige competition but did not win the award, initiation of total quality management actions led to improved employee relations, greater customer satisfaction, improved quality, lower costs, and improved market share. These companies began their QI efforts in the mid-1980s and on average had improved their performance in two and one-half years (U.S. General Accounting Office, 1991).

Many American manufacturing and service companies have embraced customer-driven quality and use the Baldrige criteria as a strategy for increasing productivity. Evidence has shown that a consistent strategy for improving quality increases productivity, lowers costs, provides job security, and affects the competitive practices of American enterprises. In addition, the publicity surrounding the creation and awarding of the MBQA has been used effectively by proponents to further their cause. For the 1991 award cycle, nearly *double* the number of companies applied as compared with the previous year. While the number of applications has fallen in recent years (to 76 applicants in 1993 and 71 in 1994), the Baldrige Awards, like the Deming Prize and ISO 9000 certification, are likely to continue to evolve and increase in importance and prestige. In an effort to reflect the changing environment, the Commerce Department has proposed opening the award competition to healthcare and educational institutions. Beginning in 1995, organizations from these sectors may submit applications and receive feedback, although no awards will be given until these pilot applications are evaluated.

Perhaps as important as the number (quantity) of firms applying for awards is the fact that many of the companies that have applied now conduct business only with other (quality) companies that have applied for the Baldrige, Deming, Shingo Prize, or other juried quality awards. In addition, there are many other (equally successful) public and private organizations that practice customer-driven quality on a daily basis without the need to apply for recognition. This is further proof that a quality consensus is emerging within the United States, reflecting a visible commitment to established quality management principles based on the Baldrige or other international or national award criteria. More importantly, the principles of TQS are rapidly becoming an effective weapon for American service firms to compete internationally. Would this have happened without government involvement?

GOVERNMENT, COMPETITIVENESS, AND TOTAL QUALITY SERVICE[9]

Should governments promote TQS in the private sector, in partnership with the private sector, in their own agencies, or not at all? At first glance, TQS does not appear to require government involvement, at least in relation to what the private sector does to build its own markets. The case can be made that private companies have better information than the government about what is needed to compete effectively, and they will adopt this strategy if and when they decide that it is in their interest to do so. There is no evidence of a lack of information about quality principles, at least on the part of large multinational manufacturing companies. In fact, government promotion of TQS may hinder its diffusion because of the negative corporate stereotype of government by some large corporations. It could be argued that time itself will determine whether theories are as effective as claimed; early efforts to promote service applications could prove a waste of resources if expectations are unwarranted (the FPL syndrome).

The preceding views generally reflect a conservative ideology that the role of government in promoting economic competitiveness should be very limited. Government should act as an "invisible hand" to protect free markets and should limit itself to promoting policies that indirectly affect competition, such as better education, reduction of tariffs, and low interest rates (Porter 1990). While these activities are important, the role of government can also be cast more broadly as looking after the competitiveness of domestic industries, especially their long-term development. Thus, what government does for the private sector is equally important as an individual corporation's QI strategy. This role is reflected in government strategies that "push, challenge, and nurture" industries. Indeed, many Japanese companies grew under substantial pushing, challenging, and nurturing of government programs in the 1950 and 1960s (Prestowitz, 1988). Should the federal government adopt a more aggressive strategy for the promotion of TQS?

The implementation of TQS principles is a very serious long-term commitment that requires substantial training and start-up resources. Return on investments in TQS training may be difficult to estimate. While some returns become evident during the early phases, most returns only become apparent after two to three years, when commitment to continuous improvement is reflected in improved customer satisfaction and market share. Thus, TQS techniques are challenging to implement in the current service environment because they simultaneously require an overhaul of existing planning processes and the institutionalization of new operational procedures and reward structures. Long-term competitiveness requires a sustained effort to transform organizational cultures. U.S. corporate and political leaders do not always act with foresight until profitability is under pressure, at which time it is often too late to seek improvements through long-term commitments.

Several other practices of American companies often deter such investment in long-term competitiveness:

1. Traditional attitudes (such as "if it's not broken, don't fix it") deter objective assessment of current performance levels and discourage the adoption of alternatives

2. Profit-driven strategies, which may reduce costs without improvements in process or quality to promote short-term profitability, but are less likely to improve competitiveness in the long term

3. Reluctance to abandon productivity-based quantitative measures over strategic vision and responsiveness to customers

4. A lack of knowledge about applications in specific services because of a shortage of trained consultants

Many of these obstacles overlap somewhat, but they support the contention that private companies are often run on the basis of short-term profitability, in both theory and practice.

What can government do to overcome these tendencies? Clearly, many actions are of necessity indirect, because public policy cannot, both legally and practically, intervene in the internal management of companies in any direct way. Instead, there are three main approaches that the government might use to promote quality: (1) provide information, (2) fund education and research, and (3) set standards. The rationale for each of these approaches is as follows.

First, while there is no evidence of a lack of general information regarding the importance of quality for U.S. long-term competitiveness, it is nonetheless reasonable to assume that many companies, in part because of their small size and limited resources, are not fully aware of the organizational changes required to launch a full-scale effort. Indeed, management in many medium or large-sized companies may be unaware of these new practices or may have beliefs about them that are false. Thus, dissemination of information, either directly or indirectly through support of conferences and symposia, can be an important strategy. Baldrige Award winners are required by law to hold public briefings outlining the basis for the award. These are particularly useful for companies in the same industry seeking advice and direction for their QI efforts.

Second, supporting research is useful for generating new applications and for verifying the success of existing ones. Education and training are also necessary to ensure an adequate supply of trained consultants and engineers. In the absence of such expertise, businesses often accomplish little more than heightened customer awareness in marketing and sales. Current levels of research and education are not well known but, as in other fields of science, government subsidies are generally required to achieve reasonable levels of output.

Third, standards are often used to alter the way in which goods and services are delivered. The federal government mandates that its defense contractors adopt total quality management (TQM) in order to reduce costs and improve the quality of supplies (Kelman, 1990). By requiring TQM, the government has *de facto* created a TQM industry of consultants, which may, at some later point in time, help spread quality consciousness to the civilian non-defense sector as well (detailed in Chapter 7).

Omitted from the preceding list are other approaches such as accreditation standards, tax incentives, subsidies, and trade policies. Traditionally, the United States has tended to rely more on incentives, while international competitors have been more inclined to practice restrictive trade practices. One competitive disadvantage to this strategy is that incentives, such as tax credits and subsidies, aim to affect production output. In this sense, direct incentives may not apply to TQS, which is a factor leading to increased production. Similarly, while procurement has been the preferred tool for promoting competitiveness in industries ranging from agriculture to space to computers and aircraft, it is not easily applied to QI because, except for training, TQS is not a procured good, but rather a service provided to government agencies.

Finally, through tariffs and buy-domestic policies, trade policy is also sometimes used to restrict competitiveness. However, because the United States remains committed to global free trade (with the exception of threatened industries such as automobile manufacturing), it seems unlikely that special policies will be enacted to include the promotion of American or America-based companies that apply TQS principles. Thus, traditional approaches are not necessarily applicable to the promotion of TQS. While current government promotion of TQS increases U.S. competitiveness, further initiatives may be called for, especially in small to medium-sized companies. One emerging approach is the use of accrediting standards against which public or private organizations can measure themselves. The strategy commonly used in Europe and increasingly being adopted in the United States is known as the International Standards Organization or ISO 9000.

ISO 9000 AND EMERGING GLOBAL QUALITY STANDARDS

The shift in power from those selling to those buying services is an irreversible trend that affects all world markets (Toffler, 1990). The deployment of telecommunication systems, satellites, fiber optics, videoconferencing, and other advanced technologies has drastically reduced prices and shortened distances between buyers and sellers. Power has shifted to consumers because more people can shop internationally for the highest quality, lowest price products and services. What were previously defined as "local" services now compete for customers worldwide. The driving forces begin these changes are customer demand for high quality, technology, and breakthroughs in communications.

Many services depend on communication linkages and are already applying TQS principles to improve customer service. Overnight package delivery companies, for example, guarantee customers next-day delivery and that they can locate packages anywhere in the system in less than 20 minutes or they will refund the cost of the service. Similarly, automobile repair services, banks, hotel chains, rental car companies, and airlines and related travel services depend on instantaneous communication. Even "local" institutions such as financial services, hospitals, and universities are utilizing technological innovations to compete for customers worldwide.

In most local markets, government regulations and monopolies protect services from international competition. Many are still protected, but increasingly less so. As the distance between the production and consumption of the world's commercial enterprises shrinks, standards for quality are becoming more visible. Quality standards are merging worldwide with the application of the Baldrige Award, Deming Prize, and International Standards Organizations (ISO 9000) criteria.

Quality improvement has become a priority for many organizations, and the ISO 9000 and 9001 Series criteria are being used as benchmarks to gauge progress. The International Standards Organization, based in Geneva, Switzerland, has developed standards for quality in both manufacturing and services. Initially, ISO certification was geared toward merging European markets, but it has been expanded to include many North American firms as well. ISO certification is voluntary and is similar to accreditation standards for education and healthcare. To date, fewer North American than European firms have applied for ISO certification. Requirements for ISO registration in Europe are limited to a few industry segments (medical, toys, and telecommunications), but the potential for growth in both Europe and North America is enormous as quality standards merge worldwide (Mauch et al., 1994; Voehl et al., 1994).

High-quality services were always available to those who could afford them. Now, with the decreasing cost of communication and transportation, more people can take advantage of higher quality, less expensive services. Mercy Hospital in Coconut Grove, Florida utilizes a satellite link to offer continuing medical education to doctors and health professionals in Central and South America. The University of Miami School of Business Administration operates a full-service undergraduate and graduate program in the Bahamas. The Cleveland Clinic and the Mayo Clinic of Rochester, Minnesota offer specialized medical procedures and advertise in local newspapers in urban locations throughout the nation. Today, as the cost of accessing high-performance services declines, more and more individuals can avail themselves of the higher quality service at competitive prices.

One consequence of the deregulation of domestic economies is the internationalization of the world service economy. In major international travel destinations such as Tokyo, Frankfurt, New York, London, Miami, Los Angeles, and Paris, comparisons of service quality are now routinely made between airports, hotels, rental car companies, airlines, and leisure services. Moreover, as the cost of air travel diminishes in relation to other services such as education and healthcare, more schools, clinics, hospitals, and specialized managed care facilities are marketing their services worldwide. Soon, comparative quality assessments similar to those available to consumers of airline travel services, hotels, and restaurants will be available to consumers of healthcare and other formerly domestic isolated services (see *Consumer Reports*, July, August, and September 1992 for comparative health service rankings).

Global comparisons are now regularly made between high-, median-, and low-performance manufacturing and service firms in Canada, Germany, Japan, and the United States (American Quality Foundation and Ernst and Young, 1992). Within a few years, these same types of comparisons will be available for those regulated, non-market educational, governmental, and healthcare agencies that seek to become high-performance service organizations (Thompson, 1993).

During the past two decades, telecommunication, air travel, and transportation costs have declined, and the trend is likely to continue into the 21st century. Several U.S. telecommunications firms such as AT&T, MCI, and Sprint offer satellite telephone communication systems that allow anyone anywhere in the world to access the U.S. telephone system. This further increases access by foreign providers of services to U.S. markets. Likewise, U.S. software service firms are marketing their services in Europe, Asia, and Latin America. In effect, these innovations eliminate regional and geographic definitions of service quality and thus introduce competition, which forces providers to respond to customer demands.

SUMMARY AND CONCLUSIONS

Government quality initiatives evolved gradually without large-scale industry support or interest group pressure. Private industry did not forcefully lobby Congress for the Baldrige Award, and it is doubtful that it would have if necessary, notwithstanding the benefits that some firms now realize from it. The Defense Department's Deming-based procurement requirements also were not structured around industry support. In fact, they were imposed as a consequence of downsizing and retrenchment. The initiative was further justified as a potentially cost-saving and budget-reducing measure for taxpayers, and it followed widespread allegations of defense contractor overbilling and complaints about poor quality military hardware. Similarly, it seems unlikely that the defense industry would lobby for increases in quality education and research, although it would likely benefit from such programs. Unfortunately, funding for new interdisciplinary program initiatives is scarce at both the National Science Foundation and the U.S. Department of Education.

Two important political constraints affect the formulation of new service quality policies that would potentially affect competitiveness: (1) the absence of positive business–government relations and (2) widespread industry views that favor a limited role of government in competitiveness. These constraints often obstruct more comprehensive change efforts, because they inhibit the formation of industry interest groups in support of government competitiveness programs. While many industry interest groups support lower taxes and less regulation, very few espouse other competitiveness initiatives. The presence and success of industry representation is very important in getting programs passed and implemented. This is particularly important when "distributional benefits" or government support is involved. When funding is involved, internal competition among interest groups is often keen, and a presence in Washington is often a prerequisite for obtaining federal funds. Clearly, a large, broad-based competitiveness constituency has yet to be formed.

There are no easy solutions to this political dilemma of industry support. Negative views about the role of government in promoting competitiveness are widespread among many private sector executives. At the same time, private sector efforts often do not succeed in demonstrating a sustained commitment to total quality principles. In the long run, the solution may be that American citizens will have to petition their representatives in Congress and the state legislatures to invest in their future, through quality and competitiveness. The importance of such a policy may increase through a heightened social concern for education, homelessness, poverty, and income inequity; increased competitiveness may come to be seen as a means to resolving these dilemmas. As more and more Americans realize that their jobs, their family incomes, and their economic futures are at risk, the likelihood of their representatives in Congress listening to a quality constituency increases. The importance of rewards and recognition will expand because service quality is increasingly judged less by the reputation of the provider than by comparable quality standards as determined by juried awards or independent evaluations. In a competitively benchmarked private market, high-performance service firms must respond to all customer definitions of quality. Comparative quality measures differentiate key competitors and exert a profound impact on bottom-line profits and losses. Changing organizational cultures to consistently improve customer service quality levels not only requires leadership, teamwork, and customer orientation, but requires training, knowledge, process improvement, and application of statistical quality principles to monitor results as well. Rewards must be provided to offer incentives to meet the new customer-directed goals. External standards can also be used to promote quality monitoring capacity. Academic, hospital, legal, and medical accrediting commissions and other professional regulatory boards identify external quality standards such as ISO 9000 for public and private agencies. The key to continuously improving performance, however, is to focus on the quality of processes common to internal systems within an organization.

ENDNOTES

1. Deming Prize Committee, *The Deming Prize Guide for Overseas Companies,* 1986, p. 2.
2. Deming Prize Committee, *The Deming Prize Guide for Overseas Companies,* 1986, p. 16.
3. Formed in 1984, FPL Group, Inc. is a holding company with both utility and non-utility operations. The utility operations segment comprises the activities of FPL Group's primary subsidiary, Florida Power & Light Company, headquartered in Juno Beach, Florida. FPL was established in 1925 and has mushroomed into the fourth largest investor-owned electric utility in the United States and the fastest growing in terms of the number of new customer accounts. Its service territory, with a population of approximately 5.7 million people, covers an impressive 27,650 square miles, about one-half of the state of Florida. In its 13 operating plants, 7 operations offices, 45 customer service offices, 72 service centers, and 397 substations, FPL employs nearly 15,000 people and handles over 3 million customer accounts.
4. Florida Power & Light Company, "Energizing for Excellence," 1987, p. 4.
5. Deming changed the cycle from "check" to "study" in 1990 to reflect his concern that checking was equated with inspection.
6. In 1987, QITs submitted 942 QI stories for review, and most were accepted. Success stories abound. One QIT from the Coral Gables office was able to reduce meter reading

errors by 50 percent by using the QI Story approach. This reduction also resulted in fewer customer complaints to the Public Service Commission relating to incorrect bills. Another QIT placed first in a competition sponsored by the Houston chapter of the International Association of Quality Control. The corporate dosimetry team (dosimetry is the measurement of radiation absorbed per unit of time) topped a number of quality teams, including groups from NASA and Rockwell International. The top team from the Fort Myers FPL power plant traveled to Tokyo in November 1987 to present their successes at an international quality conference. (Florida Power & Light, "QIP in Perspective," *Sunshine Service-News,* Vol. 49, No. 1, 1988, p. 15.)

7. Florida Power & Light, "QI Story and Techniques," *FPL Quality Improvement Program,* 1987, p. 6.

8. The award is named after a U.S. Secretary of Commerce in the Reagan Administration who was killed during a rodeo accident. He was a strong advocate of quality management as a means of competing in world markets.

9. Adapted from Evan Berman and Michael Milakovich, "Increasing Global Competition Through the Promotion of Total Quality Management" in *Productivity and Quality Management Frontiers III,* David J. Sumanth, Johnson A. Edosomwan, D. Scott Sink, and William B. Werther, Jr. (Eds.), Norcross, Ga.: Industrial Engineering and Management Press, Institute of Industrial Engineers, 1991, pp. 477–487.

6

MONITORING PROCESS, COST, QUALITY, AND PRODUCTIVITY

Consistently delivering services at levels of performance that anticipate and exceed all customers' quality requirements is challenging for even the most experienced and best-trained managers under the most favorable market conditions. Success requires assuming new (and often unfamiliar) roles, creating opportunities for genuine empowerment, and altering organizational relationships between management and labor, individuals and teams, and suppliers and customers.

Service quality must be demonstrated on the basis of total quality indicators that are comparable, based on fact, and consistent with other providers. This, in turn, requires the design of internal management systems that are capable of setting quality standards, defining customer requirements, monitoring them accurately, and providing continuous statistical feedback to eliminate the underlying causes and costs of poor quality. The losses associated with not knowing how much money is wasted as a result of poor quality vary among services. Some losses are inevitable, but most are caused by the system. They occur because of differences in the complexity of services provided, the sophistication of technology used, and the reliability of performance monitoring systems. Nonetheless, it is impossible to add value to processes without controlling costs.

Case Study 6.1

Shabby Customer Teaches Bank a Lesson

Report from Washington

AP Spokane, Washington. A bank learned an expensive lesson by refusing to validate a 50-cent parking slip for a destitute-looking man who retaliated by withdrawing his million-dollar account.

"If you have $1 in a bank or $1 million, I think they owe you the courtesy of stamping your parking ticket," John Barrier told the *Spokane Spokesman-Review* this week.

The 59-year-old man said he was wearing his usual clothes—wrinkled old jeans, a cap with old grease stains, and shabby sneakers—when he pulled his pickup truck into the Old National Bank parking lot.

He paid a quick visit to his broker, cashed a check at the bank, and headed back to his truck.

The lot attendant said that there was a 50-cent parking fee but that Barrier could take his slip inside to get it validated.

No problem, Barrier thought, because he had done business at ONB (now U.S. Bank of Washington) for more than 30 years. But a teller took one look at his grubby clothes and refused to stamp the parking bill.

The millionaire asked the teller to call a bank manager, who also refused.

"He looked me up and down and stood back and gave me one of those kinds of looks," Barrier said, turning up his nose to imitate the manager. "I said, 'Fine. You don't need me, and I don't need you.'"

Took His Money Down the Street

Barrier withdrew all his money and took it down the street to Seafirst Bank.

"The first check he brought me was for $1 million," said Dennis Veter, the vice-president of Seafirst's main Seattle branch. "You'd never know by looking at him, but you and I should be so lucky."

The incident has allowed Barrier's new bank, Seafirst, to puff out with pride. Not only did Barrier defect, but his son and daughter also bank there now.

As previously discussed, eliminating non-value-added (poor quality) costs is heavily influenced by the training of human sensors who act as system monitors. To detect problems and prevent them from worsening, sensors perform the vital early warning function. Not unlike highly sensitive instruments, the measurement characteristics they monitor must be precise, valid, reliable, and easily understood by those who must perform critical tasks within tolerable limits of bias, error, and precision. Case Study 6.1 illustrates how poorly trained monitors can impose extreme costs on organizations.

The customer's goal can be something as simple as getting a parking ticket stamped or as complex as repairing an automobile. The degree of complexity in no way diminishes the importance of monitoring results. On the contrary, everyone's attention should be focused on the process improvements necessary to satisfy customer needs. Monitoring progress requires a process or team focus, as opposed to an individual or goal-directed focus, and ends with the application of appropriate statistical tools and techniques to reduce variation and eliminate non-value-added costs. The objective of statistical analysis is to make decisions about a process under conditions of uncertainty and imperfect information. Statistical analysis plays an important role, especially for airports, banks, financial institutions, hospitals, and governments, where intensive customer contact and massive paper flow are involved. This, in turn, leads to lower costs, increased quality, and productivity gains.

The service quality revolution is accelerating process improvement within all types of organizations. Understanding processes as a means to transform knowledge and respond to customers faster than the competition is at the heart of total quality service (TQS). Reducing even a small portion of the generally accepted 20 to 30 percent non-value-added waste and unnecessary expenses can accrue enormous and immediate benefits for most organizations. Prevention and control of variation is stressed because operational systems in all types of service industries are highly complex and variable. Although statistical process control techniques can be applied to reduce variation and improve service quality, special care must be taken to first identify and then monitor valid customer measures. Although process improvement is a transformational activity that involves teams, work groups, and customer-focused systems, what is evaluated under a TQS model are the **quality characteristics** of the process. Valid customers requirements are often referred to as quality characteristics of the product or service being measured. Quality characteristics are attributes of a process or service deemed important enough to warrant some control. By analyzing and understanding the distribution of these factors, the entire process can be studied and better understood.[1]

Valid customer characteristics are **operational definitions** or **operational measures**[2] of what is needed to fulfill customer requirements. These measures are usually well-known by end users or **external customers**, the final recipients of a service produced by a work unit. For example, operational measures could include the number of units sold per month, budgetary figures, or the complaint rate per number of customers. In addition to the traditional measurement elements (specification, test, and criterion), definitions must also be **SMART:** specific, measurable, accountable, realistic, and team based. All services need to improve in order to stay in business, but the rate of process improvement increasingly separates high performers from adequate providers.

The speed at which organizations can eliminate non-value-added costs and improve processes increasingly determines winners and losers in competitive markets. When responding to valid customer demands, it is as important to have both internal and external measures of performance. Often overlooked in a service environment are the needs of **internal customers** who receive a (partially finished) product or service (forms, data, orders) produced by another work unit within the organization.[3] The rate of process improvement can also be accelerated by organizing quality control circles, work groups, or self-managed work teams and training them in the use of problem analysis tools. These groups may be formed as needed to resolve specific problems. A quality improvement (QI) "swat team" is a project team composed of line employees and technical support people; it is formed to study and solve a specific problem and then disbanded. These activities only work when there already is a company-wide commitment to quality, when the circle includes a customer (as the recipient of output from the last process), and when the group is assigned problems rather than left free to select its own topics for study.

In a TQS environment, everyone either already owns or is working toward becoming an owner of a process or set of processes. Generally, the greater the number of processes under one's supervision, the higher the level of responsibility and compensation. The challenge of leadership for TQS (see Chapter 9) is to direct these activities without interfering with the team's enthusiasm to define and solve problems.

PROCESS CONTROL TECHNIQUES

What is a process? A process is simply a transformation of *inputs* (such as materials, manpower, and equipment) into *outputs* which meet or exceed customer quality requirements. Process-oriented managers constantly seek better ways to control and improve the quality of goods and services provided to customers. They continually seek methods and tools to stabilize processes which, in time, improve a system composed of many interconnected processes. In this way, organizations, like individuals, learn to adapt to their environments and change as necessary to learn, grow, and survive (Senge, 1990). All modern QI theories stress a process or systems focus. Operational processes are complex, because they are composed of interrelated elements which interact to determine the performance of organizational subunits and systems.

Statistical process control (SPC) techniques have been used in manufacturing for decades. The classic study of modern methods of quality and reliability, published by Walter Shewhart (1931), identified the seven common elements that constitute a process:

1. **Materials:** raw materials or components
2. **Manpower** or personnel: the human factor
3. **Methods:** product and process design
4. **Machines:** tools and equipment necessary for processing
5. **Measurement:** techniques and tools used to gather data on process performance
6. **Maintenance:** providing care for process variables
7. **Management:** policy, work rules, and environment[4]

Understanding how these elements interact with the work force is the key to improving processes. All organizational processes may be viewed as unique sets or groupings of elements stemming from the seven M's. Financial management processes, for example, are a series of repetitious operations that are performed under conditions presumed to be identical for each operation. Ordering laboratory tests in a hospital, processing requests for parking vouchers, or grading student papers is unique because each impacts just one individual. Yet all are still transformation processes, which do not change wherever the provider is located (illustrated in Figure 6.1).

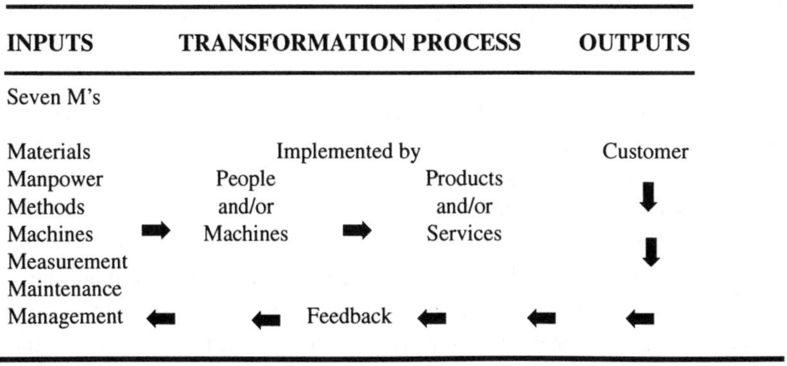

INPUTS	TRANSFORMATION PROCESS		OUTPUTS
Seven M's			
Materials	Implemented by		Customer
Manpower	People	Products	
Methods	and/or	and/or	⬇
Machines ➡	Machines ➡	Services	
Measurement			⬇
Maintenance			
Management ⬅	⬅ Feedback ⬅	⬅	⬅

FIGURE 6.1   Basic Transformation Process

While all processes transform inputs (the seven M's) into outputs (results), applications within different services vary considerably. Processes exist in administrative systems, sales, employee training, personnel, and buyer–seller relations. Processes vary in the volume of transactions and the speed at which information (throughput) is available to the next customer. Validating a parking ticket or cashing a check, for example, involves millions of separate processes, and the potential for error is extreme. Diagnosing a medical problem, giving legal advice, and grading student papers, in contrast, are labor-intensive and customized activities. The relatively distinct process of filling out an insurance claim for a disaster victim is less prone to error, however, but no less complicated. Thus, while inputs, speed of processing, and volume differ, the common elements of each process for several types of transactions can be identical for various service providers. This provides the theoretical basis for **comparative benchmarking** of processes among different service delivery organizations.

All quality characteristics used to monitor processes exhibit a certain amount of variation. Think about getting to work on time, for example. Various predictable and unpredictable factors, such as your alarm clock, your car, traffic, road conditions, and the weather, influence when (or if) you leave and whether or not you arrive on time. Therefore, efforts to improve processes must first aim at reducing controllable variation within preset or known limits. (If your car is slow to start, have the battery checked. If it is raining, leave home a few minutes early.) These are relatively predictable causes of variation. Two types of variation occur in all processes: **common** (random but predictable) and **special** (less predictable) variation. It is vital to distinguish between the two, because appropriate action in response to each type of variation is quite different.

Variation Due to Common Causes

This category of variation is inherent in any process and is caused by minute changes in one of the seven M's: raw materials, worker behavior, calibration of machines, design products, and so on. Common variation results from the inability of any process to execute the same precision, or exact duplication, on each successive output unit. Common variation exists even when processes are in statistical control, because small fluctuations in a process are difficult to detect and remove. Common variation arises from so many sources that even if the sources were found and eliminated, the overall effect would be negligible. Common variation may be due to a specific component of a machine, defective material, or a definable local condition. It has been estimated that about 85 percent of process problems stem from common variation, whereas the remaining 15 percent are caused by special variation.

Variation Due to Special Causes

When all common causes of variation have been removed, a process is said to be in a state of statistical control or simply in control. Special (random) variation results from some specific fault or malfunction which occurs *outside* a process. Unexpected causes may affect systems and processes at any time. For example, even if you left for work early, the weather or an accident on the road may still cause you to be late. The discovery and removal of special causes is the responsibility of those closest to the source, usually line workers. They should consider whether special causes occur gradually over time or are abrupt and infrequent. Various tools such as run charts and control charts are useful for this purpose.

Previous discussions have centered on process stabilization using statistics and measurement to uncover common or assignable causes of variation. Process improvement is primarily concerned with managing special variation. A broader set of problem-solving and decision-making tools are used to identity process improvement opportunities. When common variation is distinguished from special causes of process variation, then management can stop blaming employees and focus on eliminating quality problems through organizational change and the application of SPC methods.

Statistical Process Control

Walter Shewhart's SPC model helps managers control the quality of output in any process and respond appropriately to different types of variation. As mentioned earlier, an important component of the SPC model is a monitor who determines whether a process is stable or out of control. The monitor distinguishes between the many small, random fluctuations that perturb the process (but do not affect output) and the relatively large or unexpected causes of variation that could affect system operations. Something can and must be done about special causes because they are unwanted and identifiable. The SPC model establishes a procedure for monitoring processes and removing common or assignable causes of variation, such as tellers deciding whether or not to validate parking slips based on how a customer is dressed.

At the same time, it is equally harmful to confuse the two types of variation. The monitor, who may be a receptionist, police officer, salesperson, or bank teller, uses SPC methodology to observe that something seems to be changing— that the process is no longer following an established (stable) pattern. When properly trained, the monitor can recognize which type of variation exists. Once identified, common causes can be reduced and special causes can be removed or anticipated.

It is vital that customer-contact personnel distinguish between the two types (or causes) of process variation and recognize the difference. Management must guide workers in eliminating both causes of variation. In the example given in Case Study 6.1, the errant bank teller and the manager should have known that all requests for parking validation would be honored (as common variation), regardless of the demeanor of the customer. Instead, the teller and the manager treated the customer differently, as a special cause in need of differential treatment. If they had acted properly, the bank would be financially healthier today.

Process monitoring techniques include flow charts, cause-and-effect diagram, run charts, check sheets, Pareto analysis, histograms, and scatter diagrams. A process **flow chart** identifies how a service is delivered so that each step may be analyzed as a possible cause of error. A **cause-effect** or **fishbone diagram** displays a main quality characteristic as the spine on a drawing that resembles a fish skeleton. The chart focuses attention on the sources of defects, which may then be plotted on a **run chart** and/or a **check sheet** to isolate unusual or out-of-control factors. **Pareto analysis** is a powerful problem-solving and priority-setting tool in which the causes are arranged on a **bar chart** or **histogram** from most to least frequent. The most frequent causes can then be given the greatest attention. A **scatter diagram** correlates changes in process inputs and shows whether a relationship exists between two or more process characteristics. Using team problem identification and resolution techniques, these basic tools provide the process monitoring necessary to instill an attitude of TQS among all owners. Less attention is paid to statistics in this section because the subject is highly technical and requires specialized training (for details, see Omachonu and Ross, 1994; Gitlow et al., 1989; Swanson, 1995).

Processes in statistical control are predictable. After process control has been achieved, process capability analysis is used to compare actual process performance to desired customer specifications. Buyers, for example, may use capability index values to rate supplier performance. Work continues on statistically controlled processes; reducing the remaining (common) variation by achieving breakthroughs to higher service levels is a goal.

ESTIMATING THE COST OF POOR QUALITY

Anyone familiar with the day-to-day operations of any type of business knows the value of service quality, but many still think of the concept in abstract, subjective, and vague terms. A few still think that quality, like beauty, is in the eyes of the beholder and cannot be precisely quantified. Costs, revenues, and "hard" productivity measures, rather than quality indicators, tend to be more immediate drivers for many organizations, especially in the eyes of budget or financial officers. As long as quality is defined in "softer," less quantitative terms, integrated process-focused TQS systems are less likely to be regarded on equal terms with financial measures.

For most firms struggling to stay ahead in a competitive market, subjective measures have nothing to do with the harsh realities of the bottom line, traditionally defined as profits or losses.

Costs may be more tangible, but not necessarily more accurate, indicators of an organization's fixed expenses, growth potential, or total productivity. Most concerned managers also acknowledge that the value of any business is more than what is represented on a financial statement or an organizational chart: human resources interact with complex processes, subject to cost restraints, to form interdependent networks of people, materials, methods, and equipment that support a common purpose and mission. Thus, many of the most costly determinants of low productivity are hidden below the surface" (see Figure 6.2) and are inaccessible to most financial management systems.

Most managers admit, at least privately, that they lack a thorough understanding of the losses incurred as a result of poor quality practices. The "hard numbers" approach prevails because the total cost of inputs, labor, average workload per capita, and value of outputs can be more accurately estimated for each work unit. Implementing TQS can substantially reduce the cost of poor quality by eliminating non-value-added expenses. Thus, making the transition to a quality-managed, cost-effective, and continuously improving service culture requires an understanding of the complex interaction between cost, quality, and productivity.

Cost of poor quality analysis is a financial accounting methodology for estimating how much an organization spends, as a proportion of either total sales or gross income, on direct and indirect losses incurred for non-value-added activities. Non-value-added activities include excess paperwork and documentation, correcting defective outputs, inspection, risk management and liability costs for defective products or services, lawsuits, litigation insurance and retainers, customer allowances, warranty and guarantee costs, low employee productivity, absenteeism, stress-related health insurance costs, and lost sales or discounting to clear excess inventories. **Non-value-added** costs are all expenses for processes that can be eliminated without loss of value in delivering the final product or service to the customer.

The costs generally associated with poor quality practices have been used in the past to establish manufacturing guarantees and warranty charges. Rather than adding value or continuously improving processes, a service contract or warranty is a potential future expense which covers the customer (and producer) against excess costs of repairs. Since customers pay for service calls and most warranties are time dated or capped, the potential future risk to manufacturers is limited. While useful in marketing, they provide less incentive for providers to continuously improve process quality, which would make the guarantee unnecessary in the first place.

Like their manufacturing counterparts, managers of service firms recognize that errors made continuously throughout the assembly process require substantial and costly rework to correct. In healthcare, for example, the costs of administrative errors, malpractice insurance premiums, and duplicate inspections are the expensive consequences of poor process control, which may require costly and unnecessary rework. For special causes of variation, such as a malpractice suit against a hospital, the costs of legal fees and documentation alone could far exceed the insurance reserves set aside for such a contingency. Rather than issuing a warranty, it is far less expensive to prevent the occurrence from happening in the first place. It is very difficult, however, to train service workers to think in such preventive terms.

As mentioned earlier, when business is good, there are fewer incentives to measure the costs of poor quality and to take actions to eliminate the need for rework. Thus, hidden losses attributable to poor underlying process quality are routinely covered by expanding revenues. When you are making money, who cares how? Just make more! Thus, it may appear to be less costly in the short term to bury the causes of poor quality processes in obscure accounting systems or to ignore quality problems altogether by denying that they exist.

Quality costs are influenced not only by the training and motivation of employees, but by the perception of service quality by customers and the sensitivity of management systems used to monitor progress as well. In addressing these behavioral quality measurement issues, the essential differences between manufacturing and service quality control are almost negligible, since most manufacturing companies also compete for business by defining after-sales service as one of their primary products.

Measuring Poor Quality: Getting Below the Surface

In order to use quality as a strategic management tool, managers must first acknowledge the existence of visible (above the surface) and hidden (submerged) poor quality problems, as illustrated in Figure 6.2. Next, measurement systems must be designed to accurately translate these costs, establish measurement characteristics for each quality function, and designate and carefully train sensors to monitor progress. This recognition phase precedes the design and implementation phases and must involve the entire organization in the critical task of identifying which system characteristics not now being monitored must be measured. Critical but less quantifiable factors such as relationships between headquarters, suppliers, and ancillary service staff often loom beneath the surface as well. Managers must strive to go "below the surface of the iceberg" to accurately diagnose the impact of hidden costs on the financial health of the organization.

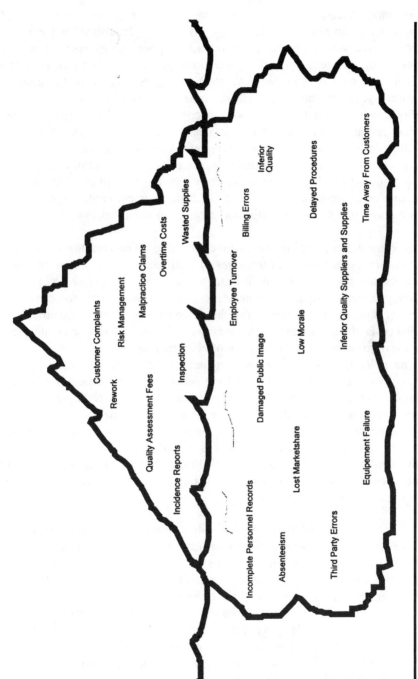

FIGURE 6.2 Visible and Hidden Costs of Poor Quality

To more accurately assess the impact of ignoring poor quality costs, Philip Crosby developed the **Eternally Successful Organization Grid** (see Appendix A), which illustrates the impact of poor quality costs at various stages within different types of organizations. His concept is based on variations in the level of understanding most managers have about the costs of poor quality. Organizations are classified as being at different stages of the quality spectrum, ranging from total uncertainty to absolute certainty. Most services are at the first stages of the quality grid (uncertainty), where there is little comprehension of quality as a management tool, the costs of poor quality are hidden, quality measures do not exist, and problems are resolved as they occur or their existence is denied in the first place. The ultimate objective of initiating a TQS planning and management control system is to reduce poor quality costs, perhaps not to zero, but at least below the 5 percent range.

To some extent, these problems are common to all organizations that focus only on profits and losses as measures of well being. Nearly all professional organizations, for instance, initially deny the existence of quality problems or narrowly define quality as conformance to accepted professional standards. For purposes of understanding the relationship between costs, quality, and productivity, the costs of quality can be conceptually divided into two areas: (1) the price of non-conformance and (2) the price of conformance.

The **price of non-conformance** includes all expenses accrued by doing things wrong, often repeatedly, for long periods of time. Healthcare service examples run the full gamut of routine activities, from correcting incomplete purchase orders, to scheduling and laboratory errors, to the need to keypunch orders a second or third time, to the more time-consuming and damaging liability costs and subsequent litigation incurred as a result of administering the wrong medication to a patient.[5] Joseph M. Juran (1988) offers a chilling example of the possible consequences of not having a quality monitoring system to discover such problems in a hospital:

> For years the hospital industry had only the vaguest idea of the extent of errors in the process of giving medication to patients. All hospitals posted rules requiring nurses to report medication errors promptly...however, in many hospitals the nurses had learned that when they made such reports they were often subjected to unwarranted blame. Hence they stopped making such reports. In due course a classic study made by a qualified outsider showed that (1) about 7 percent of the medications involved errors, some quite serious, and (2) the bulk of the errors were management-controllable, not worker-controllable (Juran, 1988, p. 95).

The **price of conformance** is what it would cost to do things right in the first place; examples include most professional quality assurance functions, education and training, all prevention efforts, and actions to improve supervisory skills. In an organization with a reasonably high degree of certainty about its quality costs, these expenses represent between 10 and 15 percent of total expenses. Previously discussed tools and techniques such as Pareto analysis, control charts, quality control circles, team brainstorming sessions, and surveys of internal and external customers are useful in identifying and reducing these non-value-added costs. It is important to employ these techniques and collect appropriate data so that the organization will have baseline information for determining where the most effective and least costly opportunities for preventive action exist.

Direct Quality Costs

In order to measure total losses due to poor quality, organizations must further analyze the costs that go into efforts to repair defective work. In general terms, these quality losses can be broken down into direct and indirect costs. Direct quality costs can be broken down further into (1) controllable costs, which include prevention and appraisal costs, and (2) resultant costs, which include internal and external error costs.[6] **Controllable** (or assignable) quality costs are those over which management has direct control to ensure that only prescribed services are delivered to customers in an acceptable manner. They can be either prevention costs, which are necessary to help an employee do the job correctly every time, or appraisal costs, which are expended to determine if a standardized activity was done properly every time. Typical prevention costs are those incurred for developing and implementing a data collection and reporting system, quality-related training, specialty training, vendor surveys, packaging inspections at the shipping–receiving docks, and preparation and documentation for outside inspections.

Probably the most effective way any organization can spend its limited resources is to invest in preventive actions. Unfortunately, most facilities neglect these investments because (1) they are time consuming and (2) the expense, as opposed to equipment or personnel costs, is often considered by budget and financial officers to be too difficult to tie to a tangible return on investment. Consistent with the example of a malpractice lawsuit cited earlier, the rewards of prevention can far exceed the cost of paying for errors. With effort, quality characteristics can be developed to complement financial and personnel measures. The underlying problem is generally not lack of technical competence, but too much concern about visible numbers and not enough attention to customer service quality.

Appraisal costs are an example of rework expended to determine if an activity was done right every time. These costs include outside audits, financial reports, approval signatures on various interdepartmental documents, outside endorsements (such as those from Underwriters Laboratories), maintenance and calibration of laboratory instruments, inspection of equipment, payload audits, and proofreading letters and memos. One reason why appraisal costs are necessary is that management is often not 100 percent confident that the money and time already expended in prevention costs has eliminated the possibility of error. Similar to inspection, appraisal costs tend to be both wasteful and too little too late. They often reflect a poor understanding of basic system processes yet are necessary as an inspection measure to prevent further waste of resources. They do little to identify and eliminate the causes of errors or to prevent them from recurring.

The resultant costs of poor quality make up a second broad category of direct costs and include all of the expenses that result from errors and all of the money spent because activities were not done right every time. These costs are called **resultant** because they are directly related to management decisions made in the controllable poor quality category. They can be divided further into subcategories of internal and external error costs. Internal error costs occur before a product or service is accepted by a customer because everyone did not do the job right every time. They are preventable, under control of management, and include examples such as:

1. A customer's refusal to submit a completed application because it was neither explained properly nor done according to an acceptable schedule

2. Costs of accounts receivable due to the billing system not producing bills on time

3. Mistakes on documents and computer reruns

4. Returning to a construction work site for a second or third time because the previous work was not performed to the customer's satisfaction.

External error costs stem from outside sources due to poor quality work by insufficiently trained service personnel. The most familiar example is a malpractice suit, but others include loss of package delivery contracts and revenues due to poor financial analysis of proposals, late delivery of supplies, and poor record keeping. With properly developed measurement characteristics, all these costs could be incorporated into an integrated TQS monitoring system.

Indirect Quality Costs

More difficult to measure, but equally important to monitor, are the *indirect,* below-the-surface costs. They are not directly measurable on a profit–loss ledger, yet are attributable to lack of quality control. Most of the indirect costs of poor quality are related to customer dissatisfaction with employee behavior and the resultant erosion of market share from dissatisfied customers, who complain to their friends and relatives. The lack of systems to monitor even relatively minor inconveniences at a critical time in a customer service encounter can escalate into major problems. Law enforcement and other public service agencies must pay special attention to these indirect costs due to the extraordinary legal, financial, and social costs incurred when something goes wrong during a citizen–police encounter.

Customer evaluation of a service will reflect a combination of expectation and perception of the quality of service given by a provider. Regardless of the quality assurance systems in place, if service levels do not meet customer expectations, any facility can incur indirect hidden costs by losing customers to other competitive providers. Dissatisfied ex-customers who tell others about their negative experiences can create a negative ripple effect, which is very difficult to counteract. Recall that reliable estimates of the cost of this negative ripple effect suggest that as many as ten potential customers, immediate family members, or friends can be influenced by a single negative evaluation. Worse yet, as many as nine out of ten dissatisfied customers fail to complain to the offending provider, in which case there is no voice of the customer to alert management that a problem exists. This can devastate the reputations of small or medium-sized facilities and can dramatically reduce repeat visits. Since these word-of-month evaluations affect attitudes and perceptions of total quality at the facility as a whole, loss of a good reputation affects all other goods and services as well.

Rather than waiting for and responding to complaints, customer dissatisfaction can be prevented by using process flow checklists or carefully designed surveys administered at appropriate intervals following delivery of service. Service providers find TQS attractive because it helps them to better understand the full range of customer needs. This can help avoid the tendency to design customer service systems around the small portion of customers who do complain. At Toyota Motors, for example, each time a customer brings his or her car in for service, a representative from the dealer will call the customer within 48 hours for an evaluation. Training in the latest theory and techniques of customer service is provided for customer service workers by Toyota personnel twice a month. Customers not only receive a phone call, but are mailed a detailed survey questionnaire to indicate their level of satisfaction with services received. This survey is mailed to the service center, not the dealer. Individual dealers and service advisors are evaluated by this independent monitoring. Toyota commits verbally and in writing to fixing the problem. If service was unsatisfactory, the customer is asked to bring the car back for same-day service to complete the work or a loaner car is provided. The standard is to complete the service on the same day.[7]

In summary, an accurate picture of the absence of total quality improvement is the price of non-conformity or the cost of continuing to do things wrong. As outlined here, these costs can be subdivided into various categories of prevention, appraisal, and failure to comply with standards and may have both direct and indirect consequences on customer service evaluations. Measurement characteristics can be established to monitor the overall costs of quality and to determine the current status of specific services or procedural compliance. These measures can be used initially to guide management in targeting areas for quality and productivity improvement. Refined systems may be used later for independent monitoring and improved implementation actions and as visible proof and recognition of productivity improvement (Milakovich, 1991b).

DEFINING IMPROVEMENT OPPORTUNITIES AND RAISING THE PRODUCTIVITY CEILING

Productivity is a commonly used term which means many different things to different people. What does it mean to be productive? Productivity is simply a ratio measure of how much an organization makes, divided by how much it costs to make the goods or services it produces. The less it costs to produce a good or service, the higher the productivity; the more it costs or the less efficiently an organization makes a product, the lower the productivity. Productivity can be raised by lowering costs or increasing efficiency, or some combination of both approaches.

    D. Scott Sink, Director of the Virginia Productivity Center, offers a seven-part productivity index to measure items such as the cost of quality, innovation, inventory, time to process a travel claim, and leadership (Sink, 1991). David Sumanth (1984) advocates the use of a total productivity model (TPM), which includes tangible output, human input, material input, capital, and energy costs to measure productivity. Productivity is defined in this chapter as the complex interaction among these and other factors, including:

■ Efficiency (the ratio of outputs to inputs)

■ Effectiveness (the effects of a job, task, or project on bottom-line profits, the local economy, society, or the environment)

■ Cost containment or reduction of expenses

■ Employee benefits, goodwill, and morale

■ Growth of a work unit's power base and/or budget

■ Ability to coordinate between work units

■ Stability and/or equilibrium (minimization of worker and managerial absenteeism, stress, conflict, and turnover)

The objective of any productivity improvement strategy is to balance the resources available with the level of service needed to satisfy the valid requirements of all internal and external customers. Listening to both types of customers is equally important in improving productivity. The only difference between an internal and an external customer is that the former receives a product or service produced by another work unit within the same organization, while the latter receives a product or service produced by another organization. All organizations strive to meet the valid quality requirements of both types of customers, albeit differently. Recall that valid customer requirements are "SMART" operational measures which reflect both the voices of the process (i.e., profit–loss statements, financial costs, overtime, healthcare benefits, fixed expenses) as well as the voices of the customers (i.e., sales, output, contracts, grievances, survey results, customer needs and complaints). High-performance services strive to raise productivity levels to meet higher customer satisfaction standards with the same or fewer resources.

In any organization, there is a theoretical limit above which productivity cannot rise using established and well-defined systems, even under perfect conditions. In quality terminology, such a system is predictable or in control. Traditional productivity improvement tools alone cannot raise productivity above the **productivity ceiling.** However, when SPC and TQS tools and techniques are combined, the ceiling can be raised. TQS sets a higher ceiling where only 75 to 85 percent of the old level of inputs is necessary to produce 85 percent of the old level of workload, which results in the following improvements: (1) a work unit can either reduce inputs or utilize excess inputs to expand operations or diversify, (2) quality of daily worklife is improved through a reduced workload, and (3) more of the workload is shifted from invisible to visible output done right the first time, so that output substantially increases.[8]

MERGING COST, PROCESS, QUALITY, AND PRODUCTIVITY DEFINITIONS

Improving service processes requires successive cycles of analysis, measurement, performance evaluation, and controlling for consistency (see Figure 2.4). Ideally, these cycles should never end, although the amount of measurement may decrease over time as procedures for measuring consistency are standardized and the whole system improves. This results in less labor content, fewer defectives, better communication, and more efficient processing. Process measures and customer satisfaction indicators must be reliable and valid. The objective is to eliminate non-value-added elements from a process. When a process is fully improved, only the essential or value-added elements remain.

Productivity improvement is a systematic strategy for increasing a work unit's ratio of inputs to outputs using some combination of the following: cost–benefit analysis, needs assessment, work redesign, process improvement, incentive systems, job enrichment, labor–management committees (less commonly called labor–management task forces), flextime, and quality control circles. The basic tools of statistical process and quality control, numerical goals set by those who have to meet them, new technology, organizational restructuring, interorganizational agreements (in both the private and public sectors) to pool resources, resource reallocation, employee retraining, and modification of perceptions, attitudes, and authority systems can also be used (Sedell, 1991). Some of these methods have been previously described and others are self-explanatory.

When facing budgetary reductions, privatization, or increasing market competition, many service managers discover that the means listed above are necessary but insufficient to achieve desired quality or productivity goals. When traditional tools prove insufficient, managers increasingly turn to extended versions of the tools. For example, quality control circles can be combined with *kaizen* or continuous quality improvement to demonstrate that everyone is responsible, including vendors, end users, and internal customers. Labor–management committees and task forces lend themselves to gainsharing or shared incentives for improvement. Groups of employees are eligible for bonuses or commissions determined by a sliding scale based on the amount of money saved or generated by cost-cutting or productivity improvement suggestions. When applied in one federal government agency, self-managed task forces were allowed to keep one-half (50 percent) of any savings they generated. It is important to creatively combine these tools to fit the organizational culture and meet local service delivery requirements.

PRODUCTIVITY IMPROVEMENT AND TOTAL QUALITY SERVICE

Service managers increasingly recognize that quality-of-life issues, the interrelationship between employees and their families, and non-monetary rewards affect recruiting, retention, morale, and productivity. Benefits such as flextime, parental leave, employee assistance plans, and care for children and elderly parents are becoming as important to raising productivity as the statistical measurement of output. Many benefits that cost very little on a per-employee basis, such as non-monetary awards presented by a supervisor in front of an employee's peers, can raise productivity on a limited budget. Increasingly, management in both the private and public service sectors has found it profitable to tailor benefits packages to the needs of their employees and have thus invested in long-term family care and other non-monetary benefits as a means to improve work performance.

Productivity improvement systems that encompass these elements are consistent with elements of total quality management (TQM), defined as strategies which (1) attempt to prevent defects instead of catching them after they have been made, (2) employ true participatory management practices, (3) are oriented toward identifying and satisfying both internal and external customers, (4) drive out fear, and (5) establish pride of workmanship (Milakovich, 1990a). The first two components of this definition are considered to be state-of-the-art in productivity improvement.

The other three components, however, have also increased productivity by eliminating non-value-added costs. For example, in terms of satisfying internal customers, if a form can be rearranged so that all of the data that unit X requires remains on the form, but unit Y's time to fill out the form is reduced with no impact on the time that it takes unit X to process the form, then why not rearrange the form? If unit X requires information from unit Y about project 1, and the information is on two forms, why can't the two forms be merged into one form? Does a certain project required by standard operating procedure still have a purpose or has its purpose been superseded by changing times? In order to add value to processes, a TQS manager asks: (1) Is there something I can do to reduce the receiver's time and cost which would cost the organization less if it were done upstream? (2) Is there something I can do to reduce the supplier's time and cost which would cost the organization less if it were done downstream (Sedell, 1991).

Driving out fear is compatible with removing dissatisfiers (hygienic factors) such as those mentioned in the earlier discussion of Frederick Herzberg's dual factor theory. Removal of dissatisfiers does not in itself provide productivity incentives to employees (Herzberg, 1966). However, removing dissatisfiers is as necessary as providing incentives in order to motivate employees; this second point is often either forgotten or overlooked by management. Applications in both the private and public sectors in the United States, Canada, Japan, and Mexico have shown that there are alternatives to punishment-based Theory X management, which not only increase productivity but actually improve managerial control by preventing the time-consuming special causes that prompt angry phone calls from superiors and/or important customers.

The fifth component is to establish pride of workmanship. William L. Ginnodo, Director of the American Productivity and Quality Center in Houston, Texas, offers a ten-point plan to establish pride of workmanship (Ginnodo, 1989):

1. Developing a mission statement and then sticking to following the *intent* of the statement
2. Emphasizing continuous improvement
3. Employee involvement
4. Eliminating anything that keeps people from performing at their best
5. Measuring and sharing results of comparisons between work units within the organization and results of interorganizational comparisons
6. Gainsharing, incentive, and recognition systems where rewards are presented to an employee by his or her supervisor in front of his or her peers (even if the reward is symbolic, such as an extra vacation day)
7. Identifying issues to be addressed
8. Championing causes about which subordinates and staff will be enthusiastic
9. Starting small
10. Managers getting employees (both in a manager's own work unit and in other work units) to identify barriers to pride in workmanship and, where it would improve the productivity of the manager's own work unit, helping employees to eliminate those barriers

To improve productivity and simultaneously reduce costs, needs assessment and process reengineering are done at both the design and implementation stages, periodically, or both. Identification of fraud, waste, and abuse is done on an irregular basis. State-of-the-art productivity improvement efforts are ongoing processes conducted by every employee using participatory management, needs assessment, work redesign, and the identification of poor quality costs. New technologies, organizational restructuring, and resource reallocation, where appropriate, are usually byproducts of adopting QI even if they are not part of the original initiative.

The cost, productivity, and quality control concepts mentioned above originated in manufacturing; they can, however, be applied in the service sector. The following case study illustrates their application in construction management, one of the nation's largest service industries

PRODUCTIVITY AND QUALITY IMPROVEMENT IN THE CONSTRUCTION INDUSTRY[9]

The construction industry has traditionally represented 9 percent or more of the U.S. gross national product. Although construction activity has declined in recent years, statistics published by the Bureau of Labor Statistics (BLS) indicate that 4 to 5 percent of the total non-farm working population was employed in an area of construction in 1991 (compared to approximately 7 percent in 1979). The BLS cautions that it has not been able to publish reliable data on construction productivity since the early 1980s, but a clear trend indicates an ongoing reduction in U.S. construction labor productivity since 1965. This declining productivity is cause for concern.[10] The trend indicates falling activity levels due to several factors: higher operating costs due to increased regulation; reduced domestic spending; decreased private spending for plants, buildings, and housing; reduced government spending; inflation in construction costs; poor quality cost practices; and foreign competition, both in domestic and overseas construction. Not unlike other services, company-level efforts to improve productivity do not conform to a standardized approach.

The construction industry is truly diverse. The BLS refers to three main categories: general building contractors, heavy construction (except building), and special trade contractors. These categories are further subdivided into 11 subheadings, of which four major groups are involved in construction and have a major influence on productivity as a result of their actions:

1. **Owners:**   Originate the need for projects and determine the locations and purpose of facilities. They arrange for design, financing, and construction.

2. **Designers:**   Usually architects or engineers who interpret the owner's wishes into drawings and specifications that are used to guide facility construction.

3. **Constructors:**   Contractors and subcontractors who provide a work force, materials, equipment and/or tools, and the leadership and management to implement the drawings and specifications to furnish a completed facility.

4. **Labor force:**   Comprised of foremen, craftsmen, or journeymen and skilled or semi-skilled apprentices or helpers. Many different crafts are represented, such as masons, pipe fitters, carpenters, and electricians (Oglesby et al., 1989).

Other parties, such as financiers, lawyers, insurers, unions, manufacturers, suppliers, and transporters, also play a role, as do public and private agencies, federal and local regulators, public services, and utilities.

The Evolution of Quality Improvement in Construction

In the area of construction, the Japanese were among the first to apply quality control techniques on a large scale, although they did not embrace this concept until after the oil crisis of 1973. Prior to this time, they thought that the construction industry was inappropriate for the application of total quality control (TQC), because of the inherent variability in projects and the difficulty in defining acceptable levels of quality. In 1975, when the formerly impeccable safety and quality image of Takenaka Komuten Company, the sixth largest construction firm in Japan, was tarnished by the failure of a sheet piling system in Okinawa, the company embarked on a quality control program. It was followed by Shimizu Construction, the second largest construction firm in Japan, which established a quality control program in 1976, and Kajima Corporation, the third largest, in 1978. Subsequently, several U.S. construction companies adopted the more familiar TQM programs used by U.S. manufacturers.

Alfeld (1988) advances the view that construction very probably promises a greater payback for performance improvement than any other service industry because of its magnitude, which indicates that a minuscule improvement in performance could translate into billions of dollars in savings. Ironically, the industry has resisted change from reactive management to performance-based management systems. Despite the obvious need to increase productivity, few companies (less than 5 percent) have undertaken QI programs. Several barriers have been suggested.

1. Project Diversity. The construction environment is very dissimilar to manufacturing (and other services) in a number of respects that hinder the application of quality and productivity improvement techniques. Most projects are unique, single-order, single-production ventures. Whereas manufacturing sites can be standardized, construction sites are unique. The long production cycle makes construction projects more susceptible to external factors. In the absence of uniform standards, construction projects are often evaluated subjectively. Project participants differ for each project, and therefore little benefit is derived from standardization and repetition.

2. Management Inadequacies. The majority of construction deficiencies result from inadequacies in the management structure of the industry, lack of training, and commercial pressures that stem from the almost universal custom of awarding work to the lowest bidder. Management is generally more concerned with meeting schedules (often to avoid penalties) than with building a quality work force that will, in turn, generate construction of better quality.

3. Lack of Quality Cost Information. As noted earlier, few organizations measure the costs of poor quality, and most are unreceptive to the idea of eliminating those costs by funding staff, training, documentation, audits, etc. Quality cost information is often masked by self-protective actions by employees. For example, excessive materials are ordered in anticipation of waste and loss. Harmful trends in operating costs are masked, and management lacks the data to diagnose the need for corrective action. The cost of establishing quality systems for construction has been estimated at less than 1 percent of turnover and is less in extreme cases such as nuclear construction (Ashford, 1989).

4. Inappropriate Measurement. Traditional project management tools do not truly address productivity. They indicate schedule slippages and cost overruns. The information that schedules provides is generally after the fact and often misleading (Goodman, 1988).

5. Declining Work Force. The Department of Labor forecasts an increase of 823,000 U.S. craft jobs between 1986 and the year 2000. In order to meet that need, over 200,000 new craft employees will have to be produced annually, and a major deficit is therefore now accumulating. The current recession has probably made the situation more critical, as younger employees find construction insecure and move to other industries. This will not help an industry that will need highly trained, quality-conscious workers to be globally competitive.[11]

6. Poor Human Relations. Construction management tends to use negative reinforcement (Theory X) to motivate workers and crews to accomplish desired performance standards. Lack of fringe benefits, combined with the image of the typical construction superintendent as a "hard charger" who rules by fear and threatens to fire anyone who fails to meet expectations, discourages long-term QI. There is also a misconception in the industry that visibly hard work and appearing to be busy, as opposed to increasing effectiveness through smarter work methods, are necessary in order to remain competitive.

7. Lack of Quality Orientation. Few companies have adopted productivity/quality improvement, and the majority see the construction process as having to achieve no more than the minimum acceptable standard to meet customer expectations. Moreover, there is a tendency to minimize costs by pushing workers to the limit and using the cheapest material allowed.[12]

8. Crisis Orientation. Many writers have documented the construction industry's resistance to change. In fact, significant changes have been sparked primarily by catastrophes of one kind or another. The Japanese initiated TQC in construction management only after the 1973 oil embargo. Major revisions were made in U.S. engineering codes after the failure of a structure in the Kansas City Hyatt Regency Hotel. Major damage to buildings in South Carolina in 1989 after Hurricane Hugo resulted in changes in building codes and inspection procedures. The devastation from Hurricane Andrew in Dade County, Florida in August 1992 resulted in a major scrutiny of building codes and their enforcement. These and other crises have been expensive catalysts to the improvement of quality systems.

The Challenge of Measurement in Construction

There are probably as many opinions on how to measure quality in construction processes as there are practitioners in the field. It is generally accepted that construction processes are far more difficult to measure than manufacturing processes and that acceptance very probably lies at the heart of the industry's reluctance to apply formal productivity/quality improvement methods. To confuse the issue further, there is much disagreement on the definitions of productivity, quality, and other measures of accomplishment.

Much of the confusion stems from the differing views of quality characteristics held by various participants in the construction processes. For example, Alfeld (1988) refers to finished work-in-place (such as framing a wall) as an *accomplishment*, a construction technique as a *method*, and *performance* as a combination of both methods and accomplishment. Accomplishment is further described as being *valuable* (such as a wall being plumbed, and in the right place, which results in valuable performance). He extends the concept of value to *worth* (i.e., worthy performance occurs when the value of the accomplishment exceeds the cost of the method). Profit is the difference between the price and the cost of a job. Constructors sometimes compensate for poor accomplishment by using cheaper methods, in order to remain profitable. The continuity of this practice is encouraged by the lack of understanding by the owner and a lack of vigilance by his or her representatives, be they design or project management professionals.

Oglesby et al. (1989) define *performance* as a broad term with four main elements: productivity, safety, timeliness, and quality. Productivity is measured in cost terms and is said to be satisfactory if "work is accomplished at a fair price to the owner, and with a reasonable profit to the contractor." It measures the effectiveness with which resources—managers, workers, materials, equipment, tools, and working space—are employed to produce a finished building or structure.

Safety relates to minimizing accidents and the attendant employee suffering, as well as project interruption and higher insurance costs. The injury rate in construction is high. In 1990, 146.1 work days were lost to injury per 100 workers vs. 134.9 in 1987; 14.1 of every 100 workers were injured in 1990. With occupational illnesses included, these figures rise to 147.9 and 14.3, respectively. The BLS reports that 51.2 days were lost per 100 workers in private industry due to illnesses and injuries in 1973, and this number rose to 78.3 in 1990.[13] Timeliness influences productivity through overall completion on time and adherence of job elements to schedules. Quality is regarded as two-dimensional: (1) meeting an owner's needs and (2) minimizing rework.

The shortcoming of most measurement models now in use in construction is that they are concerned only with partial productivity. This is misleading, as high labor productivity, for example, might distract management's attention from excessive costs of capital or high energy costs, which inversely affect productivity. Essentially, the viability of the entire enterprise can only be gauged by total productivity measurements (Sumanth, 1984). Erroneous results can be produced if any of the input factors inflate or deflate during a given period.

The Construction Industry Institute conducted research on 19 construction firms to identify trends in the application of quality management systems (Burati et al., 1991). The findings were positive: 12 companies had formal TQM, 4 had quality assurance/quality control programs, and 3 had informal TQM. The motivators for these programs included increasing competition, customer pressure, and better use of human resources. Different models were used as a basis for these programs, including Crosby, Deming, Juran, and combinations thereof. The Crosby approach was used more frequently, probably due to wider marketing, while the Deming method stressed a holistic philosophy, including continuous improvement. The more successful programs resulted from an adoption of TQM to fit each organization and were tried as pilot programs. Training throughout the organization was seen as essential for success and was most effective when integrated with an employee's job functions. With regard to program objectives, safety, schedule, cost, and quality were seen as closely interrelated. Above all, commitment of top management was cited as virtually indispensable in the success of all quality management efforts.

During the past ten years in particular, efforts have been made by both the federal government and private industry to encourage research into and application of productivity/quality improvement. Expert systems have been increasingly applied to construction measurement. One type takes information from a given situation and walks the user through all the thought processes that make for optimal project planning. The other guides users, based on standard procedures in the expert database. TQM and quality assurance/quality control programs have been implemented in several large U.S. companies, as identified by Burati et al. (1991). Bechtel, Fluor-Daniel, and other large construction companies have implemented these programs, with varying degrees of success.

There is little uniformity from one organization to another in the measurement of performance or in the concept of acceptable standards, and it appears that some organizations regard such programs as "soft" and incapable of measurement.

Tools for Improving Productivity and Service Quality

Oglesby et al. (1989) describe formal and informal methods to identify improvement opportunities. They cite typical failures on the part of management to ensure that tools and materials are available and suitable, that tasks are assigned to optimize worker skills, and management as often defensive about these fundamental errors. Traditional industrial engineering applications include (1) the learning curve for repetitive projects, (2) activity sampling, (3) questionnaires, (4) interviews, (5) time studies, and (6) time-lapse recordings.

Significant advances have been made in the development of knowledge-based process planning systems for construction, although full automation has not been achieved. The CONSTRUCTION PLANEX system is a knowledge-based expert system that generates activity plans for the excavation and structural erection of concrete or steel frame buildings. Although this system is limited in application to specific detailed designs, it can select construction technologies and assign crews to project activities. It can calculate work quantities, for example, by referencing a column footing of a given volume. Research and development need to focus on knowledge-based systems so that less experienced project planners will be able to use these systems with good results in the near future (Zozoya-Gorostiza et al., 1989).

Several work sampling studies focusing on task-based productivity measures, as opposed to firm-level productivity, have been done in recent years. This is probably due to the greater ease of measuring labor productivity as compared to total productivity. Many construction projects have begun to explore the partnering concept, whereby an ongoing working relationship is established between an owner, a general contractor, and specific subcontractors, construction managers, and design professionals. There is evidence, albeit unquantified, that the element of trust leads to better, more cost-effective construction, which is the result of improved communication and a less bureaucratic structure. Bechtel Group, Inc., for example, engaged in a partnering relationship in a major project in Japan in 1982. Overseas Bechtel, Inc., the company's Tokyo-based subsidiary, obtained a one-tenth share of a $254 million contract from Nippon Telephone and Telegraph as part of a six-member consortium. Through the partnering approach, Bechtel was able to take advantage of a joint Japan–U.S. agreement by operating cost effectively in a traditionally forbidden market.

Conferences on teamwork between owners and construction professionals have become an increasingly visible way to promote a win–win approach between contract parties and to promote trust and teamwork.

Recommendations for Quality Improvement in Construction

Many observations are self-evident in a review of available literature and form the basis for a number of recommendations. It is important to note that none of the literature suggests that TQS approaches are being used in U.S. companies. Various measures of labor output could be said to represent partial and labor productivity. While human input is considered, the combined effects of material and capital are not. The following recommendations are made:

1. Consumers of the goods and services produced by the construction industry need to be educated. In the manufacturing arena, consumers have the protection of agencies such as Underwriters Laboratories. Manufacturers are educated consumers of components and subassemblies provided by

vendors and require statistical proof of compliance with required quality levels. This situation is not duplicated in the construction industry, beyond a requirement that minimum design standards be met for items such as reinforcement, fire resistance, and electrical and plumbing codes. This compliance in no way ensures quality. Quality management professionals such as industrial engineers need to play a leadership role in this process and educate the populace to recognize specific indicators of quality compliance.

2. There needs to be a "meeting of the minds" among all parties involved, including industrial engineers and researchers, to develop uniform models for measuring productivity and monitoring quality. Only with a unified approach can the many subgroups and specialty enterprises in the industry build on each other's experiences in the spirit of continuous improvement in order to compete on a global scale in the construction arena.

3. Construction companies (constructors) need to aggressively adopt quality/productivity to emphasize building in quality. A culture needs to be developed whereby constructors do not comply with codes out of fear, but instead strive to attain quality.

4. Design professionals, architects, and engineers need to stress life cycle costing to clients, so that they gradually adopt Deming's fourth point: End the practice of awarding business on price tag alone. Value engineering should be encouraged as an adjunct to this process, but it should be practiced by properly trained individuals.

5. Quality management professionals need to take the lead in breaking down the barriers to communication and the adversities that have historically existed between the parties to a construction contract: the owner, the constructor, and to a lesser extent the designer.

6. Trade school curricula should be updated to include quality and productivity management principles. This will engender in workers greater pride in the level of their craft. Educated workers will be more likely to "build it right the first time," even without the extensive scrutiny of inspections. Trades will become more professional as opposed to being a way station for the marginal. This is especially important in light of the forecasted shortfall in the work force size, if competitiveness is to be improved.

7. Project management curricula should be more aggressively updated to include productivity and quality management principles. Not only should the quantitative aspects be taught, but human relations training should be

strongly emphasized as well. A point of balance between meeting expected costs, schedules, and building performance needs to be cultivated in project managers and constructors.

8. Dialogue needs to be pursued between lawyers, architects, engineers, constructors, owners, and government agencies having jurisdiction over regulation of the construction process. The general provisions of the standard form of a contract need to be modified to put more emphasis on incentives and less on penalties. Only when these barriers are reduced will there be a concerted move toward developing the caliber of construction that will increase global competitiveness.

9. Ongoing research needs to be funded and pursued more aggressively at several levels: industry, university, and federal. Industrial engineering approaches need to be better integrated so that "high tech" and "high touch" can blend harmoniously. There should be less reliance on catastrophes to catalyze action.

10. High-profile awards should be created to recognize substantiated productivity and quality in the work force. This will engender a less adversarial attitude on the part of workers toward management and registered professionals, and vice versa. By the same token, the industry should develop a national award for construction excellence. It cannot be expected to start at the level of the Deming Prize or Baldrige Award, but it should encourage the construction industry to strive for excellence. Many methods and techniques have been identified to improve construction productivity and quality, ranging from simplified work sampling to the application of knowledge-based project scheduling systems. The application of any of this broad range of tools and techniques is at such a fledgling stage that major gains in construction productivity and quality can be derived merely by implementing the simplest and most accessible of them. However, quantitative productivity measures should be recognized and encouraged in order to prevent programs from degenerating into slogans. Several researchers have documented positive perceptions from companies on their QI efforts, as opposed to concise productivity statistics. The common experience of researchers is that communication problems and the lack of good human relations are among the greatest and most intractable obstacles to higher productivity and, ultimately, to our competitiveness.

11. A national policy should provide incentives for companies to have better access to productivity improvement hardware and software. There should be a rating system for products, such as material handling systems for

better on-site productivity, to improve confidence in such new technology. Subsidies or tax incentives should be studied for possible implementation in this area, especially for smaller companies that have less capital.

12. Construction industry research on productivity and quality is fragmented at best, although its quantity and depth have increased in recent years. There is a general perception, from government agencies such as the BLS and the Department of Commerce on down, that construction productivity is elusive and almost impossible to measure. Standardization of research design, such as establishing specific building and facility configurations for study, should be considered in order to build a national database to aid quantification, similar to the way in which various classes and types of motor vehicles are tested. This will make studies reproducible and more usable for further development.

13. Job safety takes a high toll in terms of worker productivity. BLS reports show a marked increase in injuries and job-related illnesses over the years, at the same time that healthcare and insurance costs have risen disproportionately. These trends affect all companies, but especially smaller construction companies. It may be argued that if workers perceive that management does not appear to provide safe working conditions, then they are far less likely to offer high-quality workmanship. Stronger state or federal support may be needed in this area.

14. In recent years, many construction failures, from both natural disasters as well as unassisted causes, have revealed either inadequate design or improper interpretation of adequate designs. Today's contractors seem to be more concerned about quality, but only efforts at the federal level to better enforce construction codes are likely to reverse years of neglect in this area.

SUMMARY AND CONCLUSIONS

There are almost as many definitions for productivity as there are people who want to improve it. As a ratio of inputs to outputs, productivity is the complex interaction of efficiency, effectiveness, cost containment or reduction, employee goodwill and morale, growth of a work unit's power base and/or budget, ability to coordinate, and stability and/or equilibrium. SPC and TQS can work together to improve productivity.

Productivity improvement is generally defined as the systematic study of a work unit's output using some combination of TQC, SPC, and TQM concepts and tools. Understanding the costs of poor quality practices is essential to integrating quality and productivity improvements as well as raising an organization's productivity ceiling. Organizations are typically run on "hard" numbers such as costs and expenses, probably because there is less understanding of the actual losses from continued poor quality practices.

Without using SPC and TQS, there is an upper limit or ceiling on how much productivity can be raised using traditional productivity tools. Thus, components of SPC and TQS become logical and applicable extensions of traditional productivity improvement tools. Combining SPC and TQS with traditional tools leads to a higher productivity ceiling, but other tools may also be used to raise productivity beyond that ceiling. There are many examples in the private, public, and non-profit sectors of efforts to raise productivity, increase outputs, and either reduce inputs or utilize excess capacity to expand operations or diversify.

TQS can serve as a bridge between traditional methods and two other international QI strategies: total productivity improvement and company-wide quality improvement (the mainstream management philosophy in the Japanese private and public sectors). Merging definitions of quality and productivity concepts makes TQS, together with SPC, effective tools for organizational cost control and productivity improvement.

The U.S. construction industry has displayed a growing interest in the improvement of quality and productivity, but the ascendancy to world-class performance can only come when all involved achieve congruence in several main factors: uniform definitions of productivity and quality, consistent systems of measurement (to enable the necessary process of continuous improvement), the professionalization of construction staff, and a shift in focus from a need for mass inspection to a culture of "building it right the first time." Efforts to date represent a jigsaw puzzle with many pieces missing. Industrial engineers and other quality management professionals should heed the call to use their expertise as change agents to supply the missing pieces and pave the way for global competitiveness. Above all, top management of all organizations involved— owners, designers, constructors, and construction management companies— must be committed to the concepts of productivity/quality improvement and must provide the necessary funding and staff support to ensure success.

Whatever the future may bring, TQS is likely to be one of several pillars, because high quality, low costs, and consumer satisfaction are important components of competitiveness. Furthermore, government officials, in partnership with industry leaders, are likely to exert more influence on decisions regarding quality strategies. In theory, quality also has features that are attractive for policymakers: it is virtually impossible to argue against quality, and the costs of government programs to promote this goal are relatively small. Indeed, new programs in education, research, and small business need not require extensive bureaucratic approval, but only that of concerned elected officials, city managers, and state program officers. As we shall see in the next chapter, coalitions among these various quality interests are promoting efforts to reinvent customer-focused quality at all levels of the public sector.

ENDNOTES

1. Analysts often use two numbers—the mean and the standard deviation—to represent the performance of an entire process. This is a simple, inexpensive, and effective way to understand and improve processes. Once the mean or average process characteristic is determined, then the standard deviation (upper and lower limits) around the mean can be calculated.

2. An operational definition has three components: specification, test, and criterion. For example, a room is operationally defined as "stuffy" if the oxygen content falls below 20 percent (specification) and a specific sensor gives an accurate reading (test) below 19.99 percent (criterion), which allows for the uncertainty in the measurement.

3. A work unit is the component of an organization that is taken as a unit and analyzed. It can be a team, office, department, division, or even (in some cases) the organization as a whole.

4. The environment in which decisions take place is often included as one of the common process elements as well.

5. For details on methodologies for analyzing poor quality costs in healthcare, see the section on adapting QI principles to medical service and hospital settings in W. Edwards Deming's *Out of the Crisis* (1986), pp. 199–206. For an elaboration of the concept of how to define the needs of extended customers, see Joseph M. Juran's *Juran on Planning for Quality* (1988, pp. 17–59). These sources are particularly useful for managers as step-by-step guides for designing total quality measurement systems.

6. H. James Harrington, *Poor Quality Costs,* Milwaukee: Marcel Dekker-ASQC Press, 1987.

7. Conversations with customer service representative, Kendall Toyota, Miami, Florida, February 24, 1994.

8. For example, if 60 percent of the portion of the workload that previously produced invisible output now produces "visible" output with a pre-TQM cost of poor quality of 30 percent, then only 85 percent of the old input level would be needed to produce an output of 100.3 percent of the pre-TQM output level, even without any changes in productivity. The output/input ratio would increase by 18 percent with a 0.3 percent increase in output and a 15 percent reduction in input. (Example provided by Ken Sedell, unpublished paper, 1991.)

9. This section is abstracted with permission from Lincoln Forbes, from his paper published in John S.W. Fargher, *Proceedings of the Second International Symposium on Productivity and Quality Improvement with a Focus on Government,* Norcross, Ga.: Industrial Engineering and Management Press, September 8–10, 1993.

10. *Engineering Research News* (May 25, 1992, p. 88) describes a serious shortfall in the generation of new contracts for the 400 largest construction companies. In 1991, the 50

largest builders received $34.7 billion in new domestic contracts, $5 billion less than in 1990. The top 400 companies declined in revenue in the same period, from $67 billion to $48.5 billion. The industry is consolidating, with larger companies acquiring smaller ones, and in turn diversifying into new areas unrelated to commercial construction. This consolidation is likely to require fewer workers in the overall industry.

11. Japanese firms have also had difficulty in attracting younger workers to the construction industry. The situation is critical in light of the fact that the number of workers over 50 years of age has increased from 19 percent to 29 percent of the work force.

12. In Dade County, Florida, which has some of the strictest building and zoning laws in the country, structural investigations of damage following Hurricane Andrew in 1992 revealed a shocking disregard for existing building codes by some developers/constructors. While the intensity of the hurricane was unprecedented, the patterns of destruction indicated vast differences in the durability of buildings in the same area, which pointed to poor construction quality. There were many examples of unbraced roof trusses and plywood that was not nailed to trusses in buildings that had supposedly been inspected. Many of these defects were not detectable through the standard form of inspection, and from all appearances, the constructors had no interest in an internal quality control system.

13. According to industry statistics published in *ENR*, December 16, 1991, p. 23.

7

MANAGING QUALITY IN THE PUBLIC SECTOR

There is a pervasive need to improve quality in all types of service organizations. Despite this need, few of the over 87,000 governments in the United States, among the largest and most complex service organizations in the world, have undertaken steps to eliminate poor quality costs, empower employees, increase productivity, or respond to customer complaints about poor service. Recent trends, however, are very encouraging.

From the White House, to statehouses, to city halls and the courthouses of America, total quality service (TQS) principles are being applied by governments as part of the extensive reinvention, revitalization, and redesign now taking place everywhere in the public sector. When separated from the legislative priority-setting and policy-making process, quality improvement is one means to achieve the illusive, yet important, goal of improving the performance of public services.

In the political arena, the perennial debate over the role of government in stimulating the economy and providing jobs will continue forever. There is less disagreement, however, over one of government's basic purposes: to create a sound environment for economic expansion. In many regions of the country, "politics as usual" is giving way to new concerns about efficiency, cost effectiveness, and productivity of vital public services such as education, healthcare, law enforcement, transportation, and environmental protection. Governments at all levels find TQS techniques well suited for transforming public agencies into mission-driven, quality-focused, results-oriented, decentralized, customer-responsive (citizens and taxpayers) service organizations.

Only a few years ago, there was little discussion about quality issues, customer satisfaction, empowerment of public employees, or delayering government bureaucracies. This has changed in recent years and promises to change even more as we move into the next century. There has been even less dialogue about the role of government as a leader in the movement to make U.S. industry more competitive in world markets. As indicated in the previous chapters, policies involving research, training, and recognition of quality efforts are now being widely debated.

The current explosion of interest in the application of TQS concepts and techniques provides a promising model for a non-partisan, quality-driven, customer-focused change in public management practices. TQS offers a strategy for the quality transformation of American government at all levels. The keys to success are leadership and commitment in establishing adequately funded training to address specific problems as defined by suppliers and consumers of government services.

The complex interrelationships between the political and management sciences of public administration are discussed in this chapter. Descriptions of how TQS concepts are being applied in governments and how barriers can be overcome are provided. The chapter concludes with an overview of current implementation efforts in selected federal, state, and local government agencies.

WHY THE CHANGE?

While no single dramatic event foreshadows the service quality revolution in government, several trends have contributed to its widespread application:

1. Since the late 1970s, there has been increased publicity about the fiscal and environmental consequences of waste and inefficiency in the public sector. As a result, taxpayers in many regions have refused to approve tax increases.

2. Fiscal crises and taxpayer discontent have encouraged some governments, especially at the local level, to experiment with customer-friendly ways to deliver better quality services.

3. Privatization and deregulation were proposed in the 1980s to divest public agencies of inefficiently managed programs. Private businesses, however, were (and still are) reluctant to assume the non-profitable functions of government.

4. Changing leadership at the local, state, and federal government levels has encouraged experimentation and innovations in management. These changes, in turn, have led to benchmarking the best practices in organizations with similar processes.

5. Public and private service managers are placing less reliance on traditional top-down, control-oriented management practices and are focusing instead on better ways to respond to customers and measure results.

6. Federal executive agencies have been implementing productivity and quality programs since the mid-1980s, and recent policies have encouraged long-term planning, mission-driven results-oriented budgeting, and reduced dependence on annual performance review.[1]

7. Since 1988, traditional budgetary, cost control, inspection-based, and control-oriented management hierarchies in the federal government have been replaced by a total quality management strategy.

8. The release of the National Performance Review in the first year of the Clinton administration has prompted all federal and many state and local agencies to become more customer directed and results oriented (Gore, 1993).

The results of the 1992 presidential and 1994 congressional elections offer an unprecedented opportunity for the widespread application of these and other fundamental changes in the direction of public policy. To translate words into actions, however, and to sustain a long-term public service TQS effort, basic system changes coupled with new management practices are needed.[2] Opportunities for such changes are extremely rare in the public sector. Despite this positive evidence of progress, many governments still lack incentives to become more efficient and customer focused.

When compared with the private sector, decisions in the public sector are more complex and affect more interests; rewards tend to be less immediate and leadership is less stable. In the past, when governments made the effort to become more efficient, elected legislatures simply reduced their budgets. In short, there is no equivalent to the bottom-line market determination of quality progress in the public sector. The focus of public budgeting and financial accounting is (naturally) on inputs, or appropriations, rather than outputs or results. Government agencies must develop new ways to measure customer-driven service quality and monitor results based on measurable outputs rather than inputs.

For decades, productivity management tools and methods have been widely and ineffectively used in the public sector. They have tended to stress control, individual performance, and accountability, but failed to eliminate the causes of inefficient programs and wasted resources. Several national commissions, established to examine these issues, report widespread public dissatisfaction with the treatment received at the hands of public servants.[3] They also offer specific recommendations for change that reflects TQS applications and principles. Complaints about government services are nothing new. What is new is the recognition that government employees can do something to correct the problems.

Negative public stereotypes about the unresponsiveness of bureaucracies and the poor quality of government services are reinforced by media reports and official misconduct. The 1991 budget gridlock between Congress and the President, the staggering costs to bail out the savings-and-loan industry, mounting federal debt and deficits, and the Iran-Contra and congressional check-kiting scandals reinforce negative stereotypes of government failures. Despite these revelations, the vast majority of public officials are committed to raising the quality and productivity of vital public services such as education, law enforcement, healthcare, housing, national defense, and public transportation. Once policy decisions have been made by elected officials, there is a need for a better methodology to achieve these purposes.

Traditionally, public administrators have attempted to maintain control and accountability by emphasizing training in core functions such as personnel administration, performance appraisal, budgetary and financial management, decision-making skills, methods of goal setting, and **individual productivity measurement** such as management by objectives, POSDCORB, and planning-programming-budgeting-system. These sincere attempts to improve productivity have not seriously impacted the quality of public services. In recent years, public sector productivity improvement efforts have emulated private firms and offered employees bonuses for goal achievement and merit increases and have ranked employees for pay purposes. There is little evidence that these attempts have either improved performance or increased productivity.

Increasingly, elected and appointed public officials realize that such individual productivity methods *alone* do not automatically lead to service quality improvement. To continuously improve service quality, new management practices combined with better measures of customer satisfaction are being implemented in federal, state, and local governments. Application of TQS techniques provides a promising model for a revolution in thinking about current public management practices. If successfully implemented, TQS offers a road map for the transformation of American public administration at all levels. As their counterparts in other services do, public managers must carefully listen to and appropriately respond to all their customers, including elected officials.

THE POLITICS OF QUALITY IMPROVEMENT

The terms *politics* and *quality* together no longer form an oxymoron. Achieving quality and productivity without increasing costs (higher taxes or user fees) is more difficult, but not impossible, in the public sector because of (1) the decisive role played by politicians as the co-owners and final decision makers and (2) the complex relationship between elected officials and the appointed administrators who actually implement decisions. The two groups live in separate but often overlapping worlds of influence.

In general, elected representatives are concerned with immediate political rewards rather than long-term professional–administrative values such as efficient use of resources and increased productivity. (There are always exceptions, but annual budget cycles and pressures to be re-elected tend to reinforce a short-term perspective.) Instead of responding to customer service quality and productivity problems with new management approaches, most elected officials claim to be frustrated by bureaucratic resistance (some are actually frustrated). At the same time, however, some avoid political accountability for results by blaming public employees or prior administrations for failure to improve conditions. Public administrators are no less accountable, even though most are protected by collective bargaining or civil service rules. Buffeted by changing political ideologies and weary of taxpayers' wrath, many appointed public officials, affectionately referred to as bureaucrats, are acutely aware of the limitations of current public management practices but claim to be powerless to change them without political approval. This "blame and claim" strategy has become a vicious circle with no winners and only losers—especially the taxpayers and recipients of inefficiently managed government programs (Gordon and Milakovich, 1995, p. 392).

TQS offers an opportunity to change the very nature of the political game by emphasizing process improvements, empowering public employees, and meeting citizen/customer needs while simultaneously reducing costs. Everyone wants to see more value for their tax dollars. Ideological issues affecting vital public services are becoming less divisive; there is no inherently Republican or Democratic way to manage vital public services. Stated simply, TQS represents a better way.

Reconciling the competing demands of diverse interest groups forces politicians to reconcile multiple, vague, and often conflicting goals. Under such conditions, there is always the temptation to distribute resources broadly rather than target high-priority problems. Thus, there is a basic conflict between the quality approach, which stresses the 85/15 Pareto rule for problem identification, and the political–distributive model, which tends to disregard the most difficult problems or spread resources among the many interests represented in the political process. Often, the net result is that nothing gets done.

Larger numbers of constituencies in the political arena not only complicate decision making but increase the importance of skillfully implementing strategies designed to measure and improve the quality of all public services. Concerns about equality and redistribution of public resources inhibit but do not *prohibit* the application of market-based, entrepreneurial, or for-profit approaches such as deregulation, privatization, and contracting out government services to private firms.

In their best-selling 1992 book aimed at changing the priorities of public officials, David Osborne, a journalist and advisor to President Clinton, and Ted Gaebler, a consultant and former city manager of Visalia, California, propose ten principles (see list) for reinventing government. Many of these recommendations parallel the TQS approach (indicated with an asterisk) and stress the need for quality and productivity improvement in government.

Principles for Reinventing Government

---

*1. Government should act as a catalyst to "see to it that services are provided" (New York Governor Mario Cuomo)

*2. Empowerment and community ownership

3. Managed competition rather than monopolies

*4. Mission rather than rule-driven governance

5. Focus on outcomes, not inputs

*6. Meet citizen customer needs

7. Foster entrepreneurial enterprises

*8. Stress prevention, not cures

*9. Decentralization, participation, and teamwork

10. Market-oriented government

---

* Denotes total quality service and continuous improvement principles.

Source: Osborne and Gaebler (1992).

Given the size and diversity of the U.S. federal system of divided government, it is encouraging that some of these recommendations are being implemented by many governments. Most public agencies, however, still lack the capacity to simultaneously increase productivity, reduce costs, and motivate public employees to provide service to customers (taxpayers) in a timely, polite, efficient, and cost-effective manner (Milakovich, 1990a). Public agencies, especially large federal government departments, suffer from poor quality, which necessitates major cost increases and requires more and more borrowing to meet current expenditure levels.

In other sectors of the American economy, maintenance of *individual* productivity measures over *total system* and *process improvement* approaches has been linked to declines in both the quality of service and the productivity of employees. As a result, these approaches have been discarded and replaced with newer, customer-driven, system-focused strategies which foster teamwork, improve internal processes, reduce costs, and increase productivity. These strategies achieve quality *and* productivity goals—without appropriating additional resources—by examining the relationships between existing management systems, enhancing the capacity for individual agency-wide cooperation, increasing customer service, and continuously improving processes (Milakovich, 1991a).

TQS concepts and techniques preserve a public service manager's ability to reward truly extraordinary individual performance, yet enhance the capacity for agency-wide cooperation, continuous process improvement, and policy innovation.

WHAT IS TOTAL QUALITY PUBLIC SERVICE?

Reflecting a long-term trend toward decentralization and participatory management in American society, TQS is public policy based on the theory that the greater the commitment an employee has in determining organizational goals, the harder he or she will work to achieve them. To increase the success of the entire enterprise, TQS encourages customer focus, continuous involvement, teamwork, and better quality of results by providing incentives for participation, such as empowerment, gainsharing, and advanced training in statistical methods for process monitoring.

In the federal government and in most of the 50 states, as well as thousands of local governments, some form of quality management is being implemented. Strategies vary almost as much as the number of governments in the decentralized American democracy. While there are fewer than 87,000 different ways to improve quality, many encourage active employee participation, utilize the human resource changes outlined in Chapter 4, and employ the process control and cost reduction methods noted in Chapter 6. Key elements of a typical TQS system are listed in Table 7.1. Note the similarity to Deming's Fourteen Points (see Appendix B) and the quality improvement (QI) guidelines (Chapter 4).

These principles address not only structural but also attitudinal and organizational barriers that inhibit TQS efforts in government. Just as quality assurance or control does not necessarily result in QI, merely training employees to apply quality principles does not automatically guarantee a quality service or process. Total quality systems cannot be installed like a telephone or a computer network. All of these elements (see Table 7.1) are necessary, but are not sufficient by themselves to achieve transformation. Training must be accompanied by leadership to reduce structural and attitudinal barriers in any sustained QI effort (see Chapter 9).

TABLE 7.1 Guidelines for Public Sector Quality Improvement

1. Make customer satisfaction the primary goal and ultimate measure of service quality.

2. Broaden the definition of a "customer" to include both those *internal* to the organization (e.g., employees in other departments) and those *external* to it (vendors, taxpayers, contractors, regulators, suppliers, etc.).

3. Develop a common vision of the mission of the organization based on extended customer requirements.

4. Communicate a long-term commitment to all customers, reward teamwork, and encourage process improvement and innovation efforts at all levels.

5. Provide expanded education, training, and self-improvement opportunities in supervisory and leadership skills in order to *exceed* valid customer requirements.

6. Ensure individual involvement by establishing and supporting organization-wide process improvement teams.

7. Recognize, support, and acknowledge employee loyalty, trust, and team participation.

8. Eliminate fear in work and remove barriers to developing pride in service (i.e., "empowerment").

9. Provide the proper tools and training for everyone to respond to extended customer requirements.

10. Make the *necessary changes in public organizations* to successfully implement the preceding goals.

Source: Milakovich (1990a, p.22)

The preceding principles represent only general TQS guidelines and must be customized to fit individual public services, which vary according to the (1) branch of government (executive, legislative, or judicial), (2) type of governing board (elected or appointed), (3) agency size and geographic distribution of services, (4) primary function (e.g., airport, health service, education, transportation, civilian, or military), (5) level of government (federal, state, or local), (6) sources of revenue (totally tax-supported, mixed revenue sources, or totally user fee based), (7) level of technology required to deliver service, and (8) relationship with the private and non-profit sectors. Alternatives must be discussed; measurement characteristics defined, operationalized, and validated; empirical studies conducted; and the results of implementation studies now being conducted published before the transition to a customer-focused total quality public service is complete.

CURING PAST SINS OF PUBLIC ADMINISTRATION

U.S. government agencies have been concerned with program management, productivity, and political issues for over a century. For most of early American history, there was no distinction between politics and administration. Indeed, politics was administration and vice versa. All jobs were filled by patronage for the loyal campaign workers and followers of elected politicians. Following the assassination of President Garfield by an individual rejected for federal government service, the Pendleton Act was passed by Congress in 1883. It created the Federal Civil Service System and attempted to insulate administrative decision making from political influences. The act provided for a neutral public administration and sought to increase government productivity by raising the competence levels of U.S. government employees. The Brownlow Committee (1937) and the Reorganization Act of 1939 committed the federal government to efficiency, economy, reduction in the number of separate agencies and in staffing, and elimination of duplication between agencies. Some state and a few local governments followed the federal government's lead. In 1982, the Reagan administration's Grace Commission offered over 400 specific recommendations for increasing the efficiency of federal government operations. The National Performance Review (Gore, 1993) is thus the latest in a series of efforts to improve the efficiency, manageability, and responsiveness of public services.

Management expert Peter Drucker was concerned with the same issues over a decade ago and identified six barriers to improvement in the public sector: (1) lack of clear performance targets, (2) trying to do too many things at once, (3) solving problems by throwing people at them, (4) lack of an experimental attitude, (5) lack of evaluation so that nothing is learned from experience, and (6) reluctance to abandon programs. He asserted that these "sins" lead to program failure if two or more follow simultaneously (Drucker, 1980). Many of these "deadly sins" are still widely committed today and inhibit the successful transformation to a TQS environment.

Governments are now learning valuable lessons from earlier manufacturing efforts and are building upon the successes of their own demonstration projects (Carr and Littman, 1990; Cohen and Brand, 1993; Hunt, 1993; Hunter et al., 1987; Gilbert and Nelson, 1991). In addition, there are secondary, more subtle consequences of neglect in the public sector: increased privatization, neglect of quality concepts in professional journals, and creative (risky) financing of public services.

1. Privatization of Public Services. Evidence of recent customer (taxpayer) dissatisfaction with the quality of public services has existed since the tax revolts of the late 1970s. In response, some public services are being privatized (leased or sold to private contractors) or increasingly supported by mixed sources of public and private revenues. Formerly all-public functions have been privatized on the theory that efficiency increases as competition among affected public agencies is introduced. This competitive entrepreneurial approach is now typical of capital improvement projects and is being used more often to finance such human services as healthcare, public education, sanitation, and even some criminal justice functions such as corrections. The decline in federal grants to state and local governments in the 1980s combined with the fiscal policies of the Reagan–Bush administrations have not only created opportunities for greater privatization, but have stimulated the need for creative financing of projects that were once safely subsidized by public resources.

2. Neglect of Quality Concepts in Professional Journals. Despite the fact that various governmental agencies have been experimenting with QI concepts and methods for nearly a decade, few articles on the subject were accepted in the leading academic journals until the early 1990s. Quality-related articles existed as early as 1980, but in very small numbers, and dealt only with specific substantive areas such as air, water, and environmental quality control. Without publication of research results by academicians, is it surprising that practitioners are reluctant to change management practices? While the number of articles on service quality has increased since 1990, there are still few application cases.

3. Creative (sometimes risky) Financing of Public Services. Governments today increasingly depend on borrowing or special funds drawn from non-income or sales tax sources. These include user fees, long-term bonds, leisure taxes, impact or development fees, hotel/motel taxes, and casino gambling, parimutuel betting, and lottery proceeds. This trend continues because voters are more willing to approve tax increases for special projects than to support higher taxes for undesignated local and state government general funds. Faced with increasing service demands and taxpayer unwillingness to increase taxes, states such as California, Florida, New York, and New Jersey are coping with massive budgetary crises. Bond ratings are being downgraded as states are forced to select riskier alternatives to raise the revenues necessary for government operations. The Orange County, California debacle is a direct result of speculation in risky "derivatives" used to finance capital improvement projects in 180 California local governments. The resultant $2 billion loss will hamper growth and lower the quality of life for millions of unsuspecting taxpayers in the affected regions.

IMPLEMENTING TOTAL QUALITY PUBLIC MANAGEMENT

In the 1980s, productivity improvement efforts focused on saving money and reducing the growing federal deficit. Such efforts produced some results, but they were usually short lived and quickly replaced by other short-term ideas, such as zero-based budgeting. In recent years, however, there has been a growing recognition of the need for a long-term strategy to bring about a more permanent and sustained improvement. President Bill Clinton is firmly committed to quality and productivity improvements. As governor or Arkansas, his administration was the first to publicly acknowledge the value of total quality management (TQM) for states and local governments. Leadership is a critical issue at all levels as government quality and productivity efforts are increasingly vital to the economy as a whole.

All three levels of government are implementing quality concepts. The federal government has applied TQM since the late 1980s and the results thus far are encouraging (Milakovich, 1992; Federal Total Quality Management Handbook, 1992).

Quality Management in the Federal Government

The federal government has acknowledged that TQM is the most effective way to continuously improve the quality of customer service. The Office of Management and Budget (OMB) provides central leadership, coordination, and technical assistance by monitoring agency progress, integrating productivity plans into the budget process, providing information on strategies for improving quality, and sponsoring conferences on quality-related topics. The Office of Personnel Management (OPM), Federal Quality Institute (FQI), and the President's Council on Management Improvement (PCMI) also provide leadership, support, and technical assistance. The OMB and the agencies participating in the PCMI have initiated actions over the past few years to promote quality awareness.[4] These actions include creation of the FQI Quality Improvement Prototype case studies, special workshops offered to agency representatives, and annual conferences focusing on quality and productivity improvement issues.

The OMB director is responsible for the direction, coordination, and review of agency productivity improvement efforts as well as the identification and future elimination of any statutory or regulatory barriers to productivity improvement efforts in each agency. The results of the barrier reduction review are then reported to Congress. The Director of the Office of OPM is responsible for reviewing federal personnel and incentive policies, proposing possible changes in policies, and offering federal employees training that will promote quality and productivity improvements. The OPM director recommends changes in policies and programs for federal workers who may be displaced by such improvements, thereby reducing any possible negative effects on the federal work force as the result of a productivity improvement program. The directors of the OPM and OMB, with the cooperation of agency and department heads, are responsible for the effective implementation and administration of a government-wide productivity improvement program.

The FQI began operations in the spring of 1988 after an OMB task force recommended its creation. The FQI, a quasi-independent body, has a seven-member board of directors who are responsible for oversight, with OMB handling all the administrative responsibilities. Hoping to avoid congressional oversight, the FQI initially sought operating funds from its prospective clients, namely federal executive agencies. The FQI is a primary source of information, training, and consulting services concerning TQM. Federal agencies are encouraged to make use of the FQI and its resources. The FQI may be of assistance in four major areas: quality awareness seminars and follow-up assistance to top officials and executives, a roster of qualified private consultants, the operation of a TQM resource and referral service, and policy guidance in the implementation of the National Performance Review (NPR). The FQI is now a major player in efforts to improve productivity and quality and has assumed a major role in implementing the specific goals of President Clinton's National Performance Review (Gore, 1993).

The goal of the FQI is to increase awareness of TQM and to help implement NPR principles and techniques. Its main tool in its quest to spread the news about TQM is its one-day Executive Overview Seminar, during which agency participants are introduced to TQM and how it specifically applies to their respective agencies. The creation of the FQI is further proof that federal executives realize that many current management practices are outdated and in some cases even harmful to customer-focused quality and productivity improvement efforts.

The PCMI is comprised of key career and non-career executives at the assistant secretary level from 23 federal agencies and departments who are responsible for overseeing the management of those divisions. The PCMI provides support and leadership for major government-wide initiatives to all the federal government's agencies and departments. It is a partnership between agencies that facilitates the sharing of information and experience among departments and encourages agencies to collectively work to improve federal management. With its corps of high-level bureaucrats, the PCMI provides leadership and broad directives for mandated policy. Similarly, the PCMI will also make recommendations to the OMB and specific agencies concerning improvements that can be made in their respective programs.

The federal government's pursuit of quality formally began on April 27, 1988 with the issuance of President Reagan's Executive Order 12637. Entitled "Productivity Improvement Program for the Federal Government," it covered all executive departments and agencies and established a program to improve the quality, timeliness, and efficiency of services provided by the federal government.[5] In this hierarchical top-down effort, executive department and agency heads were required to identify and review all appropriate functions to be included and to establish goals for improving services. Bureau chiefs were similarly required to annually submit a productivity plan to the OMB. These productivity plans included each agency's goals and objectives, with yearly expansion priorities to include all appropriate functions. Proposed actions contained a description of methods for service improvement or privatization, efficiency reviews and cost comparisons, and a description of systems used to measure efficiency, timeliness, and quality of service. Once programs were reviewed by the OMB director, agency heads were required to implement them, annually assess the agency's progress including any cost savings, and report the findings to the Executive Office of the President. Senior officials were appointed to guide the program and inform all employees of their quality and productivity improvement responsibilities. Performance appraisals of managers and supervisors were expanded to include productivity and quality improvement goals. Employee participation was encouraged through the use of training, involvement in decision making, incentives, recognition, and rewards. Concepts of productivity, timeliness, and quality were introduced to all executive branch employees so that all appropriate services were covered by the mandated improvement programs of each agency.

The OMB, in compliance with Executive Order 12637, issued Circular No. A-132 on April 22, 1988. Entitled "Federal Productivity and Quality Improvement in Service Delivery," the circular established operational guidelines for the development and implementation of federal productivity and quality improvement. The goals of the program were more clearly defined in this circular than in the Executive Order. All federal agencies were required to establish quality and productivity principles and techniques to assure "continuous, incremental improvements in quality, timeliness and efficiency of services" (OMB Circular A-132, p. 1). While productivity was defined in the same terms as used in the Executive Order, the circular went further by adding definitions for quality and quality improvement. The circular also stated that:

> [I]mproved quality of a product or service nearly always results in improved productivity. Quality is obtained when a product or service is designed and produced to meet all requirements that a customer specifies or expects. Inherent in a quality design and production process is the avoidance of any rework or returns due to errors, unclear procedures or any other cause. Resources saved by "doing the right thing right the first time" translates into improved productivity (increased outputs and/or reduced inputs). Having a *quality focus* [original emphasis] implies that an organization is making continuous improvements in reducing cycle time, eliminating non value-added work and thus, reducing overall costs.

The circular stressed that doing things right the first time and avoiding rework and returns conserves resources and increases productivity. In total compliance with Executive Order 12637, Circular A-132 added the concept of continuous quality improvement to the mandate of federal productivity efforts. By more clearly defining the relationship between productivity and quality, it prevented employees from increasing productivity while ignoring quality. This new focus on quality required certain specific practices and techniques to be employed in the productivity programs of each agency.

Executive agencies are responsible for the development and implementation of their own programs to improve productivity, but in an effort to support agencies, the circular outlines ten productivity and quality management practices that must be included in any such improvement program:

■ Top-level support and commitment

■ A customer orientation

■ Written productivity and quality goals and an annual improvement plan

■ Productivity and quality measures and standards that are meaningful to agency programs

■ The use of the improvement plan and measurement system to hold managers and employees accountable

■ Employee involvement in productivity and quality improvement efforts

■ Rewards for quality and productivity achievement

■ Training in methods for improving productivity and quality

■ Retraining and placement of employees affected by improvement efforts

■ Reducing barriers to productivity and quality improvement (OMB Circular A-132, pp. 3–5)

Less than two years after Circular A-132 was issued, the OMB drafted a replacement that for the first time specifically defined and explained TQM. "Developing High-Performance Organizations to Improve the Quality of Government Products and Services" committed the executive branch to adoption of TQM as part of its Productivity Improvement Program (PIP). Each federal agency must have a TQM coordinator in addition to a PIP coordinator and is required to implement TQM as part of the ongoing efforts of all agencies. The first circular defined quality, while the later one added a definition of TQM based on the quality principles of Deming and Juran. The circular defined TQM as "a total organizational approach for meeting customer needs and expectations that involves all managers and employees in using quantitative methods to improve continuously the organization's processes, products, and services." In addition to this definition, the revision included two attachments that outlined how to assess implementation in an organization. The OMB now maintains that reliance on TQM techniques and practices will not only result in improved quality, but would also increase productivity (Milakovich, 1992).

The introduction of TQM greatly simplified the OMB's task of ensuring the effective implementation and administration of government-wide productivity and quality improvement by requiring that it be implemented in all agencies, thereby reducing the possibility of different programs working against each other. TQM allows for customized improvement programs while at the same time ensures that every agency is pursuing the same goals of efficiency, effectiveness, timeliness, and quality.

The new circular made extensive modifications to and enlarged the role of the OMB to provide policy guidance and coordination in creating "an atmosphere of positive reinforcement for TQM implementation" and monitoring the progress of each agency in achieving TQM goals. OMB oversight consists of review of each agency's annual progress reports, management reviews of selected agencies involving top management, and on-site quality review. These reviews are conducted by the OMB with the cooperation of public and private sector managers familiar with TQM; they help to assess the progress of improvement programs, develop future goals, and serve as a source of new ideas based on the previous experiences of these public and private sector managers.

Successes in the Federal Government

The federal government has documented several successful quality applications since 1989. Numerous case studies are available to other agencies. Among the recognized achievements are reduced costs, better service to customers, and faster processing of claims and grant applications. The Social Security Administration (SSA) has initiated a number of changes that have improved service to customers. Interviews with clients can now be scheduled by appointment, office hours have been expanded, and a national toll-free number has put over 60 percent of the nation directly in touch with the SSA. The SSA has also developed a quality measurement system in the Retirement and Survivors Insurance Program to track dollar accuracy of payments. The Department of Education awarded over 7700 discretionary grants during 1988; over 77 percent were awarded by June 30, 1988, compared to only 60 percent by that time the previous year. The Department of Housing and Urban Development's Single Family Application Processing showed considerable improvement in both timeliness and quality. In addition, three federal agencies have been designated as Quality Improvement

Prototypes in recognition of their TQM efforts: The Equal Employment Opportunity Commission, the Internal Revenue Service, and the Naval Aviation Depot at Cherry Point, North Carolina.

It was expected that nearly 700 program services, covering more than two million employees, would be included in federal agency improvement efforts by 1992 (Burstein and Sedlak, 1988). The long-term implications of this change are even more positive: "As more and more federal employees adopt the precepts of TQM, it is expected that significant changes will be made in operating philosophies and systems affecting...structure and service delivery" (Burstein and Sedlak, 1988, p. 132). The improvements cover a wide range of areas from barrier identification to capital investments and, as noted in the following examples, are being implemented on a broad scale.

The Treasury Department

In January 1986, Internal Revenue Service (IRS) Commissioner Lawrence B. Gibbs established the Commissioner's Quality Council. After consultation with quality experts, the council recommended and established a QI program based on the principles of Dr. Joseph M. Juran. Dr. Juran conducted a two-day quality training seminar for all IRS executives, who were then responsible for establishing QI teams in their respective departments. The OMB has designated the Fresno, California and Ogden, Utah IRS centers as Quality Improvement Prototypes (U.S. Office of Management and Budget, 1989a, 1989b). The Fresno Service Center processed 32 million tax returns in 1989. Gainsharing gave out $63,802 in awards and saved taxpayers $2,774,000 "in tangible savings" by 1989. TQM reduced average account problem resolution time from 45 days to 2 to 3 days, increased the capacity of the IRS hotline from 400 calls per week to 600 calls per week and reduced turnaround time for inquiries from weeks to four days, reduced interest charges to the federal government from $830,000 in 1986 to $172,000 in 1988, reduced refund queries from 102,000 in 1987 to 79,000 in 1988, was credited with a 50 percent reduction in Problem Resolution cases, increased internal and external customer satisfaction, and improved the morale of employees (U.S. Office of Management and Budget, 1989a). Another example of the IRS's approach to quality is its pilot program in San Francisco, called the One-Stop Account Service Quality Improvement Project (U.S. Office of Management and Budget, 1989a). The IRS's San Francisco District Office formed a quality team with the goal of increasing responsiveness to taxpayers and eliminating the multiple contacts that were required to solve taxpayer problems. The One-Stop Account Service was the result of the efforts of the quality team at the San Francisco office.

The ambitious goals and subsequent successes of the federal government's quality and productivity improvement efforts are not limited to the Department of Treasury. Other agencies, such as the Department of Defense, are experiencing positive results.

The Department of Defense

Since the fall of 1988, revolutionary changes have taken place within the U.S. Defense Department (DoD) to affect how the entire federal government, states, local agencies, and private defense contractors purchase nearly $500 billion worth of goods and services for American taxpayers. The DoD's effort was the first large-scale attempt to apply quality concepts to the procurement and contracting activities of the federal government. DoD began with the Model Installation Program, which permitted field commanders at selected installations to run their bases in the most efficient manner possible. The success of the program has shown that freeing people from unnecessary regulation stimulates creativity (allowing procurement officers to sole-source contracts in order to get better value for dollars spent, for example) and makes government organizations more interested in providing better service.

The Naval Publications and Forms Center of the Naval Supply Systems Command in Philadelphia improved the accuracy of customer orders from 90 percent to 99.6 percent and reduced the number of unfillable receipts due to error from 29 percent to only 9 percent. The Norfolk Naval Shipyard of the Naval Sea Systems Command reduced the reject rate for repaired relief valves from 21 percent to 0 percent and saved $4.2 million by decreasing the time needed for a complex carrier overhaul. Both were recognized as 1989 Quality Improvement Prototypes by the OMB. The Naval Air Systems Command (NAVAIR) was the recipient of the first Presidential Award for Quality and Productivity Improvement. These accomplishments illustrate only some of the numerous successes enjoyed by the DoD.

Several federal agencies have initiated their own quality efforts. One of most promising was the internal TQM effort at the General Accounting Office (GAO), the non-partisan agency which assists the U.S. Congress in evaluating executive agency performance. Not unlike its counterparts in the executive branch, the GAO will doubtless benefit from a quality focus, process improvements, and a customer orientation. In the future, the GAO may also become a model for the external customer focus and integration of political and administrative functions required to sustain a long-term TQS effort in the public sector (Milakovich, 1991a).

The DoD enlisted statistical quality consultant W. Edwards Deming to help restructure its own organization, while the Treasury Department's IRS has implemented the management techniques of Joseph M. Juran. The success of these and other award programs has provided valuable breakthroughs to encourage the proliferation of the quality movement at the state and local levels.

State Governments

With the commitment to quality at the federal level, state and local governments are also coming to realize that the benefits of TQS far outweigh its costs. This is vital to the future of the public service quality movement, since only 18 percent of all civilian public employees work directly for the federal government. The remaining 82 percent are state and local officials who are often responsible for implementing federal policies as well as their own initiatives.

Despite the impressive gains at the federal level, it is in the states, as the constitutionally mandated providers of the broadest range of domestic social services, that the most enduring breakthroughs are being made.

Most states have seen the value in a TQS approach and are now encouraging quality and productivity improvement efforts. Arkansas was the first to establish a state-wide QI agency. California, Florida, New York, North Carolina, and Minnesota have their own quality awards, patterned after the Malcolm Baldrige Quality Award (MBQA). Dade County, Florida initiated an award in 1991 (the Stirling Award), and Baptist Hospital of Kendall, Florida was one of the first winners. Governor Lawton Chiles expanded the program to include the entire state (see Case Study 7.1). Arizona, Maryland, North Carolina, Oregon, South Carolina, Tennessee, and Wisconsin have targeted state-wide services such as education, transportation, healthcare, and corrections for improvement. Florida, Oregon, and Vermont[6] have launched innovative healthcare service delivery programs involving Medicare and Medicaid recipients.

By July 1993, nearly 60 percent of the states were applying quality management principles in one of more functional areas; 34 percent had implemented quality improvements in five of more service functions (Berman et al., 1994). Functional applications include corrections, education, healthcare, transportation, and welfare assistance. Most of the state agencies began their journeys only since 1992, and many still characterize their efforts as in the beginning stages and too early to judge success. Among the internal and external factors that drive the quality efforts of states are interest by the governor and agency directors, public complaints about service, and the need for state-wide strategic planning.

Local Governments

Application of QI techniques by local agencies responds to grass roots citizen demands for better service quality, improves government's ability to effectively solve public problems, and provides a promising model for altering public management practices. QI strategies are now being used extensively to improve a wide range of public service organizations, hospitals and healthcare agencies, and public utilities, as well as police departments. According to a national survey of state and local governments, an estimated 26 percent of all cities with a population over 25,000 use TQM in at least one functional area. QI and customer service strategies are most often used in such functions as police services, parks and recreation, personnel administration, and financial reporting (West et al., 1994).

Public and private sector interorganizational agreements to pool resources are becoming the norm in the quality approach. In Madison, Wisconsin, for example, local businesses, the state, and county and local governments and their suppliers all worked together to produce the Quality First initiative (Hunter et al., 1987; Box et al., 1989). Other examples of such partnerships include those between Eastman-Kodak, Kingsport Foundry and Manufacturing, and other companies with the county board of education and the cities of Bristol, Johnson City, and Kingsport, Tennessee (Walton, 1990); between businesses, academia, the Santa Ana Economic Development Corporation, and the city of Santa Ana, California; between Globe Metallurgical and both its suppliers and their customers (Walton, 1990); and between the businesses, university, province, and city of Toronto, Canada.

In such diverse geographic areas as Jackson, Michigan; Madison, Wisconsin; Erie, Pennsylvania; the Tri-Cities (Bristol, Kingsport, and Johnson City) region of northeastern Tennessee; New York City; Santa Ana, California; West Palm Beach, Florida as well as dozens of other local communities, quality councils are being established to promote a political environment for QI (Lusk et al., 1989).

Fewer local governments have responded to the challenge to do more with less by implementing quality management. Madison, Wisconsin was one of the first American cities to become a model Center of Excellence. The Madison Area Quality Improvement Network (MAQIN), a non-profit organization, has helped people and organizations understand and apply continuous improvement methods to all types of services. Other cities such as Austin, Texas; Hampton, Virginia; and Sunnyvale, California have also been recognized as quality leaders.

Madison, Wisconsin has shown that employees can improve productivity by focusing on quality (Hunter et al., 1987). In 1983, a Madison city audit isolated poor productivity, labor–management relations, and interdepartmental communications in the Motor Equipment Division of the city's public works department. Incorporation of QI methods was recommended after repeated failures of traditional productivity techniques. Implementation of TQM methods at the First Street Garage (the division's main facility) was initiated, introduced, and in operation by March 1984. Two areas of concern were isolated: extended customer research and causes of vehicle downtime. The program split personnel into two teams, each concentrating on one of the basic areas of concern. The customer research team interviewed supervisors in five user agencies, surveyed other agency employees and managers, and then ranked repair priorities. The team found that safety appeared at the top of everyone's priorities, as opposed to repair costs. Customers also rated the duration of downtime as the division's biggest problem. Based on the success of its First Street Garage, the city of Madison expanded quality methods to its other agencies. Madison, Wisconsin credits its successes to three key areas of TQM: (1) a total transformation of management philosophy, (2) decisions based on facts and data instead of hunches, and (3) a sincere devotion to customer demands.

Joseph Sensenbrenner, the mayor of Madison, Wisconsin from 1983 to 1989 and now a consultant for public sector QI, observed that the primary motivation of implementing quality in the city was to make government more efficient (Sensenbrenner, 1992). As a former businessman, he could not understand why the local government could not balance its budget. After attending a Deming seminar, Sensenbrenner became personally involved in making the changes necessary to improve government efficiency. The first step was to form a team to gather information, determine the cause of system problems, and break down barriers. As a result, measurable improvements occurred not only in the garage, but in day care, trash collection, and the police department. Madison Police Chief David Couper was converted to quality as a means to improve government and has written a comprehensive workbook on leadership responsibilities to achieve quality policing (Couper and Lobitz, 1993).

The city of Phoenix, Arizona has implemented a total quality improvement program that includes quality control circles, a suggestion box program tied to gainsharing, and (in sanitation and recreation) a competitive bidding program in which both city agencies and private contractors bid on performing city services, with customer-satisfaction–based bonuses and penalties. In 1993, Phoenix and Christchruch, New Zealand were selected as the best-run cities in the world by the German-based Bertelsmann Foundation. The city of Fort Lauderdale, Florida instituted QI teams (adopted as part of the FPL/Qualtech model) in late 1985. Their first three solutions have saved the city $53,000 per year every year since they were adopted.

Local communities continue to discover that TQS principles and techniques can be used to transform the public sector from a costly tax consumer to an effective problem solver. People everywhere are benefitting from community-wide efforts to share resources and information. The vagaries of local politics not withstanding, there is no reason why these successes cannot be replicated elsewhere.

CURRENT GOVERNMENT PROMOTION OF TOTAL QUALITY SERVICE

The federal government has pursued four main approaches in efforts to promote quality: (1) creation of the MBQA in 1987, (2) programs since 1988 to improve federal executive management capacity, (3) imposition of standards in 1989 for government contractors to the DoD, (4) the NPR released in September 1993, (5) government-wide standards, and (6) legislation requiring performance and results measurement.

The Malcolm Baldrige National Quality Award

The MBQA has focused high-level attention on the importance of QI and has helped to spread the quality message to suppliers. The award requires applicants to implement quality on a company-wide basis and is widely regarded as very prestigious. As previously mentioned, MBQA winners such as FedEx, Motorola, and Xerox now require their key suppliers to conform to the award criteria as a precondition for further subcontracting.

Government-Wide Quality Improvement Efforts

Since 1988, the U.S. OMB has provided leadership for joint public and private sector initiatives. Recently, TQM has been designated the official management improvement system for all federal executive agencies. The FQI was established in 1988 to assist federal executives in their efforts. To foster the implementation of TQM in a variety of agencies, the federal government has organized its own quality consulting service, the FQI, to ensure expertise.

Federal Procurement Standards

Perhaps the most potentially far-reaching federal quality initiative affecting the private sector is the DoD requirement that all major contractors undergo a TQM evaluation and work toward improving their management of quality. Along with cost, quality has become an important procurement contracting criterion (Kelman, 1990). TQM is being viewed as a mandatory approach for companies, and companies are held accountable for lapses in both quality and cost. This 1989 requirement has caused a new Beltway industry of quality consultants to emerge. Thus, federal standards appear to be effective in creating change in industry, although the impact of this directive has yet to be evaluated. One limitation of the DoD approach is that its effect is limited to defense contractors, many of which no longer have civilian operations. Thus, its effect on economic competitiveness may be limited.

National Performance Review

Commissioned by President Clinton in early 1993, the NPR offers specific recommendations for streamlining government policies, putting customers first, empowering employees, and investing in greater productivity (Gore, 1993). Most of the proposed changes can and are being enacted by Presidential Executive Order; the remainder are being considered by Congress. By late summer 1994, most federal agencies had developed and published "customer service standards" against which performance could be measured. Others had succeeded in cutting red tape, empowered federal bureaucrats to resolve customer problems, and reduced regulations to enhance customer service.

Government-Wide Standards for Quality

The DoD standards for quality in procurement raise the question of whether or not they should be used by other government agencies. The DoD was motivated to mandate quality standards as a result of increasing costs, mismanagement, and concerns about performance and reliability; these factors are relevant to other departments as well. Mandatory government-wide quality practices would not only improve services and management in other sectors, such as transportation, education, the environment, and healthcare, but would result in substantial spillover to state and local governments. Clearly, such a level of commitment would induce parallel efforts in the private sector. Here, federal regulatory agencies must be careful in their application of standards so as to avoid a backlash from otherwise interested, but suspicious, private firms that are uncomfortable with what is perceived to be undue government interference with the competitive market.

The Government Performance and Results Act of 1993

The Government Performance and Results Act (GPRA) of 1993 is another step toward shifting the focus of government officials from program inputs to program outputs, implementation, and measuring results. The GPRA sets out requirements for defining long-term general goals, setting specific annual performance targets that are derived from general policy goals, and annually reporting actual performance compared to the targets. Federal managers are held more accountable for achieving *measurable* results and are also given greater discretion (empowerment) in how to manage programs for optimum outcomes. The legislation establishes various performance and budgeting concepts and sets up pilot projects that will operate through fiscal year 1999. Two sets of pilot projects are required over the next several years to test and demonstrate annual performance plans, strengthen program performance reporting, and improve managerial accountability and flexibility. Full-scale government-wide implementation of strategic planning, annual program goal setting, and annual program reporting of expenditures begins for all federal agencies in 1997. These tests will be evaluated against the goal of optimizing resources ultimately allocated for results. Full implementation of the GPRA will place much greater emphasis on the execution of programs (outcomes, outputs, and results) rather than traditional policy analysis. This could lead to demonstration projects in state and local governments, as well as more effective expenditures, as ineffective programs are either improved or terminated.

Productivity and measurement concerns will continue to be important, if for no other reason than the growing awareness of the limited resources available to successfully implement public policies. It is becoming increasingly accepted in government and elsewhere that we may have to make do with what we have. The promise of productivity efforts lies in the fact that technology has not yet been fully applied to this area, and there is a growing track record of successes, which should encourage similar efforts elsewhere.

Further research is needed to ascertain the results that are achieved and help disseminate case studies of the most useful approaches. At the present time, more is claimed about results than is documented by scientifically valid research. In the long run, this situation could itself become a barrier to diffusion, as uncertainty and anecdotal evidence reign. However, at present, very little empirical research that is focused on results has been undertaken; most research discusses management practices that encourage or discourage total quality in public services.

QUALITY IMPROVEMENT IN EDUCATION

Education for quality management is required at a minimum of four different levels. First, there is a need for specialized graduate programs that produce a corps of cross-trained professionals in the area of TQM as well as other specialized areas. Second, to ensure that their graduates possess up-to-date knowledge in this area, engineering and business schools need to adopt quality courses or modules in their curricula. Third, there is a need for post-graduate training and licensing courses through which engineers and consultants can receive training in this area. At the present time, a shortage of initiatives exists in both of these areas. Licensing may also be required. However, the pool of specialists is not easily expanded because of a lack of training opportunities in this area. Government efforts to improve this situation could include seed-money grants and fellowships, perhaps tied to industry co-sponsorship. Finally, and more importantly, elementary and secondary schools have begun to implement quality and productivity improvement concepts. TQS concepts and theories are being used in a number of schools (see Case Study 7.1) with a new generation of schoolchildren learning within an environment of teamwork, shared decision making, and collective accountability for results. Higher education institutions are initiating quality improvements as well.[7]

Case Study 7.1

1993 Stirling Award Winner: Pinellas County Schools

Pinellas County Schools officials envision the day when all facets of the community operate within the principles of TQM. Using W. Edwards Deming's philosophy as a basis, district staff are training administrators, teachers, parents, and community leaders, with the ultimate goal of producing students who are empowered, internally motivated learners. This ideal is clearly expressed in the district's vision statement: "The Pinellas County school district unites with families and the community in using continual quality improvement to provide a foundation for life that enables and challenges all students to be successful in a global and multi-cultural society."

This broad-based approach to TQM differentiates the school system's efforts from most companies that employ quality management strategies. District officials realize that in order to reach their goal, they must involve all stakeholders in the process, beginning with students and moving outward to teachers, administrators, parents, and the community at large. Total involvement of the community at large will take time, but Pinellas County Schools is committed to providing stakeholders with the training tools they need to succeed.

The District at a Glance

Pinellas County Schools is the seventh largest district in Florida and ranks 22nd in terms of size out of more than 16,000 districts in the United States. It has more than 96,000 students in 79 elementary, 21 middle, and 15 high schools, along with 5 exceptional education centers and 2 discipline centers. The district employs more than 14,000 people in full- and part-time capacities.

Education Reform

Implementing TQM strategies has made Pinellas County Schools a leader in the support and promotion of education reform initiatives such as the

Secretary's Commission on Achieving Necessary Skills (SCANS), Blueprint 2000, and accountability legislation.

In order for the state-mandated school-based management to succeed, Pinellas County Schools officials realize that stakeholders must have a working knowledge of quality management strategies.

Key Initiatives

Central administration officials determined that three initiatives were essential in order to implement quality management strategies in individual schools. First, Pinellas County Schools formed a District Quality Council to assure a common vision and constancy of purpose. The council integrated quality strategies with existing components of the comprehensive planning and budgeting system.

In the second initiative, the Collaborative Quality Council piloted a collaborative collective bargaining process. The council's members—the superintendent, a deputy superintendent, a quality coordinator, the president of the teachers' association, the executive director of the teachers' and support services' union, and the president of the county council of PTAs—worked as a unit to develop collaborative decision-making and collective bargaining processes.

Including the union in the beginning stages of the quality movement is a key step for success. Working together on mutually established short- and long-range goals allowed the two groups to come to an early settlement in their most recent bargaining process.

The third initiative involves continuous training at all levels of the organization. In collaboration with the business community, the district established a Quality Leadership Academy to support training. More than 100 businesses in the Tampa Bay area have volunteered to be a part of this effort to provide quality training for employees, businesses, and the community.

Quality in Departments

From central administration to individual schools, the district is firmly committed to TQM. Departments throughout central administration, including architects, data processing, finance, purchasing, transportation, maintenance, accounting, research, and warehousing, are in various stages of their quality journeys.

Departments begin with two full days of cross-functional training.

Participants study Deming's philosophy and learn to use the quality process tools. Working in groups of five or six, called quality teams, participants spend the last few hours of training applying what they have learned to their own situations.

Team members select a real project within their department, to which they apply quality processes. They spend the next four to six weeks developing flow charts, analyzing customer needs, discovering problems, and collecting data associated with the project.

After completing that segment of the process, the departments meet with the quality trainer again. Each team within a department makes a presentation to the department as a means of walking co-workers through the quality process for the project.

The training has helped many departments to increase efficiency and become more customer focused. For example, the central files staff processes requests for information from more than 70,000 current and former student files. Since implementing quality processes, about 95 percent of the requests are processed the day after they are received, compared to 80 percent before staff members began their quality journey.

School-Level Quality

Each school has a School Quality Advisory Council composed of parents, business leaders, administrators, and teachers. The councils develop the annual school improvement plan, which identifies concrete goals for moving each school toward the reform objectives. Council members are being trained to use quality process tools in order to continually assess their progress in relation to the objectives of the plan.

Student-Centered Efforts

All efforts in Pinellas County Schools are student-centered. Students are taught processes to continually assess their learning progress based on clear objectives. Pinellas County Schools officials use student performance stan-

SUMMARY AND CONCLUSIONS

Successes enjoyed by public sector efforts demonstrate that TQS can work if properly supported by senior elected and appointed officials. The successes

dards developed by the Florida Commission on Education Reform and Accountability, the Secretary of Labor, and members of SCANS and collect survey data from the business community to develop world-class standards for student performance.

Total Quality in Action

The district opened its first school developed within a total quality environment in the fall of 1992. The school, Majorie Kinnan Rawlings Elementary, does not teach and administer "in the "same old way." It is a model for reform in action for the district and the state. Before the building was completed, teachers began learning quality management strategies, and training continues. Teachers spend an afternoon each week in seminars. Rawlings' original teachers will eventually transfer to other schools for one year to train those teachers.

Rawlings' students are not just memorizing facts. They are learning how to learn. Students write every day in every subject and are evaluated through outcome- and performance-based assessments.

Pinellas County Schools' second total quality-based school, Joseph L. Carwise Middle, opened in the fall of 1993. It abandoned the traditional methods of school organization and embraced more innovative concepts. Carwise integrated all grade levels in all buildings. Students remain in the same building each year to build a sense of belonging.

The school has no departments or department heads and no department budgets. Instead, each teacher is a member of a team, with a specific role to play on that team. Each teacher is also given his or her own budget.

Carwise teachers were some of the first to attend the district's quality boot camp, a three-day intensive quality training program.

These new schools are just two examples of how the quality process is becoming meaningful to Pinellas County Schools students. The process will bring the district closer to its goal of graduating more internally motivated learners who can become productive members of a global economy.

already achieved have created a demonstration effect for other government agencies. Major problems remain, however, in implementing TQS improvement systems, including determining liability for private operation of public functions, team evaluations of individual performance, job security, collective bargaining agreements, defining and controlling costs, protecting minority group interests, and establishing valid customer-driven quality measurement characteristics, to name a few.

As more successful applications are publicized, fear of change will diminish. As more elected and appointed public officials realize that public sector productivity results from continuous, customer-driven, quality-based process improvement, reliance on individual performance appraisals and strict adherence to numerical goals, slogans, or arbitrarily set targets will decrease. As public officials, administrators, and taxpayers recognize the advantages of this non-partisan and *fact-based* approach to solving America's toughest public policy problems, implementing total quality customer service will be one of public administration's major challenges for the remainder of this century.

ENDNOTES

1. National Performance Review Accompanying Report, "Mission-Driven Results-Oriented Budgeting," Washington, D.C.: Government Printing Office, 1993.
2. The recommendations contained in the Report of the National Performance Review entitled "From Red Tape to Results: Creating a Government that Works Better and Costs Less" (Gore, 1993) emphasize decentralizing decision making, putting customers first, empowering employees, and simultaneously allowing for greater efficiency in budgeting, personnel, procurement, and empowerment of state and local governments.
3. Complaints about the quality of public services have been highlighted by the National Commission on Public Service, also known as the Volcker Commission (named for its chairman, Paul A. Volcker, former head of the Federal Reserve Board) (Leadership for America, 1990); the First Report of the National Commission on the State and Local Public Service, "Hard Truths/Tough Choices: An Agenda for State and Local Reform," sponsored by the Nelson A. Rockefeller Institute of Government, State University of New York at Albany, 1993; and the National Performance Review (Gore, 1993), cited in text.
4. Included in these initiatives are the Departments of Agriculture, Commerce, Defense, Education, Energy, Interior, Justice, Labor, State, Transportation, and Treasury and the Environmental Protection Agency, the General Services Administration, Health and Human Services, Housing and Urban Development, the National Aeronautics and Space Administration, the Office of Personnel Management, the U.S. Information Agency, and the Veterans Administration.
5. Productivity was defined to include the requirement that government services that produce measurable outputs must meet certain quality specifications. While the sole reliance on predetermined quality standards did not meet with the approval of all the quality experts, this definition at least introduced the aspects of quality methodology to federal public services.

6. Faced with the threat of rate regulation, hospitals in Vermont have convinced state legislators to attempt to control healthcare costs through a QI program. The Vermont Program for Quality in Health Care, a not-for-profit corporation, is sponsored by hospitals, physicians, payers, insurers, and the state. It is charged with developing physician practice guidelines to help reduce costly and inappropriate hospital care. Under the plan, the corporation will collect data on physician practice patterns and share the findings with appropriate medical specialty groups within the state. These groups will set clinical standards by medical specialty, procedure, or diagnosis. Physicians whose clinical performance deviates from the norms will be offered education and support by hospital quality assurance departments and medical specialty groups; those who continue to deviate will then be referred to the state medical board. Hospitals will benefit from the program because it will supply them with objective, comparative data to improve quality and lower costs in their institutions. The Vermont experiment demonstrates a convincing effort to improve healthcare.

7. For additional information in this area, see Ralph G. Lewis and Douglas H. Smith, *Total Quality in Higher Education,* Delray Beach, Fla.: St. Lucie Press, 1994.

8

IMPLEMENTING CONTINUOUS QUALITY HEALTHCARE IMPROVEMENT

Every American is worried about access, cost, and quality of healthcare. In the past, providers of primary care (i.e., doctors, hospitals, clinics, insurance companies, etc.) were concerned primarily with the financial and clinical–medical aspects of quality. Hospitals, clinics, and other suppliers of healthcare goods and services are now implementing total quality service (TQS), total quality management (TQM), and continuous quality improvement (CQI) as a vital part of all health service delivery functions, especially quality assurance and utilization management (Berwick, 1989; Miller et al., 1992). The prospect of managed care has encouraged most healthcare professionals to think in broader, more flexible, *customer-focused* terms in designing systems that lower costs, assure quality, and increase access at competitive prices.

One of the basic purposes of managed (as opposed to traditional) healthcare is to develop a delivery system that carefully reviews utilization of resources. Thus, it is likely that quality assurance and utilization review will become more important areas of specialization in the future. Whatever the option for guaranteeing access, healthcare systems must be monitored from three perspectives: the scientific–medical, the administrative–systems management, and from the perspective of the patient as well as other customers.

In the past, providers of healthcare services and suppliers of medical products[1] emphasized quality assurance, risk management, and utilization review[2] from strict *external* standards, usually medical–clinical or hospital accreditation. Healthcare policymakers, administrators, insurance companies, and allied health professionals have become increasingly concerned with the development of a broader set of *integrated* patient care, financial, human resource, and cost control measures. As members of a service industry under increasing political and social scrutiny, healthcare providers now have fewer incentives *not* to horizontally integrate medical, organizational, administrative, and patient satisfaction measures into a cross-functional TQS management system.

SHIFTING NATIONAL PRIORITIES FOR HEALTHCARE

Quality, together with cost and access to care, is critically important to the nation's well-being as well as the health of individual citizens. The immense size of the medical–industrial complex ($1 trillion and 15 percent of the GNP) amplifies the importance of issues such as cost containment, insurance coverage, and quality of care. Increasing numbers of citizens are worried about the spiraling costs and availability of healthcare services. With the introduction of the National Healthcare Security Act in October 1993, President Bill Clinton made healthcare reform and universal access one of the highest priorities on the nation's policy agenda. Expectations for reform have risen, as has the level of political rhetoric over various alternatives. Political mandates to improve quality, broaden access, and reduce costs were attempted even before healthcare became a Clinton administration national policy issue. Changes in public, governmental, and private health insurance policies have affected the delivery of healthcare services. Alternatives to individual physician visit (fee-for-service) delivery systems subsidized by public funds were created by federal and state statutes in the 1970s.[3] While less comprehensive than the current proposals for reform, they nonetheless attempt to achieve the same goals. Thus, many of the reform proposals have been enacted even without the formal passage of federal legislation.

During the 1980s, government reimbursement policies sought to decrease the rate of cost increase, while private insurers offered fixed-benefit insurance contracts as incentives to become more efficient. Efforts to contain costs included the imposition of regulations such as Medicare's diagnosis-related groups, resource-based relative value scales, and fixed-cost Medicare reimbursement plans. Prompted by outside regulators, most of these policies have thus far failed to reduce costs or standardize procedures and have had little impact on improving the total quality of system processes. Inflation in healthcare expenses continues to increase, and efforts to regulate the system have met with intense (subtle) resistance from those who provide healthcare goods and services. Efforts to improve quality and reduce costs by reallocating scarce medical resources have encouraged the use of competitive markets. In addition, entrepreneurship, corporate centralization, and restructuring of for-profit providers have resulted in increased efficiencies in delivering care. The application of expensive high-technology equipment, such as magnetic resonance imaging and gamma knives (devices that cost $3 million dollars and treat brain tumors without surgery), has also improved the quality of medical care for those who can afford it. At the same time, high-tech medicine, together with other factors, has fueled double-digit increases in the cost of medical procedures. Another contributing factor has been the maintenance of a non-competitive yet heavily regulated service delivery environment. For those who are uninsured or unable to pay for expensive treatment, access to *any* care is still limited. Hence, the United States shares (with South Africa) the dubious distinction of being the only advanced industrialized nation that does not provide healthcare insurance for nearly one-fifth of its citizens, many of whom are women and children.

The 1990s witnessed a shift from a physician-directed fee-for-service system to an increasingly regulated managed care environment. While far from the ideal that reformers envisioned, current reform proposals are more competitive and cost conscious in delivering health and medical care (Smith, 1992; Starr, 1982, 1993). In addition to health maintenance organizations (HMOs), preferred provider organizations (PPOs), and independent provider affiliates (IPAs), government-funded healthcare-buying cooperatives and managed competition among private providers are viewed by many as the best way to contain costs and provide universal access. Proposed reforms stress the need to continuously monitor customer (i.e., patient) indicators of the quality of service provided in the new managed, quasi-competitive system.

Without the discipline of a true competitive market, however, there were fewer fiscal incentives for healthcare providers to consider consumer satisfaction measures as equally important to financial and clinical–medical indicators.

In healthcare, patient interpretation of quality extends to more than merely clinical services. Today's educated consumer looks at efficiencies in all aspects of service, including housekeeping, nursing, and diagnostic and therapeutic care, as well as professional competence. Thus, patient satisfaction with hospital services is influenced by the response of hospital personnel to patient problems in addition to the technical competence of staff. Therefore, every employee must be trained to handle patient dissatisfaction at its source, before a complaint is filed.

During the expansion period of the 1970s and 1980s, less attention was paid to development of customer quality measurement systems. Combined with increases in the non-market (governmental) share of the nation's total medical care bill since the passage of Medicare and Medicaid in 1965, this discouraged healthcare providers from designing and integrating total clinical–managerial–customer quality measurement systems. Until recently, healthcare delivery systems have operated without incentives for customers (patients) to shop for the highest quality providers at the lowest costs, because medical care costs were paid indirectly to hospitals and doctors.

Changes in marketing strategy, increased government intervention and regulation, and greater patient awareness of costs have focused attention on the need to integrate medical–managerial–customer quality improvement systems. Ethical considerations, advanced directives, living wills, and greater patient participation in decision making have further accelerated the need for customer-driven quality improvement (Elfenbein et al., 1994). Healthcare professionals have been encouraged by voluntary hospital accrediting associations and government regulators to re-orient their systems from the delivery of care without considerations of cost to the implementation of team-oriented, cross-functionally managed, quality-oriented, and customer-focused systems.

This re-orientation requires all healthcare professionals to become far more aware of the total (visible and hidden) costs of healthcare delivery (see Chapter 6). Moreover, financial and information collection systems must be integrated to increase process efficiency. Hospitals that reduce costs by increasing the efficiency of internal medical and non-clinical processes such as admissions, laboratories, and patient services become more competitive. In addition, they will be favored by managed care providers such as HMOs, PPOs, and the newly emerging community health purchasing alliances. Federal Medicare administrators, state Medicaid programs, and private insurance companies will reward cost efficiencies and favor quality providers. Stated simply, those healthcare providers and suppliers that can demonstrate quality will increase market share and become more profitable.

Guaranteeing healthcare quality will always be a shared responsibility among physicians, nurses, senior hospital managers, federal and state watchdog agencies, insurance companies, and (increasingly) managed care providers. Hospitals have adapted TQM and CQI systems developed in other industries to meet their own special needs (Berwick et al., 1991). Pending federal legislation, continuing corporate restructuring of hospitals, insurance companies, and healthcare facilities encourages greater consumer awareness of the costs and quality of services provided. This allows informed consumers to make rational choices in selecting healthcare providers whose services meet their needs at costs they can afford. Many states have published data on the mortality and morbidity rates of various hospitals, which gives individuals and insurers more information upon which to base healthcare purchasing decisions.

Even with the increasing incentives for competition, however, healthcare providers must still conform to external standards of medical care at costs acceptable to patients, employers, and insurance companies.[4] Third-party providers and insurance companies are encouraging primary care providers (physicians, hospitals) to think in a more business-like manner, contain costs, and accept restricted (capitated) reimbursements for certain predetermined procedures. This effort will not be easy and is not without controversy. Achieving these goals is made all the more difficult by the sheer number of hospitals (5500), diversity of governing structures, and complexity of healthcare delivery in the United States.

Another obstacle to the development of a TQS culture is that physicians jealously guard the prerogative of defining clinical–medical quality standards. This affects the customer–supplier relationship. One limitation is the fact that the patient is often unaware of the appropriate treatment for his or her particular condition and depends on the physician for an accurate diagnosis. Most doctors admit, however, that a patient's attitude about the healing process greatly influences the prognosis for recovery. To overcome the tendency to minimize patient concerns because they lack the specialized knowledge to make complicated clinical decisions, patient relations efforts must be redesigned to include measurement characteristics for non-clinical service quality indicators. Changing doctor–hospital–patient responsibilities, coupled with the persistent demand for access to high-quality care at a reasonable cost, makes it even more challenging for healthcare professionals to design and implement quality improvement (QI) procedures.

When applied to healthcare services, TQS encompasses a much broader definition of quality assurance (QA) than the traditional narrow focus on professional (i.e., medical) definitions of the quality of services provided, usually through retrospective review. Surviving in the new competitive-regulated managed care environment requires providers to offer services on the basis of total quality rather than either lower cost or strictly clinically defined QA. Everyone must learn and apply TQS principles in continuously meeting or exceeding customer expectations and consistently doing the correct things right the first time.

Implementing continuous quality in healthcare requires the active participation of management and includes all traditional measures of cost and QA, cross-functional teamwork, and statistical evidence of compliance with medical standards. In addition, it requires surveys to monitor customer satisfaction and dissatisfaction and measures of the quality of goods and services provided by suppliers. The differences between traditional QA (retrospective quality assessment) and QI are listed in Table 8.1.

During the 1980s, state and federal legislation encouraged the creation of group medical practices, promoted free enterprise policies, expanded ownership of healthcare providers, and offered incentives for mergers of large hospital chains. This transformed U.S. medicine from a locally controlled, fee-for-service

TABLE 8.1 Comparing Quality Assurance and Quality Improvement

Quality assurance	Quality improvement
Vertical orientation	Horizontal orientation
Retrospective blame assignment	Concurrent evaluation
Inspection and "policing"	Team interplay
Suppresses stimulation	Promotes stimulation
Top-down communication	Up-down communication
Promotes autonomy	Promotes accountability
External standards	Internal standards

cottage industry into a national yet heavily regulated competitive industry. Why must health service providers re-orient their thinking to a TQS approach?

CHANGING ATTITUDES TOWARD MANAGED HEALTHCARE COMPETITION

International economic competition, a reputation for shoddy domestic services, and the need to increase productivity in order to decrease costs combined to motivate U.S. service providers to apply total quality concepts in the late 1980s.[5] By that time, American industry had already made remarkable progress toward achieving both higher quality and greater productivity while remaining price competitive in world markets. It became increasingly obvious that America's economic competitors and trading partners (Canada, Germany, Great Britain, and Japan) were far more efficient at delivering healthcare services. They spent one-half to one-third less as a percentage of GNP, provided universal access to care, *and* demonstrated better quality results than U.S. doctors and hospitals (Starr, 1993). These nations could thus devote a greater share of their economies to other vital areas such as education, public assistance, creating jobs, law enforcement, and crime prevention.

The vital connection between international competitiveness and a healthy work force is clearly seen in the increase in healthcare expenditures (which have risen faster than inflation) and the lack of productive employment opportunities. This has negatively affected industry's ability to compete in global markets. *Corporate healthcare benefits have soared to a point where they now consume over half of the net profit of American firms.* Obviously, senior managers in private companies have a strong profit motive for controlling healthcare costs.

Until recently, no similar motivation to change management practices existed in the public or service sector in general or in the competitive-regulated healthcare service delivery sector in particular. Large employers such as General Motors and Chrysler have taken the lead in promoting a more cost-conscious managed healthcare delivery system. To control costs and expand access, many employers favor a managed competition system dominated by large, heavily regulated HMO-type healthcare purchasing cooperatives. The state of Florida passed a law (the Florida Health Care and Insurance Reform Act of 1993) to ensure its 13.5 million residents access to high-quality, affordable health care. This measure makes Florida the first state to adopt the managed competition model of healthcare delivery and extend medical coverage to the state's 2.5 million uninsured residents.

Historically, healthcare service providers depended on third-party payors and direct consumer spending for most of their operational funds. Third parties are private insurance companies or government funding agencies, which pay 87 percent of the nation's healthcare bill. In 1960, for example, these two sources accounted for 81 percent of total revenues, with public funds contributing less than 20 percent. By 1991, the healthcare system received its largest single share of direct support—52 percent—from federal, state, and local governments. Another 35 percent came from other third-party providers, corporations, and private insurance companies, while the remaining 13 percent was paid for directly by patients (Al-Assaf and Schmele, 1993).

Clearly, this mixed system of revenue and divided accountability creates major problems in controlling costs, setting standards, and establishing and accurately measuring critical quality characteristics for both medical and nonclinical services received by patients. As many traditionally monopolistic public agencies are being privatized, functions contracted out or turned over to private healthcare providers are more dependent on mixed sources of public and private revenue. The reverse is also true in many private sector services which now receive revenue or the regulatory authority to operate directly from the public sector. This inflation in healthcare expenditures has contributed to increased indirect non-patient-care overhead costs.

The comparison chart in Table 8.2 shows how overhead or administrative (indirect) costs of providing care have increased and are likely to further increase if current trends continue.

These trends are particularly disturbing because administrative overhead costs are primarily non-value-added expenses, such as paperwork, duplicate appraisals, and insurance forms, which do not benefit patients. Worse still, in the last decade the ratio of administrative costs per patient has actually increased in the United States. If quality indicators were in place, the United States could reduce its total investment in healthcare by 5 to 10 percent without sacrificing

TABLE 8.2   The Cost of Healthcare (in $ billion)

Year	Cost ($ billion)	Percent GNP	Percent administration
1970	74	7.3	7
1992	809	13.4	20
2000 (est.)	1616	16.4	50

quality of patient care. The savings generated by reducing unnecessary overhead costs could be redirected to more than pay for the added expense of extending access to all Americans currently not covered.

If widely adopted, a TQS strategy of "customer quality as first among equals" would also begin to achieve an important secondary goal for any healthcare system: universal access (Miller and Milakovich, 1991b). Moreover, it would improve the negative image of U.S. medical care as costly, elitist, and serving too few by addressing the plight of nearly 38 million U.S. citizens, including one out of every four children, who have no health insurance.

This should be an employer responsibility, because the majority of those at risk are employed at least part-time (Starr, 1993). They are unnecessarily in danger of becoming indigent because all their financial resources would be decimated by a catastrophic illness. Those covered by universal insurance could be offered a basic package of services that meet minimum standards for care. If statistical evidence is provided that such care meets or exceeds customer care expectations, then the substantial cost savings that would result from switching to a lower cost, comparable quality approach could be applied to increasing access to all those who need treatment, without loss of acceptable levels of quality care (Miller and Milakovich, 1991a).

Past attempts to regulate, reallocate, or reduce public expenditures have been resisted by healthcare professionals. Many have responded defensively with real or threatened restrictions in access to services. Still others think of quality as a fixed commodity rather than a variable customer-defined service that is responsive to such factors as system improvement, customer quality characteristics, and reducing non-value-added (administrative) costs. Despite these self-serving objections, many healthcare experts have pointed out that cost containment policies need not result in lower quality care if appropriate systems are in place to measure and control quality results (Ullmann, 1985). Within the medical profession, there is less consensus on the role that customer (patient) satisfaction should play in the QA process. Several user-oriented studies have shown that patients perceive "good" hospitals as treatment centers or as homes away from home, thereby accelerating the treatment and healing process. Dr. Avedis Donabedian states that "achieving and producing health and satisfaction is the ultimate validator of the quality of care."[6] Comparing patient perceptions with actual clinical outcomes reveals that patients do possess accurate knowledge of the quality of care.

In summary, in order for the necessary transition in thinking about managing healthcare quality to occur, the technical language and concepts of TQS must be translated into a common set of relevant healthcare examples. Guided by quality theory and principles, these cases should illustrate the application of statistical quality tools and assist healthcare managers in their knowledge of how to improve their facilities. The essential elements of this new way of thinking are:

1. All actions must be guided by principles of CQI.

2. The providers of care must be actively involved in teams and problem-oriented work groups.

3. Decisions must be based on facts, data, outcome measurements, and statistical information.

4. Leaders must be personally involved and committed to serving customers, broadly defined as anyone impacted by the actions of the organization (Milakovich, 1991b).

With these elements in mind, we turn now to a more complete description of how TQS principles are being applied to healthcare and patient services.

WHAT IS TOTAL QUALITY HEALTHCARE IMPROVEMENT?

When applied to healthcare services, TQS is a unique combination of applied modern technology, cognitive skills, access to facilities at reasonable costs, and patient-centered high-quality primary and specialized clinical care. All of these dimensions of service are equally important. Therefore, as much effort must be devoted to the design of measurement systems which assess *perceived* quality of care provided patients as has been previously expended on the design of cost accounting or narrowly focused medical care QA systems.

Tighter external review by accrediting associations, such as the American Medical Association, the Joint Commission on Accrediting Healthcare Organizations (JCAHO), and Physician Review Organizations, as well as other means of external regulation such as Certificates of Need will encounter difficulty if the following issues are not addressed:

1. Control by physicians over admission to the medical profession, state licensing boards, and clinical medical quality standards

2. The often self-serving association—real or imagined—between cost containment efforts and "necessary" reductions in the level of care provided restricts the scope of external review

3. The application of stricter controls through external regulation only risks massive resistance from providers of care, i.e., physicians and hospitals

4. The lack of conclusive evidence that quality of patient care can be improved through tighter outside regulation

For most healthcare managers, the trauma of learning a new language (TQS) later in their professional life should be eased somewhat, because most medical facilities are already familiar, albeit not entirely comfortable, with review standards set by outside accrediting groups. Much of the information required by outside review organizations, such as the JCAHO ten-step process (Table 8.3), can provide useful self-assessment data for a hospital. Furthermore, the JCAHO has spearheaded the effort to shift the operative model from QA to QI.

As in many other services, healthcare TQS must develop from the bottom up but be stimulated from the top down. Planning must be guided by a statistically based quality philosophy and supported by massive retraining in TQS principles.

Similarly, components such as cost, medical standards, and customer satisfaction must be considered together rather than separately, as has been the approach in the past. Achieving this goal requires disciplined top management support as well as a greater degree of cross-functional coordination than exists today among most healthcare facilities. As more administrators, suppliers, nurses, and physicians realize that the tools and techniques developed in the manufacturing sector can be adapted and transferred to the healthcare service environment, more facilities are applying the systems necessary to remain com-

TABLE 8.3   JCAHO Ten-Step Process

1. Assignment of responsibility
2. Define scope of care
3. Identify what care to monitor
4. Identify what indicators will be used
5. Establish threshold and minimal standards
6. Collect and organize data
7. Assess and evaluate the care based on the standards that have been established
8. Take appropriate action
9. Assess actions and document results
10. Communicate information

petitive, increase productivity, and capture greater local and global market share.[7] Industrial quality control differs from traditional quality control and QA in the following respects:

■ The regular use of tools to understand processes and discover flaws: process flow diagrams, cause-and-effect diagrams, control charts, and data display charts such as histograms and Pareto diagrams

■ Prevention is preferable to detection

■ Focus on the system not the individual

■ Centrality of the customer (internal and external)

■ Variation is endemic

   • General cause—related to the process

   • Special cause—not endemic to the process

■ Broader definition of quality—not just patient care (Berwick et al., 1991)

Today, most healthcare professionals realize the potential value of applying TQS theories and techniques, but many lack the time or knowledge necessary to adapt these concepts to the healthcare environment. Despite the volumes of research devoted to specialized areas of statistical techniques applied to clinical medicine, there is still relatively little systematic research on customer service, TQM, and CQI concepts applied to healthcare. For this reason, as well as those discussed above, *managers who continue to maintain older systems, rather than make the training investment needed to develop a TQS system, will have no accurate means to determine whether their systems are actually producing at maximum levels of both economic efficiency and quality.* The economic as well as social implications of not knowing how many resources are lost due to poor quality care now exceed the excuses typically offered for failing to measure those costs.[8]

STRATEGIES FOR MEASURING PATIENT SATISFACTION

In most types of service industries, information about consumer attitudes regarding quality is critical for economic survival. In a healthcare organization, the patient as well as the patient's family must be recognized as consumers in the **extended definition** of a customer in the healthcare process (Figure 8.1). The key to providing quality service is to balance all customer expectations with their perceptions of quality in all related healthcare services, including nursing care, employee attitudes, technology, hospital administration, appearance of the facility, convenience/access, food service, and even the presence of the governing board. In the past, administrators focused on attracting and retaining qualified

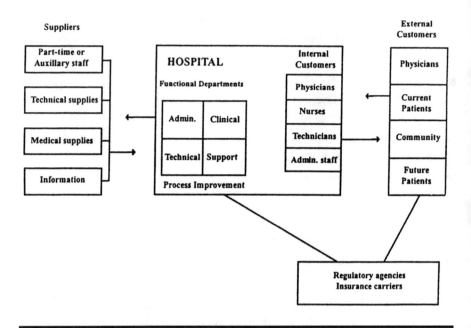

FIGURE 8.1   The Extended Customer Network in Healthcare

physicians, who in turn brought in patients. Today, however, hospitals and healthcare institutions must develop a broader range of measures that reflect patient as well as employee perceptions of care.

No QA system is perfect. Gaps can occur in systems designed to monitor quality due to the incongruence between what matters to customers and what matters to those providing service. Once expectations have been identified, gaps may still exist because of the difference between the definition of quality service and the ability of an organization to meet those standards. One way to overcome these gaps in service quality is to use the patient's knowledge to improve the healthcare process (Zeithaml et al., 1990, p. 31). Patient satisfaction also plays a vital role in establishing institutional loyalty, usage patterns, and word-of-mouth communication.

Thus, one area that holds great promise for incorporating total quality in healthcare is measurement of patient satisfaction, which refers to the recipient's reaction to critical aspects of his or her service experience. Plagued by rising costs, increasing regulations, and growing consumer interest in reducing costs, healthcare professionals can achieve gains by concentrating on patient-centered service QI, because it simply costs less to provide higher quality care than continuing to offer poorer quality. Process improvement centers on the elimination of wasteful, inappropriate, or unnecessary services while providing better clinical outcomes, fewer avoidable complications, and greater patient satisfaction. All types of service organizations can learn from patient/customer perspectives on service. Patient evaluation can lead to a more structured process for gathering patient satisfaction measures and more accurate "voice of the customer" information.

Healthcare service providers have tended to react to patient complaints rather than anticipate patient needs. Patient complaints, both oral and written, are typically handled by a single individual, usually a nurse or public relations officer, designated as the patient relations coordinator. The coordinator is responsible for resolving complaints by negotiating with attending physicians, risk managers, QA professionals, and administrators. The goal of a patient satisfaction system is to encompass all aspects of patient relations activities in a comprehensive, effective, and efficient *proactive* system that is consumer-oriented and addresses the quality of patient services.

This strategy assists healthcare professionals in becoming less defensive and more aware of patient needs and realizing how their behavior impacts the quality of healthcare services. Furthermore, listening to customers allows for evaluation of the gaps between patient and staff perceptions of service encounters. It promotes CQI rather than merely reacting to complaints.

Designing a quality patient satisfaction system involves five primary activities: (1) benchmark the best practices of one's own institution and other hospitals or related service industries, (2) obtain customer feedback, (3) consider complaints as opportunities for improvement, (4) empower a QI lead team or council, and (5) institutionalize follow-up service evaluations and surveys.

Benchmarking

Designing a patient satisfaction monitoring system could begin with a review of the facility or other business organizations outside of healthcare. Obvious related service industries are hotels and food service. Firms known for their commitment to QI, such as Hyatt Hotels, Ritz-Carlton, and Marriott Corporation, are being benchmarked for systems to (1) measure customer satisfaction from check-in to check-out, (2) train employees to become more aware of customer needs, (3) encourage customers to complete surveys, (4) develop top management commitment to quality assessment and improvement, and (5) continually adjust processes to obtain desired outcomes.

Data Sources

The second component is monitoring patient feedback on the care received while hospitalized. Consumer assertiveness has challenged healthcare professionals to devise new ways to incorporate patient input into TQS management systems.

Techniques designated to solicit patient feedback are available and have helped expand professionals' definitions of quality. Some of these data-gathering techniques are:

- Telephone interviews
- One-on-one interviews
- Complaint inquiries
- Patient and other customer surveys and questionnaires
- Focus groups made up of past, current, or future patients
- Referral information services

Patient questionnaires are generally divided into sections that coincide with a patient's experience during hospitalization, from admission to discharge. After collecting and examining patient questionnaires, the information can be used to focus on improvement opportunities. This form of **scenario writing** (see Chapter 4) aids management in eliminating the root causes of problems in specific departments or hospital services. Another advantage of using systematically collected patient input data is that by encouraging responses other than yes or no, respondents can express their true feelings and attitudes toward their hospitalization. This methodology removes the likelihood of obtaining skewed data and, when analyzed, will increase the validity of patient satisfaction data.

Redesigning Patient Relations

A third component of a successful quality patient satisfaction model is to establish an appropriate organizational center that encourages interdepartmental communication and serves to address patient complaints about healthcare services. Each complaint should be viewed as a QI opportunity. The information can be received formally from written complaints, orally from appropriate reporting personnel, or directly from patients. Patient relations problems can be reported directly to the QA director, whose mission is to integrate departments in achieving QI goals.

Quality Assurance Committee

The inherent goal of any TQS healthcare improvement effort is to positively impact the quality of health services provided to patients. In order for the process to succeed, extensive input must be gained from all individuals directly or indirectly involved in patient satisfaction. The fourth component of the proposed model is a Quality Assurance Team, which is an interdisciplinary council that addresses patient care issues. This group uses an interdisciplinary framework to monitor all patient complaints obtained from various data sources and ensures that corrective actions are implemented in a reasonable time frame. The chairperson could be the hospital CEO, and the committee could be composed of medical directors, the QA director, the volunteer coordinator, the patient relations director, and representatives from the nursing and medical staffs. In addition, because of their impact on patient satisfaction, representatives from the food services and environmental service departments could be part of a follow-up team if these areas are identified as needing improvement. Other ancillary departments are included on an as-needed basis. Lead team members serve as resource persons in identifying and prioritizing patient complaint issues, developing corrective actions, and monitoring the effectiveness of process improvements. All of the components of the model are important, but a well-functioning Quality Assurance Team may be the most important one.

Follow-Up/Evaluation

As with many other services, patient complaints are rarely even considered until a patient communicates dissatisfaction, which may not occur until after he or she has been discharged. Once a patient's hospitalization comes to an end, follow-up and evaluation of the quality of health services delivered are often neglected. In many cases, it is too late to effectively respond. Mechanisms must be put in place to anticipate patient grievances by continuously monitoring attitudes and perceptions in order to improve the quality of processes. The fifth and final component of the model is follow-up and evaluation. Automobile dealerships have been benchmarked in this area for many years. Following the purchase of an automobile and after each service encounter, service representatives personally contact customers to solicit feedback on satisfaction with service. Customers have come to expect personalized follow-up evaluation from service quality leaders and are usually willing to share thoughts and attitudes and even make improvement recommendations. This information is analyzed and integrated into the QI system. Implementing a callback system or similar methods of responding to patients in a timely fashion is critical to patient perceptions of service quality.

As mentioned earlier, the average business does not hear from 90 percent of its unhappy customers. However, the absence of complaints does not mean the absence of dissatisfaction. It has been noted that for every complaint received, as many as 6 other serious problems and 30 less serious complaints have not been expressed. In a hospital setting, this may be magnified because patients have been conditioned to believe that passive and uncomplaining behavior may be less damaging to their care.

Quality patient and other customer satisfaction is oriented toward providing timely information which can be used in an external marketing campaign. As competition increases, market segmentation in healthcare is also increasing. By offering fitness classes, post-operative rehabilitation programs, and other non-clinical services, medical facilities hope to capture distinctive markets by restructuring their delivery systems to offer alternative services. As healthcare providers attempt to develop these alternative quality systems, emphasis is on the selection, location, and availability of services. Through patient satisfaction programs, providers may discover that they would have greater success in positioning themselves in the market by addressing issues of patient–physician interaction, staff competence, and actual medical care. In the search for a market niche, knowledge of consumers and their perceptions of the facility is vital.

The rationale behind using patient satisfaction monitoring is that patient perceptions can aid healthcare organizations in a variety of ways, such as monitoring quality of care, reducing the cost of care, and providing useful marketing surveys to encourage the use of services by others. Whatever the results, these solid facts provide an excellent basis for preparing an advertising campaign. With accurate information about service quality, a hospital can differentiate itself from others in the marketplace without relying solely on reputation or specialization.

A number of forces exert increasing pressure for QI in healthcare. In addition to the previously mentioned competitive service environment, these forces include high liability insurance premiums for hospitals and physicians, tougher state regulations, and JCAHO requirements. The area of quality assessment is also a growing part of the healthcare evaluation process. The ultimate purpose of quality monitoring is to exercise surveillance so that departure from standards can be detected early and corrected, before it negatively impacts patient care.

Structured approaches to improved patient satisfaction focus on the institutional aspects of care, such as hospital policies, staff qualifications, physical facilities, and the organizational framework in which the care-giver and the patient interact. Structural evaluation focuses on the system, whereas process evaluation focuses on the implementation of care provided by a facility. The actions carried out by health professionals are measured by outcome evaluation, which stresses the end result of care or the change in a patient's health status as a result of treatment. By implementing a patient satisfaction program, a healthcare facility can monitor the quality of structure, process, and outcome from the clinical, managerial, and patient points of view.

Defining standards for quality of care requires identifying the characteristics of care as well as the criteria that constitute good care. The management of illness can be divided into two areas: the technical and the interpersonal. It is important to remember that the quality of interpersonal encounters may affect the quality of the technical care provided, in addition to eliminating expensive, below-the-surface, hidden costs of poor quality.

Patients often play an important role in defining what constitutes quality care by determining which values are associated with different outcomes. Determining patient perceptions also provides information about the performance of healthcare professionals. Without using inspection as a tool, a well-designed comments form can serve as a device to monitor the availability and performance of personnel. This adds a measure of accountability for employees, physicians, and managers in terms of meeting or exceeding the customer's technical and emotional needs. It also reduces the probability of malpractice cases and the need for risk management policies.

Patient satisfaction is promoted when healthcare service encounters are tailored to individual needs and wants. This requires that patients understand treatment options and that their expectations be both heard and acted upon. The process of shaping expectations should begin before the patient's arrival and continue after he or she is discharged. Patient participation in making treatment and other healthcare-related decisions restores a patient's sense of control and encourages the healing process.

Healthcare QI is a complex and dynamic activity which involves thousands of organizations and millions of individuals. In the next section, some of the more successful QI techniques are summarized. In indicating how they could be adapted to a hospital or healthcare environment, emphasis is on proven methods that managers can use to implement change within their own organizations.

IMPLEMENTING ORGANIZATION-WIDE HEALTHCARE QUALITY

Experience in manufacturing as well as other service organizations confirms that the best-designed QI systems are only as good as the people who implement them. This is especially true when measuring the behavioral as well as the technical quality of care. There are no significant differences between the two areas in any organization in terms of the need to measure quality, except that measurement can be more difficult when no tangible product results from a process. Measurement characteristics in service organizations are more difficult to define and monitor accurately, primarily because they rely on human sensors rather than scientific instruments for data collection and interpretation. *Human sensors must be more sophisticated and sensitive and capable of overcoming the natural tendency to make judgments according to individual biases. Careful training is the key to overcoming this tendency.*

In order for successful implementation to take place, all departments in a health service organization must be involved, but one person should initially accept the responsibility to serve as quality coordinator. Ideally, this person should be at or near the top-management level within the organization, preferably the CEO or president. As a practical matter, in light of the various routine QA data collection efforts required at most facilities, a senior vice-president or comparable appointee will typically initiate and coordinate the quality review process. As long as the person assigned the task has authority commensurate with his or her responsibilities and the effort has the full support of senior-level staff, organization-wide action can begin.

The first order of business is to create or update the organization's **mission statement**.[9] The second step in the implementation process is the formation and training of **teams** in which all units in the organization are represented. These teams will meet initially to discuss the goals and objectives of the quality review,[10] establish targets for improved process efficiency, and develop measurement characteristics appropriate for each quality function within the work unit. Several quality measurement characteristics may already be available within the existing information collection process; others may have to be created by departmental teams. In a department such as patient accounts payable, for example, measurement characteristics could include the number of rebills, number of billing delays, number of patient inquiries about mischarges, and other indices. Each departmental team member is responsible for developing a set of items that are directly related to the quality of his or her section of the work unit. Brainstorming and focus group sessions can be used to narrow and refine the team-generated lists of quality measures.

Team leaders are appointed or elected by team members and are given additional training in QI theory and techniques. They must be carefully chosen and thoroughly trained to communicate the purposes and goals of the activity to their respective work units. Team leaders must understand the concept and principles of CQI, explain the need to develop appropriate measurement characteristics, and facilitate the identification and collection of data from each department. *All members of the department, work group, or subunit must be included in the process.* Team leaders must explain the TQS concepts at the departmental level, conduct brainstorming sessions with all members to develop complete lists of quality characteristics, and represent the department or subunit in **cross-functional planning** with other units. In addition, top management must support departmental quality projects and encourage small-group quality efforts, until quality planning becomes a routine part of the quality measurement collection process.

In all likelihood, most line workers, especially nurses, are already overburdened with paperwork, filling out forms, collecting data, and other monitoring procedures. Most white-collar service employees will be familiar with such tools as control charts, but they are likely to be skeptical of additional paperwork. Thus, the purpose of a TQS process improvement exercise such as a cause-and-effect diagram as a bottom-up exercise in total organizational QI must be clearly and succinctly communicated to everyone in order to gain cooperation and sustain momentum.

Collecting data on the costs of poor quality is not an inherently difficult task, yet it is rarely done in the hospital or healthcare setting because clinical care and financial reporting requirements dominate data collection efforts. Many hospitals and other healthcare facilities fail to collect data to determine whether valid customer requirements are being met. When customer satisfaction data are collected, they are rarely integrated with clinical and financial systems. With sufficient resources to support the effort, a team can outline a TQS system in just a few months. The first data collection effort may produce only 70 to 80 percent of the total data required, but analysis of these data often provides sufficient "shock value" so that most facilities will not need the remaining 20 to 30 percent of the data for some time. As more data are collected, the quality review process can be calibrated and teams can be expanded as necessary to collect additional information.

Members of each departmental team and the team leader should discuss their list of quality characteristics with other departments. Departmental facilitators summarize and condense the lists and provide a summary of key indicators. Department liaisons or team leaders then meet with other departmental representatives during a cross-functional focus group exercise to discuss strategies for identifying the costs associated with each quality indicator. Here, representatives from staff areas such as nursing, patient relations, finance, and accounting could also be consulted as part of a cross-functional team-building exercise to attach costs to each of the measurement characteristics proposed by departmental teams.

All departmental team leaders then discuss their quality indicators with the QI coordinator, who in turn devises a monthly reporting system using feedback from each of the departmental reporting team sessions. Team members then meet and discuss progress on a continuous basis and review the statistics generated by each department. Adjustments to the process (or fine-tuning) are made as necessary, based on these statistical data. In this way, all members of the organization begin to develop fact-based approaches to the solution of departmental QI problems. Above all, the problems in the system which cause flaws, rather than the people who work in a flawed system, must be addressed (Berwick et al., 1991).

Healthcare managers must develop multiple measurement systems capable of monitoring the full range of clinical services, products from suppliers, and patient satisfaction with services. Within most medium to large facilities, it is possible to automate a good portion of the data collection and reporting effort and reduce the paperwork burden on employees. Developing a **fact-based information processing system** capable of accurately assessing various measurement characteristics is as important as the change in thinking required of all employees. To some people in any organization, the data collection and reporting steps outlined here may appear to be overly detailed and time-consuming. However, as discussed earlier, the use of organizational change strategies, training, systems thinking, and statistical methods provides everyone with a better understanding of the differences between common and special causes of variation within the system.[11]

CONCLUSIONS AND ACTION STEPS

TQS implementation and patient satisfaction plans vary from more conceptual, philosophical approaches to more detailed, hands-on approaches. Following the organization-wide commitment to TQS, decisions on the depth, breadth, and scope of the effort are made by senior management. While specific plans vary depending on the size, mission, and function of a particular facility, several general steps can be taken to strategically improve the quality of healthcare:

1. Study the literature and disseminate appropriate **case studies** of QI efforts in other settings. This is a necessary step and is not time consuming because there are still few studies in the area. CQI has been applied to service industries only since the late 1980s. Influential academic and practitioner journals are recognizing the importance of the subject and publishing increasing numbers of studies to assist professionals in all types of facilities to develop case applications appropriate to their particular institutions.

2. Personal commitment and involvement on the part of top management to QI efforts is essential to initiate and sustain the process of **top-down–bottom-up implementation**. Without top-down encouragement, efforts initiated from the bottom are more difficult to sustain.

3. Recognize **poor quality cost practices** as a necessary transition step. Integrate cost measures with patient care, financial, and clinical–medical data. Here, top management must support small-group QI efforts as part of routine information collection processes.

4. Ensure **patient privacy** as well as the **professional autonomy** of physicians, psychologists, nurses, and other state-licensed professionals; at the same time, involve all professions in QI plans.

5. Develop **bottom-up work-unit–based measures** consistent with professional discretion and patient requirements, designed to meet extended definitions of customer expectations.

6. Encourage **cross-functional coordination**, both vertically and horizontally, between line and staff functions within the facility using training and small-group problem identification techniques,

7. Implement **quality function deployment** to merge customer requirements with organizational process controls and QA standards in order to minimize costly resistance during the critical start-up phase and sustain the continuous improvement process (Omachonu, 1991).

In addition to the guidelines outlined here, healthcare administrators must communicate precisely why and how a strategy for service QI differs from other management systems. Moreover, they must stress the importance of extended definitions of customer satisfaction, assume the lead in training all employees, and develop multiple measures and key characteristics of quality (Milakovich, 1991b).

ENDNOTES

1. Including hospitals, nursing homes, health maintenance organizations (HMOs), medical laboratories, public health departments, preferred provider organizations (PPOs), medical schools, pharmaceutical manufacturers, medical device producers, and physicians in private or group practice.
2. Quality assurance in healthcare administration terminology is not the same as quality assurance in quality management science terminology. This is explained in greater detail elsewhere in this chapter. Utilization review is concerned primarily with over-utilization of hospital beds and the elimination of unnecessary and inefficient medical procedures.
3. HMOs, for example, were created in the early 1970s to reduce the costs of providing quality care by encouraging group practices, preventive strategies, internal efficiencies, and cost containment. Insurance companies and healthcare entrepreneurs have since developed other forms of managed care such as independent provider affiliates and PPOs to better serve patients while controlling costs and utilization of resources.
4. One of the more interesting strategies to combat the inflation of healthcare costs was devised by Ryder Corporation, Inc. of Miami, Florida. Ryder employees who discover any billing errors by hospitals or doctors for company-paid medical care receive bonuses or finders' fees. In addition to encouraging employees to become more aware consumers of healthcare services, the employee may keep a percentage of the incorrect bill as an incentive.
5. The leading researchers in quality theory and applied techniques include W. Edwards Deming (*Out of the Crisis*, Cambridge, Mass.: MIT Center for Advanced Engineering Study, 1986), Philip Crosby (*The Eternally Successful Organization*, New York: McGraw-Hill, 1988), H. James Harrington (*Poor Quality Costs*, Milwaukee: Marcel

Dekker-ASQC Press, 1987), Howard Gitlow (*Tools and Methods for the Improvement of Quality,* Homewood, Ill.: Richard D. Irwin, 1989), Joseph M. Juran (*Juran on Planning for Quality,* New York: Free Press, 1988), and Kaoru Ishikawa (*What Is Total Quality Control? The Japanese Way,* Englewood Cliffs, N.J.: Prentice-Hall, 1985).

6. Quoted from Paul Cleary and Barbara McNeil, "Patient Satisfaction as an Indicator of Quality Care," *Inquiry,* Vol. 25, No. 1 Spring 1988, p. 25.

7. Michael Milakovich, "Creating a Total Health Care Environment," *Health Care Management Review,* Vol. 16, No. 2, Spring 1991, pp. 9–20.

8. Suspecting it costs them substantial money and staff resources but lacking TQS systems to estimate exactly how much, most service managers [reluctantly] accept the reality of poor quality and the "rework" required to correct mistakes. Once measurement systems are in place, however, many are often disturbed when they learn what the costs actually are. The costs of poor quality may actually *increase* in the short term after a quality monitoring system is in place. Managers should be aware of this possibility and plan accordingly. It should not be surprising that these costs may go up in view of the generally accepted estimates that place the total losses from waste and inefficiency at 25 to 35 percent of total healthcare costs, or $250 to $350 *billion* for the entire industry during 1993. These are just estimates, and actual costs may be higher, because most facilities still do not understand how the costs of poor quality affect their organizations.

9. The best guidelines available to managers of any organization who want to update or develop their mission statement are the 66 questions contained in W. Edwards Deming's *Out of the Crisis* (1986), Chapter 5, pp. 156–166.

10. Some suggestions for such a quality review are provided in Appendix F (pp. 243–246) of Maasaki Imai's *Kaizen: The Key to Japan's Competitive Success* (New York: Random House Business Division, 1986).

11. Basic to any statistical process control system is the distinction between common variation (resulting from causes that are under management's control) and special or random variation (resulting from causes outside of management's control). Review Chapter 6 for a full explanation of the importance of this distinction.

LEADERSHIP
FOR ACHIEVING
HIGH-PERFORMANCE
QUALITY
IMPROVEMENT

This final chapter begins with a brief summary of the key points made in earlier chapters. After this review, barriers to achieving total quality service (TQS) are identified and discussed, followed by action strategies to overcome these obstacles. Before proceeding further, the reader is once again reminded that TQS is a continuous journey rather than a destination. Those seeking quick fixes for service quality problems will be disappointed. Instead, the leadership challenges for those who are committed to achieving TQS are presented within the broader context of developing a high-performance TQS delivery environment.

In today's competitive service markets, achieving high performance and quality means *anticipating* valid future customer needs and responding to them quickly and courteously with consistent, customized treatment. Responsiveness to customer needs for flexibility, *genuine* employee empowerment, and the capacity to *exceed* rather just meet customer expectations are required. Anticipating valid demands for better service quality further empowers everyone involved in delivering services and encourages employee ownership and confidence in responding to "their" customers' needs. In most cultures, satisfaction of employees with the way they are treated significantly improves satisfaction of customers with the services they receive. Without employee dedication, participation, and support, the best-designed and most generously funded quality and productivity improvement efforts are doomed to fail.

Leaders are not just defined by rank, but include all those who own, seek to own, or empower others to continuously improve processes within their organizations. Leaders know how to continually improve processes, systems, and services so as to anticipate customer needs. They also appreciate the complexity of strategies and tactics needed to transform existing service cultures to focus on customer-driven quality. In the competitive, profit-driven private sector, achieving customer-driven product and service quality *absolutely* determines a firm's future economic survival. Delivering TQS is no less important in the regulated, non-competitive public and non-profit sectors. It may actually be *more* important because lack of a quality focus perpetuates waste and breeds further antagonism between the paying customers (citizens/taxpayers) and those who provide services (government employees/bureaucrats). TQS principles are being successfully applied to merge thinking and guide leadership in all types of organizations—private businesses, non-profit agencies, and governments.

In our diverse free market economy, the principles of quality improvement (QI) spread rapidly, albeit unevenly, during the 1980s. Despite some early failures, false starts, and frustrations, many manufacturing companies found that application of quality theories and techniques increased efficiency, reduced waste, decreased costs, and improved customer satisfaction. Increased customer loyalty was often, but not always, accompanied by impressive gains in productivity and an enhanced global competitive position. In those highly publicized instances where quality failed to deliver as expected (i.e., FPL, McDonnell-Douglas, and Wallace Corporation), the causes could be traced to changing markets or lack of consistency and commitment on the part of leadership.

IMPLEMENTING TOTAL QUALITY SERVICE TO ACHIEVE HIGH PERFORMANCE

Specific strategies must be customized to fit to each service culture, and the successful implementation of TQS requires action in the following areas:

- Integrating management functions, promoting teamwork, and flattening hierarchies
- Defining customer quality requirements
- Strengthening customer–supplier relationships
- Empowering employees

■ Continuously improving processes
■ Understanding systems
■ Reducing poor quality costs

Prominent world-class quality theorists have contributed ideas and enhanced our knowledge of quality leadership and process improvement. Although it is important to understand the influential quality pioneers and their theories, owners of processes are best able to select and apply the appropriate elements of theories to improve their own work environments.

To understand quality leadership from the perspective of customer service, it is important to grasp the theoretical basis of the various approaches to QI and understand how those theories can be applied to change organizations. W. Edwards Deming observed that "experience teaches nothing without theory." To consistently and effectively apply theory requires an understanding of the interrelationships between the concepts and how they affect the substructure of a particular service organization. An example is the relationship between systems thinking and continuous quality improvement (CQI) (see Figure 2.7).

Regardless of size or the nature of the service provided, leading the TQS effort in any service organization is a team-based, interdisciplinary, theory-driven activity. In many respects, Xerox Corporation, the state of Connecticut, Ford Motor Company, Levi Strauss, and Metlife Insurance are similar, yet in many respects they differ. While a process orientation allows for comparisons between different types of organizations, all processes within services are slightly different. Deming also observed that "inefficiency in a service organization, just as in manufacturing, raises prices to the consumer and lowers his standard of living. The principles and methods are the same for service as for manufacturing. The actual application differs, of course, from one product to another, just as all manufacturing concerns differ from one to another" (Deming, 1982, p. 183). The purpose of service organizations generally does not include producing a standard product at a uniform cost; rather, it is to provide *customized* treatment for each recipient by emphasizing individual needs. Therefore, training in the "high-touch" human relations elements of TQS is as important as technical training in statistics and methodology.

While the major points of the world-class quality masters have been highlighted in the preceding pages, the emphasis throughout this book has been on generic rather than brand-name quality concepts. Among those elements common to all efforts are establishing better coordination between functions within organizations, promoting teamwork, focusing on customer-driven definitions of quality, maintaining closer customer–supplier relations, continuously improving everything, thinking systematically, and reducing process variation and quality cost practices. Achieving these goals on a consistent basis allows more resources to be devoted to individualizing treatment in order to address the unique circumstance of each customer.

The four key components of a TQS model are leadership, teamwork, customer orientation, and systems thinking (see Figure 4.1). They must be carefully balanced to meet the special needs of particular customers for a specific service. Successful leadership for achieving quality and productivity goals is theory based, results oriented, focused on action, and transformational. Widespread decentralized non-hierarchical participation in self-managed teams is a goal. Achieving such a cooperative work force requires a far different leadership style than that practiced in most organizations. Executives who reached senior positions under the old system may have trouble empowering those beneath them in competitive hierarchical organizations.

Transforming the behavior of individuals within service organizations is an essential leadership component of TQS, which views the human, technical, and management subsystems as team based, customer oriented, and interrelated with the organizational mission. Service processes can be constantly improved by creating opportunities for participation, stressing knowledge transfer as well as results, and using appropriate statistical methods and tools shared by the entire work force. Ten principles of human resource quality management developed by Jose Romero-Simpson (1990) guide the discussion of how to achieve the transformation to a TQS culture:

1. Anticipate customer needs
2. Obtain committed top-management leadership
3. Educate for self-improvement
4. Continuously improve processes and systems
5. Create an environment free from fear
6. Develop a stimulating work environment
7. Teach and practice teamwork
8. Stress communication, not inspection
9. Think statistically
10. Encourage personal commitment to change

These human resource training principles are particularly useful in organizations where continuous learning is valued. This strategy reflects a process where knowledge is created through the transformation of experience. Those organizations that master the art and science of knowledge transfer between component subsystems faster and more effectively than the competition increase their chances of survival. They also build the confidence levels of all participants and create a cadre of able and willing leaders upon whom quality results depend.

For those who must learn how to change faster than the competition in order to survive changing business environments, the full array of QI options can be very confusing. Various approaches with acronyms such as CQI, JIT, QA, QC, SPC, STSM, TQM, and TQC have been introduced throughout America. When applied to services, they are widely viewed as a means to achieve the elusive goals of economic efficiency and increased productivity. Too often, however, the precise meaning of these terms varies with the depth of one's own understanding or, more commonly, that of one's consultant. Talking about the rewards of improvement is less difficult than actually implementing QI systems. Advocates of the various approaches can point to success stories, usually in "another" industry. Extreme care should be taken *not* to assume that successes in one sector can automatically be applied to another.

As we have seen, rigid organizational structures and hierarchies are inconsistent with TQS. At the same time, TQS does not abandon accountability, which is the traditional justification for bureaucratic hierarchy. On the contrary, the application of TQS principles is designed to provide flexibility instead of uniform responses, allow action rather than reaction, and create empowerment to act in the customer's best interest. Effective leadership for process analysis requires both a system-wide perspective and greater team responsibility for demonstrating results. Training and empowerment permit individuals, as members of self-directed work teams made up of committed workers, to address problems at their source and respond to the expressed needs of customers, without depending on time-consuming and rigid command and control structures.

The power of QI principles depends less on the use of consultants' jargon, confusing acronyms, or complicated tools than on the capacity to learn and teach organizational change. Enhanced responsiveness to all customers and true empowerment of employees, members, or associates through teamwork, participation, and systematic analysis of task-related problems are essential in learning these concepts and applying these skills to improve processes.

TQS can improve the competitiveness of service industries in world markets and increase efficiency in domestic services as well. Multinational firms that deploy QI principles have obtained competitive advantages and cost reductions by enlisting employees, suppliers, and customers in the continuous improvement of processes. The same is true for regulated services such as utilities. Government actions to promote quality leadership include the Malcolm Baldrige National Quality Awards, the President's Productivity Awards, and various state award systems. In Europe, the International Standards Organization has performed a similar function. These actions parallel ongoing government efforts to deregulate, privatize, and devolve functions to levels closest to the customers.

Operational processes within organizations are complex and consist of the interaction of the seven M's: materials, manpower, methods, machines, measurement, maintenance, and management. Implementing TQS requires an understanding of the tools and techniques used to encourage systems thinking within process improvement work teams. Problem identification techniques such as brainstorming, nominal group technique, multivoting, and cause-and-effect diagrams can help reduce variation in existing processes. When blended together, they can yield valid service quality measurement characteristics which then become operational measures for monitoring the needs of customers. Statistical quality control tools (group decision making, Pareto analysis, cause-and-effect diagrams, check sheets, control charts, and run charts) can be used to eliminate non-value-added steps and monitor performance. Understanding the definition and application of quality measurement characteristics is at the heart of process analysis and system improvement.

The ultimate goal is to eliminate non-value-added steps in response to customer requirements. It is equally important to integrate TQS principles and traditional approaches to cost containment and productivity improvement. Numbers-driven productivity measurement is the established management method. Most managers with more than five years of experience will be unfamiliar with certain aspects of the "softer" TQS approach. Fear of change and not wanting to get caught with extensive knowledge of "last year's" fad can be barriers to implementation. Some theorists have argued that productivity cannot be raised beyond a certain level using traditional tools without applying statistical process control (SPC). There are many examples of the effective use of SPC to raise productivity, increase outputs, and either reduce inputs or utilize excess inputs to expand operations or diversify. Components of SPC are logical extensions of traditional productivity tools; combining those tools with TQS principles inevitably leads to a higher productivity ceiling. In private service industries, where competitors are making quantum leaps in productivity, a blend or mixture of the "soft" and "hard" approaches may be necessary.

TQS serves as a bridge between traditional productivity methods and two familiar perspectives: the marketing-based **customer service approach** (Zeithaml et al., 1990) and the more statistically based **company-wide quality control**, which is the predominant management philosophy in the Japanese private and public sectors (Ishikawa, 1985). Although TQS can be employed as a transitional tool, when combined with SPC it provides an effective means for organizational transformation, cost containment, and productivity improvement.

Current interest in applying TQS techniques to a wide range of public services is spreading to all levels of government, including the primary suppliers of essential education, healthcare, law enforcement, and retirement services for millions who cannot afford to purchase them from private providers. TQS provides a promising model for launching a non-partisan quality revolution for the American public and private sectors at all levels. There is an increasing need to improve customer service quality in all functions and at all levels of American public services. Despite this need, few governments have implemented the changes in attitude and culture necessary to empower employees, eliminate poor quality costs, and respond effectively to citizen complaints about service quality. Past failures of governmental productivity efforts increase the willingness of elected and appointed public officials to experiment and innovate. Still, there is as yet no reward equivalent to the bottom line (e.g., increased profit and market share) in the public service sector. Successful TQS strategies result in higher productivity per worker, greater job satisfaction, reduced waste, and lower operating costs. Citizens, taxpayers, and voters—the true customers of public service agencies—benefit from greater return on their investment in more effective governance.

Despite the prospect for change, immense challenges confront those intent on applying TQS in a health service delivery environment. Chronic waste of resources accompanies our increasingly mixed system of public and private healthcare delivery. Taxpayers now subsidize care for nearly one-half the general population: the elderly, poor, disabled, and those whose incomes fall below the poverty line. If universal health insurance is enacted through a system of managed competition, the efficiency of delivering services will become even more important. Hospital, medical, and healthcare services have traditionally emphasized retrospective quality assurance and externally imposed regulatory standards from a strict clinical perspective. Historically, health professionals have lacked incentives to integrate services into a TQS system in order to improve medical, organizational, administrative, and patient evaluation processes. Today, the complexity of measuring clinical outcomes combined with the new competitive, cost-conscious, regulated service environment requires an integrated view of quality. TQS is more than quality assurance or quality control; continuous improvement requires strategic management actions based on a clear understanding of extended customer requirements and a precise mission statement. Combined with regulation and cost competition, TQS is becoming a primary policy implementation strategy for healthcare institutions seeking to lower costs, raise productivity, and enhance profits in the ultra-competitive healthcare market of the 1990s. This is especially important in terms of the Clinton administration's pledge to control costs and provide universal access to healthcare for all Americans.

The most common barrier to achieving quality is the failure to train employees to respond effectively to customers. Not unlike manufacturing, service organizations must adopt modern training methods or risk being unable to compete in tomorrow's global marketplace. The potential impact of combining ISO 9000, the Baldrige Award criteria, and SPC with TQS is significant and impressive, especially in an environment of declining markets or shrinking resources. Using these techniques increases an organization's proportion of "visible" (useful) output and decrease its "invisible" (wasted) output (see Figure 6.2). Training must be focused on quality strategies to distinguish between value-added and non-value-added activities. Everyone must understand such concepts as variation (common and special), value addedness, and team-based evaluation; the difference between quality assurance, quality control, and QI; and how these concepts and techniques can be combined to improve productivity and better serve customers.

BARRIERS TO ACHIEVING TOTAL QUALITY SERVICE

The regulated monopolistic character of many services, especially—but not only—those offered by the public sector, has tended to discourage new ideas, competition, and innovation. Poor training, uneven knowledge, concerns about status within existing hierarchies, lack of job security, and other attitudinal barriers have inhibited customer service QI. These structural and behavioral barriers are rapidly breaking down as once-protected public and private service monopolies face the same competitive challenges confronted by American manufacturing industries in the 1980s.

There are various reasons for the failure of U.S. industries to respond to the international challenge of service QI. While their origins are complex and all the reasons have not been fully explored, the primary barriers are suggested below.

1. Dependence on Top-Down Management. Despite calls for greater employee participation and empowerment, the Weberian model, or "chain of command" hierarchy, still predominates. This management method is still taught in most business school courses and practiced in most American organizations. Based on ancient religious and military doctrine advanced to theory status in the mid-1800s, this model was applied at the beginning of the Industrial Revolution to discipline and control an illiterate work force. Not surprisingly, it actively discourages participation in customer service improvement, problem solving, and goal setting. One costly symptom of its perpetuation is divisive American labor–management relations. American industry has paid a heavy price for continued distrust between workers and owners. Dependence on top-down management is slowly declining, as evidenced by successful union–management cooperation, gainsharing in the United States, joint U.S.–Japanese ventures, and harmonious management–worker participation in Northern Europe and Japan.

Futurist Alvin Toffler underscores the importance of reducing hierarchies in all types of organizations, but especially among "knowledge workers," who work primarily in service organizations (Toffler, 1990).

2. Management by Objectives. First proposed by Peter Drucker in the mid-1950s, MBO was applied to the Department of Defense for the explicit purpose of gaining control of the defense industry work force in the 1960s. Study after study shows that MBO has failed in both goal attainment and internal process improvement. Yet, as if tradition somehow requires it, MBO continues to dominate public and private graduate management education as well as government and private industry administrative practice. Management by control must be re-examined and replaced by total quality leadership, horizontal rather than vertical management, and empowered employees trained to respond to, rather than hide from, customers. Leaders must provide a secure environment, support, resources, and education to train and empower workers and help the organization reach its goals (Greebler-Schepper, 1993).

3. Annual Review and the (De)Merit System. Prior to the re-emergence of the service quality movement in the United States, there were few incentives to change individual performance appraisal systems. The merit system currently used to set pay and bonus rates encourages destructive (I win–you lose) competition, destroys morale, creates fear, and inhibits cooperation. Employees are not rewarded based on the quality of services provided, because performance appraisal and merit selection processes (if examined at all) emphasize results and pleasing superiors instead of system improvements. Some are rewarded and others are punished without examining the underlying causes for system variation (Deming, 1986). Without statistical verification, it is assumed that greater productivity per se leads to higher quality. Peter Scholtes says flatly that individual performance appraisal is antithetical to QI (Scholtes, 1993). James Bowman argues that, if necessary at all, performance appraisal should be tied to quality evaluation (Bowman, 1994). In order to improve service quality, a thorough restructuring of the personnel system must be undertaken, in which incentives for employees to work together to uncover and eliminate non-value-added costs and the systemic causes of customer-defined problems are emphasized.

4. Overspecialization in Job Descriptions. All knowledge-based services are to some extent provided within bureaucracies which are hierarchical, specialized, fragmented, and compartmentalized to allow a professional staff or "experts" to exercise control over employees and maintain authority over customers. This is especially true in construction, healthcare, education, government, and other "credentialed" services. As long as personnel and hiring rules specify specialized skills in job descriptions, further fragmentation is likely, which makes it more difficult to promote teamwork and break down barriers to cooperation. Because of a lack of integration with other functions within organizations, overspecialization may become a barrier used by technical experts in dealing with non-specialized recipients of services. TQS principles can be used effectively to overcome overspecialization, which distances providers from those being served.

5. Ineffective Productivity Management Techniques. The widespread misuse of productivity measurement techniques in most public (and many private) organizations is a barrier to TQS. The prevailing myth that productivity declines as quality increases also inhibits change. Leaders of businesses, public organizations, and universities fear that the use of quality and productivity management techniques could render bonuses, merit procedures, step increases, and other productivity tools obsolete. Reluctance to train employees in quality concepts may reflect insecurities among well-intended senior managers who are themselves not prepared for the changes. Many leaders continue to practice the traditional methods and techniques which got them to leadership positions in their organizations. Implementation of quality is a delicate process, and its long-term success depends upon changing leadership principles, long after a particular leader has departed. The inability of senior managers to empower employees is one of the key leadership challenges in implementing TQS (Drath, 1993). Too few leaders are committed to transforming the current system in order to improve it.

6. Fear of Change. TQS must be approached with an open mind. Fear of acquiring new knowledge which conflicts with that previously learned remains one of the primary obstacles to permanent service QI. The thought of implementing new approaches disturbs many senior managers, who are either incapable of or unwilling to change their management practices. Upon first exposure to Dr. Deming's teachings, many managers dismiss his Fourteen Points as naive, utopian, overly complex, socialist, or in less flattering (and unprintable) adjectives. Most soon realize, however, that much of what they have previously learned about management is outmoded and dysfunctional. At the very least, exposure to Deming's principles causes many to question the conventional wisdom about how best to achieve quality and productivity improvement (Milakovich, 1990a).

These barriers limit the acceptance of QI theories and techniques in the service sector. To overcome them, manufacturing support and service firms have taken bold steps, including decentralizing operations and abolishing the merit system, to remove implementation barriers—with stunning success. Successful experiences in other sectors of the economy provide the broad policy guidelines for achieving the transformation of the service sector.

ACTION STRATEGIES FOR SERVICE QUALITY IMPROVEMENT

1. **Consistent with the mission of the organization, flatten hierarchies that discourage teamwork and create barriers between departments.** If each department and every individual within each department acts to optimize itself, himself, or herself, then the effectiveness of the organization as a whole is reduced. Teamwork can be achieved by implementing cross-functional management, flow charting processes, identifying internal and external customer needs, and, as necessary, using statistical tools to monitor customer satisfaction. Eliminating barriers between departments, establishing trust and cooperation rather than fear-based competition, and providing training for teamwork are all necessary to accomplish the transformation. The most challenging element in the promotion of teamwork is to create mutual respect between team members. Empowered teams are then able to eliminate the causes of variation within systems and processes. Members whose tasks are interdependent develop mutual respect for each other and, in training for teamwork, develop a shared common vision transmitted throughout the organization. Even in highly unionized organizations, it is still possible to break down barriers if TQS implementation is mutually agreed to and written into contracts. Ironically, with or without union cooperation, experience showns that middle management is more likely to resist quality implementation.

2. **Formulate a mission statement that reflects the shared values and *operationally defines* the vision of the organization.** Once the mission statement has been written, it must be published as official company policy so that each and every employee understands his or her role in accomplishing the mission. Teams can then be trained to implement their part of the mission. Senior TQS managers, who act more like coaches or facilitators than inspectors or judges, must guide the preparation of a mission statement that articulates the vision. Identifying internal customers and flow charting processes not only increases internal efficiency and defines tasks more clearly, but also empowers employees to cope with their environment as a series of interconnected processes and subsystems over which they exert control rather than "the system."

3. **Empower employees instead of threatening them.** One hospital recently decided to implement quality. In the opening training session on CQI theories and techniques, the consultant hired to conduct the quality training said, "In five years, most of you will not have a job!" This caught the audience's attention, but in precisely the wrong way to prepare anyone for the journey. On another occasion, the CEO of an organization said, "This [quality] is our goal. We may never reach it, but we are going to come as close to it as we can. We will use whatever means necessary to achieve this, and anyone who gets in the way had better join in or ship out."

During the early phases of the ill-fated Florida Power & Light (FPL) Quality Improvement Program described in Chapter 5, the chairman and CEO produced a videotape which was "required" viewing by the entire work force. The purpose of the video was to encourage the then skeptical work force to implement quality the way it had apparently succeeded in the Japanese utility used as a model for the FPL quality effort. The message was clear and professionally presented, but the ending portended the rocky road ahead. Near the end of the video, the speaker said, "The train is rolling; either get on board, or get out of the way!" With this introduction and unforgiving attitude, it was not surprising that the work force later rebelled over the amount of extra work required to please the Japanese counsellors and win the Deming Prize.

These fear-based statements reflect a dilemma shared by managers in many competitive industries: how do they empower when they have achieved rank and status by *not* sharing power or authority with others? In theory, most managers value empowerment of subordinates but have a difficult time putting the concept into practice (Drath, 1993). Making coercive statements in a service organization reflects a fundamental problem with implementing action strategies in a diverse work force. Leadership style must be consistent with the mission of the organization. If empowerment and participation are valued, then threats and intimidation are inconsistent with the mission.

4. Pay more attention to your customers and suppliers. Develop systems to survey and collect feedback from *all* customers. Do not wait for complaints, because by then it is usually too late. Even public agencies which serve large numbers of persons who cannot or will not purchase services from private providers are deregulating outmoded laws, empowering employees to act in the recipient's interest, and privatizing non-essential services. Increasingly, user fees are being charged for the delivery of basic services; when a citizen pays for a service directly, he or she has every right to demand that service be performed to his or her satisfaction. Service satisfaction measures are being widely applied in the emerging "entrepreneurial" public service sector.

5. Begin slowly and do not create unrealistic expectations. Examples presented here show numerous successful (and some less so) efforts to apply quality principles in services. Important lessons can also be learned from failed attempts. It is important to be aware of the basic tenets of quality, referred to here as TQS. In addition, the manner in which quality concepts and productivity principles are introduced is equally important. Emphasis should be on internal rather than external rewards for QI. Not every company that provides a quality service at a reasonable cost needs to apply for the Deming Prize or the Baldrige Award, nor should all quality firms invest the time or resources. Those willing to participate should be forgiven for early mistakes in judgment. The learning and organizational change process requires patience and understanding. Results will come, but slowly, as the work culture changes.

6. Anticipate and continually adapt to change. Political and social environments are continuously changing as world markets expand, definitions of product and service quality merge, and TQS strategies are successfully applied to more and more different types of services. Even those services protected by domestic regulations and tariffs are no longer immune to global competition. Failure to recognize market changes is a common reason why businesses lose market share and disappear. Learning is encouraged as organizations, just like individuals, adapt to changes in business environments. The "light at the end of the tunnel" for future service quality leaders is not a certificate, a diploma, or an award; it is the achievement of a cultural change which allows everyone to continuously improve processes.

A leadership style consistent with the changing organizational culture is as important to the ultimate success of the quality effort as listening to customers and responding to their needs. But it is only one element, along with customer orientation, learning how to change, true empowerment, and systems thinking. Leaders must strive to balance their quality and productivity improvement strategies with the needs and expectations of those who must actually deliver the service. It is always wise not to get too far ahead of those upon whom you depend to accomplish organizational goals (Roston, 1993). Without support from those who must actually make the changes and deal with customers, even the most enthusiastically supported and generously funded strategy will fail.

LEADERSHIP CHALLENGES

Never underestimate the difficulty of convincing an organization made up of diverse interests that quality is always the answer to every problem. Unless required by your mission, never threaten or intimidate people into producing more. An educated work force that delivers customer-contact airline, banking, educational, or healthcare services will resist these tactics, and both quality and productivity will plummet. Initiating permanent QI requires sound theory, consistency, hard work, discipline, and confronting realities about the basic structure of the organization which might have to be changed. Above all, a personal commitment to the success of the change is required.

During the early stages of any QI effort, some obvious areas of conflict are likely to arise, including:

■ Getting used to a participatory rather than a hierarchical managerial approach to decision making

- Developing collective team-based performance measures

- Applying CQI rather than quality control standards

- Learning to work within a more flexible yet closely monitored performance structure

All of these changes will require training within the context of a comprehensive strategic QI plan.

In the past, changes such as MBO, planning-programming-budgeting-systems, or zero-based budgeting were initiated as short-term responses to the latest financial crisis or in reaction to customer complaints. If these are the primary motives, then changes are destined to fail. In order to succeed, fundamental and lasting organizational changes must be accompanied by the resources and training necessary to achieve QI results.

Leadership for QI means motivating others to do what is best for the organization for their own reasons (creating a win–win situation). Managers should learn how to think and act like coaches, teachers, and facilitators rather than administrators, inspectors, and bureaucrats. New roles include teacher, benchmarker, motivator, mentor, and entrepreneur. Realistically, not all managers or employees are capable of the personal commitment required to learn and practice these new skills. Those who cannot commit should at least learn how to co-exist in a win–win environment and not resist the change effort (Milakovich, 1993).

Change can be frustrating. It is often hard enough to change one's own behavior, much less that of an organization made up of diverse individuals, not all of whom welcome change. How does a committed quality leader handle resistance? Not in the traditional, control-dominated, "take no prisoners," "shoot the messenger" style. Resistance from employees, like complaints from customers, is a critical barrier which cannot be ignored. Causes must be understood and action taken by empowered teams to eliminate the reasons for dissatisfaction. Understanding why some may not assist in the TQS effort will help to overcome resistance. The reasons include:

- They are afraid to speak out

- They are unaccustomed to being asked to participate

- They are afraid of appearing stupid in front of others, especially those with whom they work

- They don't believe it will do any good, so why bother

- They distrust calls for cooperation when competition has prevailed in the past

■ The new roles are uncomfortable at first

■ Those involved in the change process are not certain that the change will last

■ They don't know how to "look good" in the new roles

Overcoming these and other valid employee concerns requires committed leadership from senior officials. Leaders in quality-oriented service cultures generally adopt a tranformational leadership style, as opposed to a traditional or situational approach. The new roles for leaders to play in guiding the internal transformation are:

■ Acting as coaches for CQI teams, defining ultimate objectives, training teams, and facilitating successful performance

■ Offering constructive advice on the formulation of policy to support a TQS culture

■ Creating an environment that is free from traditional barriers and promotes open communication

Among the most important leadership challenges for success in these new roles are developing a vision of the service that is responsive to customers and implementing this strategy with the full cooperation of employees. This must be accomplished without resorting to threats of downsizing, layoffs, or sham productivity efforts which produce the same results. Important transitional steps for achieving these results are delegating responsibility to the lowest levels (empowerment) and using pilot projects on a small scale to demonstrate results.

Finally, incentives and reward systems must change to recognize, rather than punish, those willing to assume responsibility for managing non-traditional applications such as benchmarking, gainsharing, and performance measurement, heretofore untested on a broad scale in the service sector. To continuously improve service quality, new leadership styles combined with better measures of customer satisfaction are needed. Application of techniques described in this book provides a framework for rethinking current management practices. As implementation breakthroughs occur in greater numbers of services, TQS will be seen as offering an alternative road map for the transformation. Leaders in a quality-oriented service culture generally adopt a tranformational style, as opposed to a traditional or situational approach. Why is it important to transform basic structure?

It is very difficult to prepare a work force for impending changes without threatening them with dismissal if they demand to be included or raise questions about the pace of change. A backlash results from the frustrations experienced by those who must ultimately implement quality improvements. Some have criticized total quality management as a cult; others refer to their attendance at Deming seminars as a religious experience. In different ways, both observations are probably correct.

In his seminars, Deming frequently talked about recruiting "joyful bosses" and restoring "joy in work." In his sincere effort to restore everyone's reason for working, he may have been offering an operational definition of the "self-actualized" personality which Abraham Maslow defined four decades ago as the optimal goal for motivating workers and managers (Maslow, 1954). For many in today's workplace, this is a very compelling message. Beyond a certain point, most people do not work solely for money. In a fully operational TQS environment, other forms of recognition become important. This was nicely summed up by a sales executive at a seminar who described the difference as working to achieve the mission of the organization rather than just working to receive a paycheck.

Leadership is getting others to internalize opportunities to adopt cooperative win–win solutions rather than creating competitive zero-sum internal conflict. In many ways, quality leaders behave more like elected political representatives than either self-serving managers or appointed permanent bureaucrats. In an American work force increasingly made up of diverse interests and individuals, leaders must practice a form of leadership analogous to a political campaign, where broad-scale participation and assumption of individual responsibility are encouraged. Political leadership skills in dealing with varied interests and resolving conflicts peacefully among different groups are valued. As opportunities for participation increase, everyone is happier because the size of the pie being sliced is bigger.

In practice, the real power of quality theories lies not in their theoretical promise but in their proven success to positively change attitudes and opinions. A word of caution: if not properly introduced, QI could make things worse. Moreover, it requires changes in work environments which could threaten existing hierarchical relationships. In the initial stages, TQS organizations must be forgiving of mistakes, especially when all causes of system variation have not been discovered and eliminated. Individuals must not be blamed for mistakes caused by the system. Quite often, in non-TQS organizations, part or all of the blame for a mistake falls upon a single undertrained, low-paid, overworked employee. There are some simple things that any organization can do to prevent these "special causes" and assist every employee in maximizing his or her self-improvement effort.

When top management encourages every individual to improve himself or herself, the total sum of human resources available to serve customers increases, at little cost to the organization. Eliminating barriers and establishing a cooperative (win–win) work environment, rather than a fear-based competitive workplace, provides the basis for the trust and teamwork necessary to accomplish the transformation.

Examples of successful quality applications to improve products, services, processes, and systems abound. Thousands of American firms have made the commitment and are reaping the benefits of increased profits, lower costs, higher productivity, and greater market share. Virtually all American consumers are aware that "Quality Is Job One" at Ford Motor Company. At leading firms such as AT&T, Walt Disney, Citicorp, the Marriott Corporation, and Southwest Airlines, employee dedication to customer needs is expected from the beginning. At Motorola, "Six Sigma" quality (less than two parts per billion defective) has become an attainable goal as well as an operational management philosophy. At FPL, the first large American public service utility to institute total quality control, breakthroughs in service quality implementation have been incorporated into company policy. At FedEx, dedication to customer satisfaction, reliability, on-time delivery, and continuous monitoring of performance has produced measurable results.

Despite these and many other successes, the quality revolution is not yet over in services, especially in small businesses, non-profit organizations, regulated monopolies, and public agencies. Implementing the principles outlined in this book achieves demonstrable cost savings, increases the number of satisfied customers, reduces lost work time because of fewer on-the-job injuries, and offers better service reliability. When changes are made, everyone benefits as customers and suppliers of better quality goods and services for domestic and world markets.

THE ETERNALLY SUCCESSFUL ORGANIZATION GRID

	Comatose	Intensive care	Progressive care	Healing	Wellness
Quality	Nobody does anything right around here. *Price of Non-conformance = 33%*	We finally have a list of customer complaints. *Price of Non-conformance = 28%*	We are beginning a Quality Improvement Process. *Price of Non-conformance = 20%*	Customer complaints are practically gone. *Price of Non-conformance = 13%*	People do things right the first time routinely. *Price of Non-conformance = 3%*
Growth	Nothing ever changes. *Return after tax = nil*	We bought a turkey. *Return after tax = nil*	The new product isn't too bad. *Return after tax = 3%*	The new group is growing well. *Return after tax = 7%*	Growth is profitable and steady. *Return after tax = 12%*
Customers	Nobody ever orders twice. *Customer complaints on orders = 63%*	Customers don't know what they want. *Customer complaints on orders = 54%*	We are working with customers. *Customer complaints on orders = 26%*	We are making many defect-free deliveries. *Customer complaints on orders = 9%*	Customers' needs are anticipated. *Customer complaints on orders = 0%*

The Eternally Successful Organization Grid (continued)

	Comatose	Intensive care	Progressive care	Healing	Wellness
Change	Nothing ever changes. *Changes controlled by Systems Integrity = 0%*	Nobody ever tells anyone anything. *Changes controlled by Systems Integrity = 2%*	We need to know what is happening. *Changes controlled by Systems Integrity = 55%*	There is no reason for anyone to be surprised. *Changes controlled by Systems Integrity = 85%*	Change is planned and managed. *Changes controlled by Systems Integrity = 100%*
Employees	This place is a little better than not working. *Employee turnover = 65%*	Human Resources has been told to help employees. *Employee turnover = 45%*	Error Cause Removal programs have been started. *Employee turnover = 40%*	Career path evaluations are implemented now. *Employee turnover = 7%*	People are proud to work here. *Employee turnover = 2%*

Source: Philip B. Crosby, *Quality Is Free: The Art of Making Quality Certain*, New York: McGraw-Hill, 1979, p. 31.

DEMING'S FOURTEEN POINTS

1 Create constancy of purpose toward improvement of product and service with a plan to become competitive and to stay in business. Decide to whom top management is responsible.

2 Adopt the new philosophy. We are in a new economic age. We can no longer live with commonly accepted levels or delays, mistakes, defective materials, and defective workmanship.

3 Cease dependence on mass inspection. Require, instead, statistical evidence that quality is built in to *prevent* defects rather than *detect* defects.

4 End the practice of awarding business on the basis of price tag. Instead, depend on meaningful measures of quality, along with price. Eliminate suppliers that cannot provide statistical evidence of quality.

5 Find problems. It is management's job to work continually on the system (design, incoming materials, composition of material, maintenance, improvement of machines, training, supervision, retraining).

6 Institute modern methods of training on the job.

7 The responsibility of foremen must be changed from sheer numbers to quality...[which] will automatically improve productivity. Management must prepare to take immediate action on reports from foremen concerning barriers such as inherited defects, machines not maintained, poor tools, and fuzzy operational definitions.

8 Drive out fear, so that everyone may work effectively for the company.

9 Break down barriers between departments. People in research, design, sales, and production must work as a team to foresee problems of production that may be encountered with various materials and specifications.

10 Eliminate numerical goals, posters, and slogans for the work force, asking for new levels of productivity without providing methods.[1]

11 Eliminate work standards that prescribe numerical quotas.

12 Remove barriers that stand between the hourly worker and his right to pride of workmanship.

13 Institute a vigorous program of education and retraining.

14 Create a structure in top management that will push every day on the above 13 points.[2]

ENDNOTES

1. According to Deming, individual goals are necessary, but "numerical goals set for other people, without a road map to reach a goal, have [negative] effects opposite to the [positive] effects sought" (Deming, 1986, p. 69).
2. Deming has stated that if a critical mass equal to the square root of the number of people within the organization accepts his Fourteen Points, then the organization will successfully transform. However, he may have underestimated the resistance to change in many American service firms.

APPENDIX C

CROSBY'S FOURTEEN STEPS

1 **Management Commitment.** Management must commit to all parts of quality management.

2 **Quality Improvement Team.** Crosby's QITs are cross-functional management teams which consist of department heads during the first cycle and either department heads or high-level designates thereafter.

3 **Quality Measurement.** Choose the quality output measures and begin to measure them (i.e., percentage of late reports, time lost due to equipment failure, etc.).

4 **Cost of Quality Evaluation.** The cost of poor quality is the shortfall in bottom-line profits because everything is not done right the first time; it includes but is not limited to insurance protection against litigation, inspection costs, lost sales or the equivalent, and costs of providing guarantees, warranties, and allowances.

5 **Quality Awareness.** This includes but is not limited to employee training in quality; disseminating brochures, memoranda, etc. about quality; and making public within the organization the quality output measures and the cost of poor quality.

6 **Corrective Action.** Required to change organizational systems to eliminate poor quality practices.

7   Ad Hoc Committee for the Zero Defects Program.   This is an interdepartmental committee whose job is to implement **DIRFT** (**D**o **I**t **R**ight the **F**irst **T**ime) and supervise the transition to **Zero Defects Day**, the one day when the organization has absolutely zero defects.

8   Employee Education.   To define the training needed by all employees to actively carry out their roles in the quality improvement process.

9   Zero Defects Planning and Zero Defects Day.   See Step 7 for details. In addition, the CEO should give a face-to-face speech to employees on this day. The speech should be about the importance of zero defects and conformance to requirements.

10   Goal Setting.   After Zero Defects Day, every employee in the organization meets with his or her superordinate to negotiate 30-day, 60-day, and 90-day quantifiable goals. The superordinate tries to coordinate these goals to encourage teamwork.

11   Error Cause Removal.   A one-page form is disseminated throughout the organization on which every employee is asked to list in specific terms his or her greatest problems. Cross-functional groups will be established to process these forms within set time limits (24, 48, or 72 hours).

12   Recognition.   Present workers with non-financial rewards for outstanding achievement in quality improvement in front of their peers.

13   Quality Councils.   The QIT chairpersons and the quality professionals meet regularly as a quality council to discuss how to continuously improve the quality program.

14   Do It Over Again.   Reaffirm management's commitment (Step 1) and begin the cycle again.

MALCOLM BALDRIGE AWARD CRITERIA

1995 EXAMINATION CATEGORIES/ITEMS

1.0	**Leadership**	**90 points (9%)**
	1.1 Senior executive leadership	45
	1.2 Leadership system and organization	25
	1.3 Public responsibility and corporate citizenship	20
2.0	**Information and Analysis**	**75 points (7.5%)**
	2.1 Management of information and data	20
	2.2 Competitive comparisons and benchmarking	15
	2.3 Analysis and use of company-level data	40
3.0	**Strategic Planning**	**55 points (5.5%)**
	3.1 Strategy development	35
	3.2 Strategy deployment	20
4.0	**Human Resource Development and Management**	**140 points (14%)**
	4.1 Human resource planning and evaluation	20
	4.2 High performance work systems	45
	4.3 Employee education, training, and development	50
	4.4 Employee well-being and morale	25

5.0	**Process Management**	**140 points (14%)**
5.1	Design and introduction of products and services	40
5.2	Process management: Product and service production and delivery	40
5.3	Process management: Support services	30
5.4	Management of supplier performance	30
6.0	**Business Results**	**250 points (25%)**
6.1	Product and service quality results	75
6.2	Company operational and financial results	130
6.3	Supplier performance results	45
7.0	**Customer Focus and Satisfaction**	**250 points (25%)**
7.1	Customer and market knowledge	30
7.2	Customer relationship management	30
7.3	Customer satisfaction determination	30
7.4	Customer satisfaction results	100
7.5	Customer satisfaction comparison	60
TOTAL		**1000 points**

Note: The relative weights given to each examination category can change annually, at the discretion of the MBQA Board of Overseers. The revised weights for the 1995 criteria reflect a *decrease* in emphasis on leadership, human resource development, and customer satisfaction. There was little or no change in the information and analysis, strategic planning, and process management categories. The greatest *increase* came in the category of business results, up 25% (from 180 to 250 points) from 1992 to 1995.

BIBLIOGRAPHY

Al-Assaf, A.L. and June A. Schmele, *The Textbook of Total Quality in Healthcare,* Delray Beach, Fla.: St. Lucie Press, 1993.

Albrecht, Karl, *The Only Thing that Matters,* New York: Harper Business, 1992.

Albrecht, Karl and Ron Zemke, *Service America!: Doing Business in the New Economy,* Homewood, Ill.: Dow Jones-Irwin, 1985.

Alfeld, Louis Edward, *Construction Productivity,* New York: McGraw-Hill, 1988.

American Quality Foundation and Ernst and Young, "The International Quality Study Best Practices Report: An Analysis of Management Practices that Impact Performance," Cleveland: Ernst and Young, 1992.

Ashford, John L., *The Management of Quality in Construction,* E.& F.N. Spon, 1989.

Bassett, Glenn, *Operations Management for Service Industries,* Westport, Conn.: Quorum Books, 1992.

Bennis, Warren and Burt Nanus, *Leaders: Strategies for Taking Charge,* New York: Harper and Row, 1986.

Berman, E. and M. Milakovich, "Increasing Global Competition through the Promotion of Total Quality Management," in *Productivity and Quality Management Frontiers III,* David J. Sumanth, A. Johnson, D. Edosomwan, Scott Sink, and William B. Werther, Jr. (Eds.), Norcross, Ga.: Industrial Engineering and Management Press, Institute of Industrial Engineers, 1991, pp. 477–487.

Berman, Evan M. and J. West, "Municipal Commitment to Total Quality Management: A Survey of Recent Progress," *Public Administration Review,* Vol. 55, No. 1, January–February 1995, pp. 57–67.

Berman, Evan, M. Milakovich, and J. West, "Implementing TQM in the States," *Spectrum: The Journal of State Government,* Vol. 67, No. 2, Spring 1994, pp. 6–12.

233

Berry, Thomas, *Managing the Total Quality Transformation,* New York: McGraw-Hill, 1991.

Berwick, D.M., "Continuous Improvement as an Ideal in Health Care," *New England Journal of Medicine,* Vol. 320, 1989, pp. 53–56.

Berwick, D.M, A.B. Godfrey, and J. Roessner, *Curing Health Care,* San Francisco: Jossey-Bass, 1991.

Block, Peter, *The Empowered Manager,* San Francisco: Jossey-Bass, 1991.

Block, Peter, *Stewardship: Choosing Service over Self-Interest,* San Francisco: Barrett-Koehler, 1994.

Boseman, Barry, *All Organizations Are Public,* San Francisco: Jossey-Bass, 1987.

Bowman, James, "Quality Circles: Promises, Problems and Prospects in Florida," *Public Personnel Management,* Vol. 18, No. 4, 1989, pp. 375–403.

Bowman, James, "At Last, An Alternative to Performance Appraisal: Total Quality Management," *Public Administration Review,* Vol. 54, No. 2. March/April 1994, pp. 129–136.

Box, G.E.P, L. Joiner, S. Rohan, and F.J. Sensenbrenner, "Quality in the Community: One City's Experience," paper presented at the 1989 American Quality Congress, Toronto, 1989.

Broadhead, James S., "The Post Deming Diet," *Training,* Vol. 28, No. 2, February 1991, pp. 41–43.

Brown, Stanley A., *Total Quality Service: How Organizations Use It to Create a Competitive Advantage,* Englewood Cliffs, N.J.: Prentice-Hall, 1992.

Burati, J.L., M.F. Matthews, and S.N. Kalidindi, "Quality Management in Construction Industry," *Journal of Construction Engineering and Management,* Vol. 117, No. 2, 1991, pp. 341–359.

Burstein, Carolyn and K. Sedlak, "The Federal Productivity Improvement Effort: Current Status and Future Agenda," *National Productivity Review,* Spring 1988, pp. 122–133.

Camp, Robert, *Benchmarking: The Search for Industry Best Practices that Lead to Superior Performance,* Milwaukee: ASQC Press, 1989.

Carlzon, Jan, *Moments of Truth,* New York: Balinger, 1987.

Carr, David and Ian Littman, *Excellence in Government: Total Quality Management in the 1990s,* Arlington, Va.: Coopers and Lybrand, 1990.

Cleary, Paul and Barbara McNeil, "Patient Satisfaction as an Indicator of Quality Care," *Inquiry,* Vol. 25, No. 1, Spring 1988, p. 25.

Clemmer, James, *Firing on All Cylinders,* Homewood, Ill.: Business One Irwin, 1992.

Cohen, Allan, Stephen L. Fink, Herman Gordon, Robin Willits, and Natasha Josefowitz, *Effective Behavior in Organizations,* Homewood, Ill.: Irwin, 1992.

Cohen, Alfie, *Punished by Rewards,* Boston: Houghton Mifflin, 1993.

Cohen, Steven and Ronald Brand, *Total Quality Management in Government,* San Francisco: Jossey-Bass, 1993.

Consumer Reports, July, August, September 1992.

Couper, David C. and Sabine Lobitz, *The Quality Leadership Workbook,* Madison, Wisc.: Madison Police Department, 1993.

Crosby, Philip B., *Quality Is Free: The Art of Making Quality Certain,* New York: Mentor, 1979.

Crosby, Philip B., *Quality without Tears,* New York: New American Library, 1984.

Crosby, Philip B., *Completeness,* New York: McGraw-Hill, 1992.

Day, Ronald G., *Quality Functional Deployment,* Milwaukee: ASQC Press, 1993.

Deming, W. Edwards, *Some Theory of Sampling,* New York: Wiley, 1950.

Deming, W. Edwards, *Quality, Productivity, and Competitive Position,* Cambridge, Mass.: MIT Center for Advanced Engineering Study, 1982.

Deming, W. Edwards, *Out of the Crisis,* Cambridge, Mass.: MIT Center for Advanced Engineering Study, 1986.

Deming, W. Edwards, *The New Economics for Industry, Government, Education,* Cambridge, Mass.: MIT Center for Advanced Engineering Study, 1993.

DiIulio, John J., Gerald Garvey, and Donald F. Kettl, *Improving Government Performance: An Owner's Manual,* Washington, D.C.: The Brookings Institution, 1993.

Dobson, Eric, "Designing and Implementing a State Quality Award," Washington. D.C.: National Institute of Standards, U.S. Department of Commerce, 1993.

Drath, Wilfred H., *Why Managers Have Trouble Empowering: A Theoretical Perspective Based on Concepts of Adult Development,* Greensboro, N.C.: Center for Creative Leadership, 1993.

Drucker, P., "The Deadly Sins in Public Administration," *Public Administration Review,* Vol. 40, No. 2, March/April 1980, pp. 103–106.

Elfenbein, Pamela, Jack B. Miller, and Michael E. Milakovich, "Medical Resource Allocation: Rationing and Ethical Considerations," *Physician Executive,* Vol. 20, No. 2, February 1994, pp. 3–8.

Federal Total Quality Management Handbook, "Education and Training for Total Quality Management in the Federal Government," Washington, D.C.: U.S. Government Printing Office, 1992.

Feigenbaum, Armand V., *Total Quality Control,* 3rd ed., New York: McGraw-Hill, 1983.

Finn, Chester and Theodore Rebarber (Eds.), *Education Reform in the 1990s,* New York: Macmillan, 1992.

Forbes, Lincoln, "What Do You Do When Your Organization Isn't Ready for TQM?" *National Productivity Review,* Vol. 13, No, 4, Autumn 1994, pp. 467–478.

Fromm, William and Len Schlesinger, *The Real Heros of Business and Not a CEO Among Them,* New York: Currency/Doubleday, 1994.

Gabor, Andrea, *The Man Who Discovered Quality,* New York: Times Books, 1990.

Galloway, Robert A., "Quality Improvement and Heightened Self-Esteem: The Brighton Police Story," *National Productivity Review,* Autumn 1992, pp. 453–461.

Gartman, Col. J.B. and John Fargher, "Implementing Gainsharing in a Total Quality Management Environment," *Proceedings of the International Industrial Engineering Conference,* 1988.

Garvin, David A., "What Does 'Product Quality' Really Mean," *Sloan Management Review,* Vol. 26, No. 1, Fall 1984, pp. 25–43.

Garvin, David A., "Competing on the Eight Dimensions of Quality," *Harvard Business Review,* November/December 1987, pp. 101–109.

Garvin, David A., *Managing Quality,* New York: Free Press, 1988.

Gass, Gerald L., "Measuring TQIM Efforts: Management By Fact," Total Quality Insurance Conference, Orlando, Fla., June 4–5, 1992.

Gilbert, Ronald, *The TQS Factor and You,* Boca Raton, Fla.: Business Performance Publications, 1992.

Gilbert, Ronald and D. Nelson, *Beyond Participatory Management,* Westport, Conn.: Quorum Books, 1991.

Ginnodo, William L., "How to Build Commitment," *National Productivity Review,* Vol. 8, No. 3, Summer 1989, pp. 249–260.

Gitlow, Howard S., *Planning for Quality, Productivity, and Competitive Position,* Homewood, Ill.: Dow Jones-Irwin, 1990.

Gitlow, Howard, Lecture on "Deming's Management Method," University of Miami Quality Institute Forum, March 1991.

Gitlow, Howard and Shelly Gitlow, *The Deming Guide to Quality and Competitive Position,* Englewood Cliffs, N.J.: Prentice-Hall, 1987.

Gitlow, Howard S. and Shelly Gitlow, *Total Quality Management in Action,* Englewood Cliffs, N.J.: RTR Prentice-Hall, 1994.

Gitlow, Howard S., Shelly Gitlow, Alan Oppenheim, and Rosa Oppenheim, *Tools and Methods for the Improvement of Quality,* Homewood, Ill.: Irwin, 1989.

Golden, Malcolm, "Quality Concepts, Statistical Analysis and Modern Techniques of Quality Improvement," unpublished paper, Management Science Department, University of Miami, Coral Gables, Fla., 1990.

Gordon, George and Michael E. Milakovich, *Public Administration in America,* 5th ed., New York: St. Martin's Press, 1995.

Gore, Vice President Albert Jr., *From Red Tape to Results: Creating a Government that Works Better and Costs Less. Report of the National Performance Review,* New York: Times Books, Random House, 1993.

Greebler-Schepper, Carol, "The Psychology of Continuous Improvement: Understanding Human Behavior; The First and Most Critical Step," personal correspondence, October 1993.

Griffin, A. and H.R. Hauser, "The Voice of the Customer," *Marketing Science,* Vol. 12, No. 1, Winter 1993, pp. 1–27.

Groocock, J.M., *The Chain of Quality: Market Dominance through Product Superiority,* New York: John Wiley & Sons, 1986.

Hammer, Michael and James Champy, *Reengineering the Corporation,* New York: Harper Business, 1993.

Hauser, J.R. and D. Clausing, "The House of Quality," *Harvard Business Review,* Vol. 66, No. 3, 1988, pp. 63–73.

Herzberg, Frederick, *Work and the Nature of Man,* Cleveland: World Publishing, 1966.

Hodgetts, Richard M., *Blueprints for Continuous Improvement: Lessons from the Baldrige Winners,* New York: American Management Association, 1993.

Hudiberg, John, *Winning with Quality: The FPL Story,* White Plains, N.Y.: Quality Resources, 1991.

Hunt, V. Daniel, *Quality in America: How to Implement a Competitive Quality Program,* Homewood. Ill.: Business One Irwin, 1992.

Hunt, V. Daniel, *Quality Management in Government: A Guide to Federal, State, and Local Implementation,* Milwaukee: ASQC Press, 1993.

Hunter, W.G, J.K. O'Neill, and C. Wallen, "Doing More with Less in the Public Sector," *Quality Progress,* July 1987, pp. 19–26.

Hyde, Albert C., "Reserving Quality Measure from TQM," *The Bureaucrat,* Vol. 19, 1990–91, pp. 16–20.

Imai, Maasaki, *Kaizen: The Key to Japan's Competitive Success,* New York: Random House, 1986.

Ingraham, Patricia W., Barbara S. Romzek, and associates, *New Paradigms for Government: Issues for the Changing Public Service,* San Francisco: Jossey-Bass, 1994.

Ishikawa, Kaoru, *What Is Total Quality Control? The Japanese Way,* translated by David J. Lu, Englewood Cliffs, N.J.: Prentice-Hall, 1985.

Johns, Gary, *Organizational Behavior: Understanding Life at Work,* Glenview, Ill.: Scott, Foresman, 1988.

Johnson, H.T. and R. Kaplan, *Relevance Lost,* Cambridge, Mass.: Harvard Business School Press, 1987.

Joiner, Brian L. and Peter R. Scholtes, "The Quality Manager's New Job," *Quality Progress,* Vol. 19, No. 10, October 1986, pp. 52–56.

Juran, Joseph M., *Managerial Breakthrough: A New Concept of the Manager's Job,* New York: McGraw-Hill, 1964.

Juran, Joseph M., *Juran on Planning for Quality,* New York: Free Press, 1988.

Juran, Joseph, *Juran on Leadership for Quality,* New York: McGraw-Hill, 1989.

Juran, Joseph M. and Frank M. Gryna, Jr., *Quality Planning and Analysis: From Product Development through Use,* 2nd ed., New York: McGraw-Hill, 1980.

Juran, Joseph M., Frank M. Gryna, Jr., and R.S. Bingham, Jr., *Juran's Quality Control Handbook,* 4th ed., New York: McGraw-Hill, 1988.

Kano, N., "A Perspective on Quality Activities of American Firms," *California Management Review,* Vol. 35, No. 3, Spring 1993, pp. 12–31.

Kano, Noriaki and Howard Gitlow, "Lectures on Total Quality Control and the Deming Management Method," unpublished lecture notes, University of Miami Quality Program, Coral Gables, Fla., 1988–89.

Katzenbach, J.R. and D. Smith, *The Wisdom of Teams,* Cambridge, Mass.: Harvard Business School Press, 1992.

Keehley, Patricia, "TQM for Local Government," *Public Management,* August 1992, pp. 10–16.

Kelman, Steven, *Procurement and Public Management: The Fear of Discretion and the Quality of Government Performance,* Washington, D.C.: AEI Press, 1990.

King, B., *Better Designs in Half the Time: Implementing QFD in America,* Metheun, Mass.: Goal/QPC, 1987.

Kolb, David A., *Experiential Learning: Experience as a Source of Learning and Development,* Englewood Cliffs, N.J.: Prentice-Hall, 1984.

Kolb, David, Irwin M. Rubin, and James M. McIntyre, *Organizational Psychology,* 2nd ed., Englewood Cliffs, N.J.: Prentice-Hall, 1984.

Kravchuk, Robert S. and R. Leighton, "Implementing Total Quality Management in the United States," *Public Productivity and Management ▪ Review,* Vol. 17, No. 1, Fall 1993, pp. 71–82.

Kreitner, Robert and Angelo Kinicki, *Organizational Behavior,* Homewood, Ill.: Richard D. Irwin, 1989.

Kujawa, Duane. *Japanese Multinationals in the United States: Case Studies,* New York: Praeger, 1986.

Kujawa, D. and Bob Daniel, *American Public Opinion on Japanese Direct Investment,* Survey Report of the Japan Society, July 1988.

Latzko, W.J., *Quality and Productivity for Bankers and Financial Managers*, New York: Marcel Dekker/ASQC Press, 1986.

Leadership for America: Rebuilding the Public Service. The Report of the National Commission on the Public Service and the Task Force Reports to the National Commission on the Public Service, Lexington, Mass.: Lexington Books, 1990.

Levin, Martin A. and Mary Sanger, *Making Government Work: How Entrepreneurial Executives Turn Bright Ideas into Real Results*, San Francisco: Jossey-Bass, 1994.

Lillrank, Paul and Noriaki Kano, *Continuous Improvement: Quality Control Circles in Japanese Industry*, Ann Arbor, Mich.: Center for Japanese Studies, University of Michigan, 1989.

Liswood, Laura, *Serving Them Right: Innovative and Powerful Customer Retention Strategies*, New York: Harper and Row, 1990.

Lusk, K., M. Tribus, C. Schwinn, and D. Schwinn, "Creating Community Quality Councils: Applying Quality Management Principles in a Political Environment," paper presented at the William G. Hunter Conference, Madison, Wisc., April 19, 1989.

MacGregor, Douglas, *The Human Side of Enterprise*, New York: McGraw Hill, 1960.

Mann, Nancy, *The Keys to Excellence: The Story of the Deming Philosophy*, Los Angeles: Prestwick, 1985.

Maslow, Abraham, *Motivation and Personality*, New York: Harper and Row, 1954.

Masternak, Robert L., "Gainsharing Boosts Quality and Productivity at a BF Goodrich Plant," *National Productivity Review*, Vol. 12, No. 2, Spring 1993, pp. 225–239.

Mauch, Peter, James Stewart, and Frank Straka, *The 90-Day ISO Manual*, Delray Beach, Fla.: St. Lucie Press, 1994.

McCormick, Betty L. (Ed.), *Quality and Education: Critical Linkages*, Princeton Junction, N.J.: Eye on Education Press, 1993.

Milakovich, Michael E., "Total Quality Management for Public Sector Productivity Improvement," *Public Productivity and Management Review*, Vol. XIV, No. 1, Fall 1990a, pp. 19–32.

Milakovich, M.E., "Enhancing the Quality and Productivity of State and Local Government," *National Civil Review*, Vol. 79, No. 3, May–June 1990b, pp. 266–277.

Milakovich, M.E., "Total Quality Management in the Public Sector," *National Productivity Review*, Vol. 10, No. 2, Spring 1991a, pp. 195–215.

Milakovich, M.E., "Creating a Total Quality Health Care Environment," *Health Care Management Review*, Vol. 16, No. 2, 1991b, pp. 9–21.

Milakovich, M.E., "Total Quality Management for Public Service Productivity Improvement," in *Public Productivity Handbook*, Marc Holzer (Ed.), Milwaukee: Marcel Dekker, 1992, pp. 577–602.

Milakovich, M.E., "Leadership for Public Service Quality Management," *The Public Manager,* Vol. 22, No. 3, Fall 1993, pp. 49–52.

Milakovich, M.E., "How Quality-Oriented Have State and Local Governments Really Become?" *National Productivity Review,* Vol. 14, No. 1, Winter 1995, pp. 73–84.

Milakovich, M.E. and S. Dan, "Achieving Quality at Florida Power and Light: The Pursuit of the Deming Prize," *Quality Digest,* Vol. 10, No. 11, November 1990, pp. 38–50.

Miller, J. and M. Milakovich, "Total Quality Management and the Utilization Review Process," *Physician Executive,* Vol. 7, No. 6, November–December 1991a, pp. 8–11.

Miller, J. and M. Milakovich, "Improving Access to Health Care through Total Quality Management," *Quality Assurance and Utilization Review,* Vol. 6, No. 4, November 1991b, pp. 138–141.

Miller, J., M. Rose, M. Milakovich, and E.J. Rosasco, "Application of TQM Principles to the Utilization Management Process: A Case Report," *Physician Executive,* May 1992, pp. 10–16.

Moss Kantor, R., *The Change Masters: Innovations for Productivity in the American Corporation,* New York: Simon and Schuster, 1983.

Murgatroyd, Stephen and Colin Morgan, *Total Quality Management and the School,* Buckingham, England and Philadelphia: Open University Press, 1993.

National Commission on the State and Local Public Service, *Hard Truths/Tough Choices: An Agenda for State and Local Reform,* Albany, N.Y.: Nelson Rockefeller Institute of Government, 1993.

New York State Police, The Governor's Excelsior Award, 1992 Public Sector Award Winner, Interview with Col. John Wallace, New York State Police, June 21, 1993.

Oglesby, C.H. H.W. Parker, and G.A. Howell, *Productivity Improvement in Construction,* New York: McGraw-Hill, 1989.

Omachonu, Vincent, *Total Quality Productivity Management in Health Care Organizations,* Norcross, Ga.: Institute of Industrial Engineers, 1991.

Omachonu, Vincent K. and Joel E. Ross, *Principles of Total Quality,* Delray Beach, Fla.: St. Lucie Press, 1994.

Osborne, David and Ted Gaebler, *Reinventing Government,* Reading, Mass.: Addison-Wesley, 1992.

Ouchi, William, *The M-Form Society,* Reading, Mass.: Addison-Wesley, 1984.

Parker, Glenn M., *Cross-Functional Teams: Working with Allies, Enemies, and Other Strangers,* San Francisco: Jossey-Bass, 1994.

Peters, Tom, *Thriving on Chaos: Handbook for a Managerial Revolution,* New York: Knopf, 1987.

Peters, Tom, *Liberation Management: Necessary Disorganization for the Nanosecond Nineties,* New York: Fawcett Columbine, 1992.

Peterson, K., *The Strategic Approach to Quality Service in Healthcare,* Rockville, Md.: Aspen Publishers, 1988.

Porter, Michael E., *The Competitive Advantage of Nations,* New York: Free Press, 1990.

Presidential Award for Quality, Federal Quality Institute, "Ogden Internal Revenue Service Center," Washington, D.C.: U.S. Government Printing Office, 1992.

Prestowitz, Clyde, *How We Let Japan Take the Lead,* New York: Basic Books, 1988.

Rabbit, John T. and P. Bergh, *The ISO 9000 Book: A Global Competitor's Guide to Compliance and Certification,* White Plains, N.Y.: Quality Resources, 1993.

Rivlin, Alice, *Reviving the American Dream: The Economy, the States and the Federal Government* Washington, D.C.: Brookings Institution, 1992.

Romero-Simpson, J. Eulogio, "A Quality-Improvement Oriented Organizational Behavior Course," paper presented at the OBTC Meeting, University of Richmond, Va., June 13, 1990.

Rosander, A.C., *The Quest for Quality in Services,* Milwaukee: ASQC Quality Press, 1989.

Roston, Gordon, interview at American Society for Public Administration Meeting, San Francisco, July 1993.

Rounds, J.L. and Chi Nai-Yuan, "Total Quality Management For Construction," *Journal of Construction Engineering and Management,* Vol. VIII, 1985, pp. 117–129.

Ryan, Kathleen D. and Daniel Oestreich, *Driving Fear Out of the Workplace,* San Francisco: Jossey-Bass, 1991.

Scherkenbach, W.W., *The Deming Route to Quality and Productivity,* Washington, D.C.: CEEP Press, 1988.

Scherkenbach, W.W., *Deming's Road to Continual Improvement,* Knoxville, Tenn.: SPC Press, 1991.

Schmidt, Warren H. and Jerome P. Finnigan, *The Race without a Finish Line: America's Quest for Total Quality,* San Francisco: Jossey-Bass, 1992.

Scholtes, Peter, *The Team Handbook: How to Use Teams to Improve Quality,* Madison, Wisc.: Joiner Associates, 1988.

Scholtes, P., "Total Quality or Performance Appraisal: Choose One," *National Productivity Review,* Vol. 12, No. 3, Summer 1993, pp. 349–365.

Scholtes, Peter and Heero Hacquebord, *A Practical Approach to Quality,* Madison, Wisc.: Joiner Associates, 1987.

Scholtes, P. and H. Hacquebord, "Beginning the Quality Transformation. Part I," *Quality Progress,* Vol. 21, No. 7, 1988, pp. 28–33.

Sedell, Kenneth, "The Relationship between Quality and Productivity" unpublished research paper, Political Science Department, University of Miami, Coral Gables, Fla., 1991.

Senge, Peter, *The Fifth Discipline,* New York: Doubleday, 1990.

Sensenbrenner, Joseph, "Quality Comes to City Hall," *Harvard Business Review,* March–April 1992, pp. 64–75.

Seymour, Daniel, *On Q: Causing Quality in Higher Education.* New York: Macmillan, 1992.

Shewhart, Walter A., *Economic Control of Quality of Manufactured Product,* New York: Van Nostrand Reinhold, 1931.

Shewhart, Walter A., *Statistical Method from the Viewpoint of Quality Control,* W. Edwards Deming (Ed.), Lancaster, Pa.: The Lancaster Press, 1939.

Shingo, Shigeo, *Zero Quality Control: Source Inspection and the Poka-Yoke System,* translated by Andrew Dillon, Cambridge, Mass.: Productivity Press, 1986.

Shingo, Shigeo, *A Study of The Toyota Production System,* translated by Andrew Dillon, Cambridge, Mass.: Productivity Press, 1989.

Shonk, James H., *Team-Based Organizations,* Homewood, Ill.: Business One Irwin, 1992.

Sink, D. Scott, "Developing World-Class Quality and Productivity Management Efforts," in *Productivity and Quality Management Frontiers III,* David J. Sumanth, Johnson A. Edosomwan, D. Scott Sink, and William B. Werther, Jr. (Eds.), Norcross, Ga.: Industrial Engineering and Management Press, Institute of Industrial Engineers, 1991, pp. 210–216.

Smith, David G., *Paying for Medicare: The Politics of Reform,* New York: Aldine De Gruyter, 1992.

Spechler, J., *When America Does It Right. Case Studies in Service Quality,* Norcross, Ga.: Industrial Engineering and Management Press, 1988.

Spechler, J., *Managing America's Most Admired Companies,* Norcross, Ga.: Industrial Engineering and Management Press, 1993.

Starr, Paul, *The Social Transformation of Medicine,* New York: Basic Books, 1982.

Starr, Paul, *The Logic of Health-Care Reform,* Knoxville, Tenn.: The Grand Rounds Press, Whittle Books, 1993.

Sumanth, David, *Productivity Engineering and Management,* New York: McGraw-Hill, 1984.

Swanson, Roger C., *The Quality Improvement Handbook: Team Guide to Tools and Techniques,* Delray Beach, Fla.: St. Lucie Press, 1995.

Swiss, James E., "Adapting Total Quality Management (TQM) to Government," *Public Administration Review,* Vol. 52, No. 4, July/August 1992, pp. 356–362.

Szilagyi, Andrew D. Jr. and Marc J. Wallace, Jr., *Organizational Behavior and Performance,* Glenview, Ill.: Scott, Foresman, 1990.

Taguchi, Genichi, *Introduction to Quality Engineering: Designing Quality into Products and Processes,* White Plains, N.Y.: Quality Resources and the Asian Productivity Organization, 1986.

Taguchi, Genichi and Don Clausing, "Robust Quality," *Harvard Business Review*, January–February 1990, pp. 65–75.

Taylor, Frederick W., *Principles of Scientific Management*, New York: Norton Free Press, 1911.

Thompson, James D., *Organizations in Action*, New York: McGraw-Hill, 1967.

Thompson, Frank J. (Ed.), *Revitalizing State and Local Public Service*, San Francisco: Jossey-Bass, 1993.

Toffler, Alvin, *Power Shift: Knowledge, Wealth, and Violence at the Edge of the 21st Century*, New York: Bantam: 1990.

Tribus, Myron, *Deployment Flowcharting*, Los Angeles: Quality and Productivity, 1989.

Tribus, Myron, interview at Deming Seminar, Costa Mesa, Calif., February 1990.

The Economist, "The Final Frontier," February 20, 1993, p. 63.

Ullmann, S.G., "The Impact of Quality on Cost in the Provision of Long-Term Care," *Inquiry*, Vol. 33, 1985, pp. 292–306.

U.S. Equal Employment Opportunity Commission, "EEOC Approach to Quality Assurance," Washington, D.C., 1985.

U.S. Executive Office of the President, "Executive Order 12637," *Federal Register*, Vol. 53, No. 83, 1988.

U.S. Executive Office of the President, "Circular A-132," *OMB Circular*, Washington, D.C.: 1988.

U.S. Executive Office of the President, "Circular to Replace A-132," *OBM Draft*, Washington, D.C: 1990.

U.S. General Accounting Office, "Management Practices: U.S. Companies Improve Performance through Quality Efforts," GAO/NSIAD-91-190, May 1991.

U.S. General Accounting Office, "Quality Management: Survey of Federal Organizations," Document GAO/Ggd-93-9BR, October 1992.

U.S. Office of Management and Budget, "Quality Improvement Prototype: Internal Revenue Service—One Stop Account Service—Department of Treasury," 1989a.

U.S. Office of Management and Budget, "Quality Improvement Prototype: Fresno Service Center, Internal Revenue Service," 1989b.

U.S. Office of Management and Budget, "Quality Improvement Prototype: Ogden Service Center, Internal Revenue Service," 1989c.

Voehl, Frank, Peter Jackson, and David Ashton, *ISO 9000: An Implementation Guide for Small to Medium-Sized Businesses*, Delray Beach, Fla.: St. Lucie Press, 1994.

Walton, Mary, *The Deming Management Method*, New York: Dodd, Mead, 1986.

Walton, Mary, *Deming Management at Work,* New York: G.P. Putnam's Sons, 1990.

Weber, Max, *The Theory of Social and Economic Organization,* New York: Free Press, 1947.

West, Jonathan P., E. Berman, and M.E. Milakovich, "Total Quality Management in Local Government," in *The Municipal Yearbook 1994,* Washington, D.C.: International City/ County Management Association, 1994, pp. 14–34.

Wheeler, Donald J. and David S. Chambers, *Understanding Statistical Process Control,* 2nd ed., Knoxville, Tenn.: SPC Press, 1992.

Whitney, John, Columbia University Insurance Study, interview at Deming Seminar, Costa Mesa, Calif., July 1989.

Woodall, Jack, "Policy Deployment: How FPL Focuses for Improvement," University of Miami Quality Program, October 1988.

Zeithaml, Valarie, A. Parasuraman, and Leonard L. Berry, *Delivering Quality Service: Balancing Customer Perceptions and Expectations,* New York: Free Press, 1990.

Zemke, Ron and Dick Schaaf, *The Service Edge,* New York: New American Library, 1989.

Zozoya, Carlos, Chris Hendrickson, and Daniel R. Rehak, *Knowledge Process Planning for Construction and Manufacturing,* San Diego: Academic Press, 1989.

INDEX